QUEER COMPANIONS

DUKE UNIVERSITY PRESS   Durham and London   2022

QUEER COMPANIONS

RELIGION, PUBLIC INTIMACY, AND SAINTLY AFFECTS IN PAKISTAN

OMAR KASMANI

© 2022 DUKE UNIVERSITY PRESS
All rights reserved
Designed by A. Mattson Gallagher
Typeset in Warnock Pro and Fira Sans by Copperline Book
Services

Library of Congress Cataloging-in-Publication Data Names:
Kasmani, Omar, author.
Title: Queer companions : religion, public intimacy, and
saintly affects in Pakistan / Omar Kasmani.
Description: Durham : Duke University Press, 2022. |
Includes bibliographical references and index.
Identifiers: LCCN 2021030522 (print)
LCCN 2021030523 (ebook)
ISBN 9781478015413 (hardcover)
ISBN 9781478018032 (paperback)
ISBN 9781478022657 (ebook)
Subjects: LCSH: Qalandar Lal Shahbaz, 1177–1274— Shrines.
| Shrine of Lal Shahbaz Qalander (Sehwan, Pakistan) |
Sufis—Pakistan—Sehwan. | Sufism— Pakistan—Sehwan. |
Fakirs—Pakistan—Sehwan. |
Sexual minority community—Pakistan—Sehwan. |
Ethnology—Pakistan—Sehwan. | Muslim pilgrims
and pilgrimages—Pakistan—Sehwan. | BISAC: SOCIAL
SCIENCE / Anthropology / Cultural & Social | HISTORY /
Asia / India & South Asia
Classification: LCC BP188.8.P182 S449 2022 (print) |
LCC BP188.8.P182 (ebook) |
DDC 297.4/3554918—dc23/eng/20211105
LC record available at https://lccn.loc.gov/2021030522
LC ebook record available at https://lccn.loc.gov/2021030523

Cover art: Photograph by Omar Kasmani, 2009.

In the company of lovers
– past, present, future –

CONTENTS

NOTE ON ORTHOGRAPHY

Transliteration of terms from oral sources remains a challenge. My interlocutors spoke Urdu, Sindhi, Punjabi, Seraiki, and Balochi. While the terms and concepts in use often bear Arabic, Persian, or Sanskrit roots, my transliterations reflect a diverse sociolinguistic ethos and privilege the colloquial and the spoken over their etymological origin or written form. I adopt fakir instead of *faqir* to better capture the term's vernacular inflection and alternate etymology in Sehwan and not to privilege or reproduce its colonial referencing. I also remain aware that an easy recourse to translated terms, or my rendering of distinct Islamic concepts such as *dargah* (threshold) as *shrine* and *wali* (friend of Allah) as *saint*, is far from ideal given their Christian connotations. For the sake of readability, I have also minimized the use of diacritics. Similarly, plurals of most non-English terms are indicated by adding *s* (for instance, *kafis* for lodges instead of *kafiyun*). I employ italics for non-English words and English words that were used in otherwise Urdu sentences as well as to indicate emphasis. All translations are my own.

ACKNOWLEDGMENTS

Stories of arrival are very often also stories of companionships. This book is somehow also propelled by a once-peripheral argument between friends. Sehwan, 2012: On a sweltering July evening in the field, Delphine Ortis and I couldn't agree less on the term *intimacy* to describe saintly religious experience. It was on that occasion, as my field notes attest, that I first brought up and defended *intimacy* in its devotional and extrasexual terms. Karachi, the following year: Shayan Rajani's otherwise simple provocation to think of my material in relation to the Pakistani state would ultimately prompt me to venture beyond the personal and to explore intimacy's public infrastructures. Zurich, 2015: Bettina Dennerlein invited me to think more politically about the concerns and contours that queer theory was introducing into my project, more broadly what queer brought to the study of religion. Her gentle nudge animates the coda to this book. Finally, Lancaster, Pennsylvania, 2018: while at the Capacious Conference, an online chat with Blake Beaver on a dating app amusingly led me to Elizabeth Ault, the book's eventual editor. Arguments, provocations, flirtations, invitations—possibly also ones I am unable to recall or reproduce here—capture the various paths, prompts, and persuasions by which this book has arrived. That this work of many years has come to fruition is also not without the systematic support and long-term care I have received from my mentors and fellow scholars, friends and lovers, whose persons and contributions I wholeheartedly acknowledge here. The book is in their and others' debt, for solitary as the experience of writing so often feels, it is that craft by which we place ourselves in companies: citational, intellectual, affective.

My greatest debt is to the fakirs of Sehwan: all endeavors toward this book would have been entirely futile without their generosity. They are the ones who opened their hearts and minds to facilitate my project even when some were not too certain of my methods, let alone my means of learning or modes of knowing. They have trusted my motivations all the same and have, with their insights, recommendations, and deeply personal stories and conflicts, led me as well as this work in new and exciting directions.

This book has found its shores in the company of many a guide, though foremost among them is Hansjörg Dilger. This book simply would not exist without him. He has most closely guided this journey and in the process also shaped me as a scholar. I am most fortunate to have had his magnanimous support and incredible care over the years. First as my *Doktorvater* (doctor father)—the academic equivalent of the Sufi figure of the guide—and then as a project leader in collaborative research, his attentive thinking and intellectual generosity have enabled me to grow in my own skin, and for that I remain in his debt. The greater part of this research was carried out in the framework of a doctoral project at the Berlin Graduate School Muslim Cultures and Societies at Freie Universität, Berlin. It was made possible by a financial grant received from the German Research Foundation (DFG). Earlier fieldwork in 2009 and 2010 was carried out with the support of Aga Khan University (International) in the UK and Mission Interdisciplinaire Française du Sindh (MIFS), respectively. I am equally grateful to all members of the dissertation commission, especially to the project's cosupervisors, Magnus Marsden and Hermann Kreutzmann.

A huge thank you to Michel Boivin. He has remained a friend, a mentor, and an inspiration for my involvement in Sehwan. I have lovingly called him my *murshid*, the master who shows the path, for in his generosity and openheartedness as a scholar, he has proven to be a guide who never stops giving. So much of my understanding of Sehwan is indebted to him; so much of this work can only proceed in light of his scholarship. To the brilliant Elizabeth Ault, my editor at Duke University Press, my heartfelt gratitude: her insightful engagement has enabled this work to prosper in decisive ways and to find its own pathways. In her editorial care, I have won myself a cothinker, and for her remarkable support and company throughout, I remain thankful. This book is equally shaped by the generosity and support that it has received from its two anonymous readers. Their careful deliberations on my work and their insightful recommendations, not least the time and energies devoted during the review process, have been truly formative. This book is richer for their interlocution.

I remain particularly grateful to all those scholars and friends who have commented on various drafts, read chapters at different stages of the manuscript, and provided me with useful feedback. A heartfelt thank you to Kamran Asdar Ali for his longtime support of my research and the anthropological *masala* he brings to life and scholarship; to the incredible Greg Seigworth for his generous endorsement of my work, and also for simply being "affectionately yours"; to Jan Slaby for the intellectual friendship he offers and the inspiration he continues to be; to the brilliant Max Schnepf for being my queer partner in anthropological crime; to Ali Raza for his capacious cothinking; and to the very inspiring Anjali Arondekar for her sharp take on everything queer. In 2009, as I was making my transition to the social sciences, Sarah Bowen Savant shepherded me through my master of arts thesis at the Institute for the Study of Muslim Civilisations in London; Schirin Amir-Moazami and Manan Ahmed Asif guided my early years of doctoral coursework in Berlin. My gratitude in no less measure goes to them and all those who have in their own ways engaged with this research at different stages of its development and have left their lasting imprints: Delphine Ortis, Bettina Dennerlein, Margrit Pernau, Rémy Delage, Jürgen Wasim Frembgen, A. Azfar Moin, Shayan Rajani, Nasima Selim, Nida Kirmani, Ward Keeler, Farina Mir, Yasmin Saikia, Babak Rahimi, Umber bin Ibad, Nigel Rapport, Almut Schneider, Peter Pannke, Sonja Brentjes, Saʿdiyya Shaikh, and Todd Sekuler. This work is no less indebted to Sara Ahmed, Lauren Berlant, Kathleen Stewart, Elizabeth Freeman, and Christina Sharpe—scholars who, though I do not know them on personal terms, have remained all the same, in spirit and thought, inspiring and intimate companions. A special callout to Amira Mittermaier for an eye-opening conversation on a Berlin U-Bahn, more generally for her inspirational scholarship; and to Dominik Mattes for our joint explorations in the study of affect. I wish to thank Sophie Reynard and Yves Ubelmann for their maps and drawings; Rubab Paracha for her illustrations; and Benjamin Kossak and Liz Smith at Duke University Press for shepherding this book through the production process.

The long road to a book invariably involves writing, revisions, and rewriting. Sections of chapter 1 appeared in "Pilgrimages of the Dream:

On Wings of State in Sehwan Sharif, Pakistan," in *Muslim Pilgrimage in the Modern World*, edited by Babak Rahimi and Peyman Eshagi, 133–48 (Chapel Hill: University of North Carolina Press, 2019); some ethnographic details of chapters 2 and 3 can be traced to "Women (Un-)Like Women: The Question of Spiritual Authority among Female Fakirs of Sehwan Sharif," in *Devotional Islam in Contemporary South Asia: Shrines, Journeys and Wanderers*, edited by Michel Boivin and Rémy Delage, 47–62 (Abingdon, UK: Routledge, 2015); and an early incarnation of chapter 5 found itself in "Grounds of Becoming: Fakirs among the Dead in Sehwan Sharif, Pakistan," *Culture and Religion* 18, no. 2 (2017): 72–89. When compared to these earlier writings, the book departs significantly in conceptual terms. It has no doubt benefited from the editorial reviews of previous publications as well as the feedback this work has received over the years at various conferences and workshops.

The field research that I have been able to carry out in Sehwan over many years is due only to the kindness and hospitality of its people: fakirs and their spiritual masters, visiting pilgrims or those employed at the shrine, policemen, Auqaf officials, contract workers, tea boys, photographers. I am particularly grateful to Sayyid Mehdi Raza Shah Sabzwari, one of the traditional custodians of the shrine at Sehwan. His hospitality and support have been exceptional. I am also indebted to Sayyid Hasan Shah Khatdhani, a prominent spiritual figure of Sehwan, for the countless evenings during which I was able to partake of his unconditional guidance, wisdom, and generosity. Worthy of mention are also the Lakkiyari sayyids, who have welcomed my research endeavors in Sehwan. I would especially like to thank Nazir Ahmed Sehwani for being ever so forthcoming with his knowledge of local sources, histories, and traditions. His support was instrumental to my early work in Sehwan. I will forever be grateful to my dearest Marvi Mazhar for helping me first get access to women in the shrine courtyard back in 2009. I have also benefited from my exchanges in the field with researchers of the MIFS. The opportunity to share fields—physical and discursive—with a scholar like Michel Boivin has greatly advanced my historical understanding of the context; with Rémy Delage I have learned to appreciate procession routes and the complex organization of fakir lodges in the town; my ongoing conversations with Delphine Ortis, a dear friend and fellow anthropologist, have taught me much about Sehwan's ritual life, and for it I have come to better read my own material. She also makes return appearances in several chapters of this book. My research stay in Sehwan was graciously supported by the

Department of Antiquities, Government of Sindh, Pakistan. I would like to thank Dr. Kaleemullah Lashari, Mr. Wasim A. Ursani, and Mr. Saeed A. Awan, who have served as department secretaries during this period and with whose approval my stay at the department's rest house in Sehwan was facilitated. I am grateful to Hamir Soomro, without whose help and interventions I would not have been able to overcome some of the bureaucratic hurdles that came with accessing state institutions and archives.

Like all research, this work has also nurtured me beyond the field, through very personal labors of life in Berlin. Jérémie Mortier, Olivier Capillon, Bani Abidi, Schokofeh Kamiz, Rachel Knaebel, Sylvia Schedelbauer, Zahra Lakdawala, and Ali Raza: to these friends, my lovelies and other lovers, who bring meaning to a life in migration, a big thank you for your enduring friendships, for listening to my endless fakir stories, for bearing with my unsolicited disquisitions on intimacy. I am grateful to my colleagues at the Collaborative Research Center, Affective Societies, in whose company I have discovered my love for everything affect-y. I also appreciate the support I have received from colleagues at the Institute of Social and Cultural Anthropology at Freie Universität, Berlin. A sincere note of thanks to people at Leuchtstoff and Myxa, two cafés in Berlin-Neukölln, for accommodating my daily spells of writing. Just as this book has arrived by many paths, it has also taken me to several places. Parts of this book were also written during writing retreats in Istanbul, Austin, Thessaloniki, and Bolzano.

"To theorize, one leaves home," notes the anthropologist James Clifford (1989, 177). Yet departures and displacements, wanderings and wayfaring that ethnographic research brings about are in some measure also in service of knowing oneself, for such forays unsettle far more than they produce, theory or otherwise. When I first arrived in Sehwan in July 2009 at the tail end of a two-year MA program in Muslim Cultures, it was three years after I had quit a five-year career in architecture. A great deal was up in the air. It was only in time and in the company of fakirs that I would come to better understand that giving up a secure course in life and taking on new ones involves pursuing an evading cluster of promises; that such wayfaring against lines means that certain destinations will fall behind us; or that arriving takes a brush with uncertainty, ambivalence, and a fear of the unknown. Thus, I remain grateful also in cognizance of those who have not only witnessed this journey but have been affected by it in personal and profound ways. I wish to wholeheartedly thank my parents, whose general skepticism about what I do or why I do what I do has compelled me to reflect on what makes this work so personal; my dearest sister, Munazza Kasmani, whose faith, despite my wanderings, has not once wavered; and not least Amna Iqbal, or Amo, with whom I once learned to cherish dreams but also, to whose disadvantage, possibly, I have questioned orientations and dispensed with inherited lines. What makes this work deeply personal is hence also that which could not be salvaged in the wake of turmoil. It warrants the acceptance that Sehwan has altered me, in ways hard to describe, let alone put to page, or that I have come into my queer self not only in metropolises—Karachi-raised, academic by way of London, Berliner-by-love—but perhaps more definingly through the unstraight persuasions of an ancient and multifaith place of pilgrimage. In some ways, this book is that intimate journey. It is still, first and foremost, a fulfillment: one promise delivered in a pursuit still unfolding.

On Coming
Close

قُرب | *qurb*
(Urdu, from Arabic) Intimacy, closeness,
affective nearness, trust

An unfolding, a bloom, an elaboration: intimacy is an inward genre with outward skins. So long as to intimate is to imply more than to tell, make known through an indirect sign, coming close is to be in the queer course of disclosure. Affect, likewise, is a felt mode of indistinct knowing. *Queer Companions* asks, what unfolds or takes hold as individuals draw close to deceased Islamic saints in the present? It ruminates on the futures that intimacies with saints afford as well as the existing sociohistorical relations their enshrined figures frustrate, make awry, or simply expand. It trails patterns, rhythms, refrains—felt and enfleshed, be they tender, tormenting, or taut—that flourish between distinct but close bodies and by virtue of their affective bonding. Crucial to such thinking by way of the intimate is the book's predominant insight that intimacy blooms, if only haltingly and piecemeal, through critical affective relations, knowings, and obstinacies. These are *unstraight affordances* in terms of this book, or those inclined prospects of futuring that are revealed or foreclosed by virtue of one's coming close to saintly objects, often at the expense of other social objects, at times simply alongside them.

Queer Companions is an ethnography. Set in the ancient pilgrimage town of Sehwan in Pakistan's Sindh Province, it narrates the life-altering paths of fakirs (also *faqirs*).[1] They are the ascetically drawn protagonists of this book who, on the basis of their growing bonds with a thirteenth-century saint, abandon home, question inherited lines, and forego straight economies of family and work. Whether in dream meetings or in the midst of busy shrine economies, via attachment to tombs or through reclusiveness, coming close in this book has world-making ramifications: intimacy textures as much one's sense of being historical as saintly affections mobilize futures in excess of ascribed lines of the social. Intimate bonds with saints, as I understand and explore through various fakir life stories, enfold and unfurl consequences that suture scales of the personal and the political in Pakistan. These are, in the book's view, affective formations that imbricate individuals, society, and the state in a public architecture of intimacy.

Part of what I am pursuing here—refracting affect through saintly archives and Sufi-religious matrices—is the epistemological work of regathering intimacy in ways that do not squarely home in its Euro-American genealogies and secular orientations.[2] Islamic saints, strangers if not anomalies to queer and affect studies, are intimate lovers and queer companions in this book, knotty fellows if you will, whose more-than-human ties and tangles with the living—fakir or otherwise—serve to affectively reappraise the world. It follows that *queer* in this project isn't strictly a figure of sexuality. It serves rather as that capacious hermeneutic by which we come to read not so much religion queerly—what a project of queering Islam might demand of us—as we advance by reading queer religiously.[3] The distinct endeavor here is to appreciate how and why the unfrequented intersections of religion and queer, no matter how notoriously difficult or haltingly adaptive, are in fact openings.[4] *Queer Companions* avails the chance to define the terms and shapes of this critical meeting ground.

A dining room conversation in Karachi had gone awry. Using the English words *line* and *cross* in an otherwise Urdu sentence, my mother thought it timely to reprimand me. A heated argument ensued about a mere photograph taken in jest at Sehwan's shrine. It was in fact a photo template in which Amin, a photographer for hire at the shrine, had artificially inserted my image alongside the saint of Sehwan through computer-aided techniques—intimate company my mother found not one bit amusing. Saints, even if ubiquitous, are divisive figures in Pakistan, though none is more vexing than the saint in question: La'l Shahbaz Qalandar (d. 1274 CE, henceforth Lal) is a thirteenth-century mystic known for his radical rejection of Islamic religious institutions, norms, and practices.[5] Paradoxically, the antinomian saint is Pakistan's most beloved figure of devotion, whose tomb-shrine in Sehwan, a town of about a hundred thousand residents, draws millions each year.[6] As a modern-day avatar of an ancient site of pilgrimage, the town by the Indus River remains a magnet for ordinary pilgrims and radical ascetics alike. Devotees come from a whole spectrum of social, religious, and ethnic backgrounds. If Sehwan attracts the poorest of the poor, Lal's followers have also included the country's former prime ministers and its top fashion models and photographers. Sufi by renown, Shivaite in heritage, and increasingly Shi'i in following, Sehwan is in many ways Pakistan at its complex best.

Back in the family dining room, the photograph featuring the saint and myself had ruffled quite some feathers. Pictures like these were otherwise popular mementos. Pilgrims in Sehwan were routinely caught in prayer-like postures at the shrine, posing with the saint as it were, facing, however, not his tomb as was customary, but the camera. Photographers carried albums illustrating a variety of available templates. For a reasonable expense of 50 rupees, one was able to place oneself in a graphic assemblage featuring not just saintly figures, sites, and symbols but also political personalities. The one featuring Benazir Bhutto and Lal was an all-time favorite. Also popular was the template with Bodlo, the saint's most favorite disciple. On the left side of this composition is a particularly affectionate scene: Bodlo has his head resting in the saint's lap while the saint's body is seen leaning forward, his palm securing the disciple's head in a loving embrace, so close that his body is almost indistinguishable from the body of the saint. Bodlo's intimacy with Lal is no accident. Believed to be his contemporary, Bodlo is the fakir par excellence whose shrine is the second most important site for pilgrims in Sehwan today.[7] The melding figures confirm Bodlo's affective closeness to the saint but also a saintly status of his own. On the right side of this template is the space where the pilgrim's figure is usually inserted. The elaborate blue-tiled facade of the mausoleum serves as backdrop, while Lal is additionally featured flying above in his popular falcon form (see fig. 1.1). What had tipped things over with my mother that night was a different iteration of this image in which Bodlo's face had been virtually replaced with mine. In this version, I was no longer just an onlooker standing next to an affectionate scene between saint and fakir. I was the one in loving embrace with the saint, my head securely placed in his lap, my body queerly close to his, arguably too close for comfort (see fig. 1.2). The ensuing argument with my mother was proof that such intimacy with the saint, even if doctored through photo software and relegated to an image, wasn't to be taken lightly.

To be fair, the risqué move of intervening in the iconography of the saint was not lost on me either. I clearly remember my hesitation in the moment the photograph was being worked over. Graphic collaging, cutout figures with changeable clothes and replaceable heads, were common features in creating poster art of the saints, items usually sold in markets adjoining shrines in Pakistan (Frembgen 2012b, 130). Still, I was not sure how a request to replace Bodlo's face with mine would fare with Amin. We were sitting in a tiny shop right across one of the shrine's secondary entrances when I spontaneously brought up the idea of tweaking the format. He had paused for a moment, asked me to confirm what I had said, then smilingly proceeded with the task on his computer. To our utter surprise, the photograph became an instant hit at the shrine as Amin proudly showed it to others. The embrace, which some at the shrine read as the saint's approval of my research, didn't really raise any eyebrows. Instead, photographers and pilgrims couldn't stop commenting on the likeness of my face to that of the saint's favorite disciple. What caused marveling at the shrine generated disturbed reactions at home. When I shared the photograph with my mother, I counted on her good humor, just as when she had responded to other templates, the one with Benazir Bhutto, for

instance. I expected her to see what people at the shrine saw: if not the saint's favor, the uncanny resemblance to his disciple perhaps. Come to think of it, my mother did see as others saw. To her, much like the shrine-goers, the saint's affection in the photograph was no laughing matter: neither dormant in any way nor a meaningless object that one might overlook. If not the power of saints, the power of intimacy was unmistakably compelling. As my mother put it that evening, *a line has been crossed.*

Then, three years into my research and hardly 300 kilometers north of Karachi, Sehwan still felt like a world farthest from where I had grown up, a distance impossible to cover in a four-hour drive to the town. That shrines were frowned upon at home was hardly news to me. Invoking saints or seeking their assistance had no place in the reformist version of Islam I had grown up with.[8] A visit to a shrine, however ubiquitous in the Pakistani landscape, never featured in our daily lives; venerating saints was, in fact, shunned at home, equivalent to the great sin of attributing partners to the one God. I was also aware that my growing involvement with Sehwan as a site of intellectual inquiry and my constant discussion of its affective-emotional lifeworlds evoked all shades of anxiety at home. Did I believe in miracles of the saint? Was I taking part in rituals? Why was there a red thread on my wrist? Had the saint appeared in my dreams? Did I consume food offerings at the shrine? These were questions regularly asked of me. Why saints make for knotty figures of the social, are anxiety-evoking and proverbially contentious, also has to do with the notion that saints as per Islamic imagination are not simply the sanctified dead, comfortably buried and done away with. Saints are literally friends of Allah—*wali* (pl. *auliya'*) in Urdu from Arabic—who, precisely on grounds of intimacy and by virtue of their closeness to God, are privy to divine knowledge and potentially active companions to the living.[9] They are, as is commonly believed, the more-than-living. Invariably, then, the hot question of correct Islamic practice, a perpetually debated and argued issue of public relevance in Pakistan, involves the contentious place and agency of saintly, noncorporeal and otherworldly beings in the world.[10] Naveeda Khan (2012) and Katherine P. Ewing (2006) have both in their own ways shown how such lines of discord have a way of cutting through Pakistani publics—workplaces, neighborhoods, families, and households—enabling at times a critical and creative space for reordering social relations through engaging in religious disputation.[11] In our home, such space for arguing *in* Islam was often found when sharing meals. Just as it is both perfectly ordinary and characteristically Islamic for Muslims to make meaning in difference from one another—a point Shahab Ahmed makes in his framework for conceptualizing Islam—the everyday object of the dining table offered a perfect setting: it laid out, if you will, for every member of the family, an individually scaled but historically given possibility and position from which to hermeneutically enter "a vast and polyphonic discursive terrain" (2016, 193). It also bears mentioning that just as Sehwan isn't simply a Shi'i place, neither entirely Sufi, whether shrine-going or otherwise, being Sunni in Pakistan is not a settled matter either. It involves navigating a range of theological opinions and doctrinal orientations from four schools of jurisprudence to Ahl-e Hadis of my family who follow neither.[12] In their religious but equally class-inflected worldview, figures like Lal were historical beings properly dead, incapable of affecting the world in the present and whose tombs drew only the uneducated, the unenlightened. Hence, it wasn't really the views on saints and shrines that struck me, but rather a profound paradox that shone through such microanxieties. Saints' allure, which my family so vehemently rejected, still harbored a futural property, as it were—enduring affects borne, if not from their remote acting beyond the grave as is commonly believed of Islamic saints, then of my more deliberate and immediate ways of coming close to them. My affinity for Sehwan, which my father had once compared to the risk of drowning, was an unfolding peril insofar as such ties introduced other historical objects or did not extend existing shapes of inheritance. Saints were risqué companions, shrines a risky business, and a simple photograph, in this instance, a harrowing record of a wayward affair.

Had I come too close? Did I go too far? I then wondered. A line or not, in moving from the right of the composition to the left in the photograph, I had indeed crossed some distance. So long as to move toward or to be close to certain objects involved a gradual becoming remote to certain others, the saint's embrace or embracing the saint were political moves with ethical stakes whose implications far exceeded a singular scene of intimacy. What such intimacy dis/closes, that is to say, what it unfoldingly affords or impedes, makes up the greater material of this book. It was in fact a woman at Sehwan's shrine who had first pointed me to the stirring effects of tarrying with saintly relations, that is to say, such intimacy's durational affects, its *long middle* so to speak, that space of feeling out before intimacy is durable enough to count as an event (Berlant and Edelman 2014, 22). Figures like her are primary interlocutors in this work: women, men, and gender-variant fakirs who leave home in pursuit of saintly objects to eventually and invariably arrive in Sehwan. They come from all over the country: from urban metropolises to small villages, from medium-sized towns to sparse settlements. Their life-altering paths in this ethnography are life stories of coming close. Whether converging at the shrine or moving through remote realms of dream, crossing material stretches or imaginal thresholds, coming close to Lal invariably involved going far along social, spatial, and temporal lines. It is in saintly trysts and fakir bonds that this book locates and sutures notions of intimacy and futurity, the latter being intimacy's capacity for forward endurance in time.[13] I argue that coming close to saints, whether or not yielding, embroils public economies and ecologies of affect. I also contend that saintly intimacy bears futural-political import insofar as it affords individuals expanded possibilities of the social and, if only durationally, authors more-than-inherited ways of being in and with the world. Long before I was to articulate this line of thinking with companions in queer and affect theory, a woman fakir had already evoked its terms: Zaheda had serendipitously, as it were, divined a prognosis of my research. Her line, much like my own, is a pathway into the book.

Our lines had first crossed on the white marble floor of the shrine courtyard in July 2009. By late afternoon that day, the heat was giving way and, suitably enough, the general mood at the shrine had turned leisurely. Clusters of women were hanging out under the open sky. As I singled out Zaheda for a chat, I had assumed her to be like other women at the shrine, that is to say, vow-making women in pursuit of healing or improvement in their everyday circumstances. Part of that expectation derived from literature on South Asian shrines and sites of ritual healing.[14] A great deal of that was true for Sehwan too. Female pilgrim narratives and women's motivations to be at saints' places were largely marked by familial disputes and personal tragedies: many of these were accounts of illnesses, afflictions, family hardships, possessions, and evil spells. Zaheda's purpose, as I would come to learn that afternoon, was unlike that of most women. She was a fakir or, better still, "in the line of fakiri," as she herself put it. *Fakir*—also the word for *beggar* in Urdu, at times an honorific for transgenders in Sindhi—here refers to persons who take up voluntary poverty as an ascetic performance of devotion. To be poor, as Delphine Ortis (2020, 317) has noted, is to embody the ideal that fakirs possess nothing, not even their own selves. Fakirs in this book are distinctive individuals who arrive in Sehwan as a result of prophetic dreams and personal callings, some in search of mystical mentors; others leave home in the face of family feuds, accidents, court cases, illnesses, disappointment in love, or simply out of severe economic or social deprivation. Many live on donations from pilgrims and devotees, but some also rely on their practice as spiritual guides and healers to run households and support families. Acquiring spiritual roles also means that fakirs earn a measure of respect, which not only comes to remedy the disadvantage that such persons might bear in terms of economic class and social status, but as in the case of women, also advances their otherwise rare prospects for a public life. In short, Zaheda's public place in the shrine was precisely a result of her fakir status.

At the time of our first meeting, Zaheda was in her early forties. She had been married for about twenty-five years, with eight children, and belonged to a middle-income household. Intrigued as I was by Zaheda's singular purpose and circumstances, I remember being equally amused by her choice of the English word *line* in an Urdu conversation. Line wasn't a limit, a thing to cross or transgress, as my mother had meant in reacting to the photograph. It was a figure of orientation in Zaheda's use, a thing that distinguished her from other women. More compellingly, in this statement of hers, to be a fakir was not so much to be someone as it was to be going somewhere, a path to something, a line, which in Zaheda's description she had been precariously attending to for over seven years. Metaphors of orientation and journeying made sense also because these were citations of what Muslims call *tariqat*, the path of the mystics.[15] More remarkable, however, was the fact that for months at a stretch, a thousand or so kilometers away from home, Zaheda spent her days and nights alone in the shaded arcades that flanked the length of the shrine's forecourt. She was regularly surrounded by women, largely visitors who would consult her on spiritual matters. Though despite their everyday presence at saints' places, lone and unchaperoned women were not a common sight in Sehwan.[16] Zaheda, too, knew well that her stay at the shrine of Sehwan at the expense of Sargodha, a city in the Punjab where her family lived, demanded explaining.

"I am very close to him," Zaheda had remarked in one of our early exchanges. What sounded like a somewhat ordinary statement carried a pronounced sense of achievement. She had backed it up with a quick *masha'allah* (what Allah has willed) as if to protect herself from her own sense of pride or the evil eye of others. Her use of the word *qarib* (close) signaled her distinction from other women and her chosen status in relation to Lal, the saint of Sehwan whom she had simply referred to in the third person (him). *Qurb*, from which the word *qarib* derives, is a concept that stands for affective nearness and conditions of intimacy. Thus, to be close in this instance is not simply to be *nazdik*, the other Urdu word for proximity, which would speak to her physical location in the shrine courtyard in relation to the tomb of the saint. *Qarib* additionally portrays Zaheda as a bearer of *qurb*, the one who has found closeness to the saint in emotional-affective terms. It is such intimacy that distinguishes fakir figures from ordinary pilgrims and enables them to perform as intermediaries with the saint and as spiritual guides to their followers. In fact, as Delphine Ortis (2020) has argued, through being in the service of saints and by virtue of their engagement with devotional artifacts, fakirs, though exclusively men in her case, are able to build themselves up into potential saints in Sehwan.

In evoking the figure of the line, not only had Zaheda evoked the question of being oriented, but being in line also meant awaiting an outcome. Being close or near in this sense was also to be nearly there. Seven years into her pursuit, Zaheda at the time of our first meeting described herself as on the verge of accomplishing her fakir goals; she anticipated that things were about to settle. In other words, to be close was to be imbued with a sense of futurity. It pointed to the impending or to that which was about to happen and thus was already a presence without yet being actually present in the present tense (Muñoz 2009, 9). What followed, however, through the course of my research was contrary to Zaheda's expectations. Her protracted stays at the shrine regularly invited her husband's displeasure, keeping her occupied with domestic trouble. In the years to come, she would question her marriage as well as her fakir pursuit. She would fear the loss of lines and the saint's affection toward her, become riddled with doubts and dilemmas, conditions I take up in chapter 3 of this book. Although even before her ordeals began, Zaheda was acutely aware that being in the line also meant a parting with other lines, other objects, other places. Far beyond her own story and circumstances, Zaheda's *qurb* with the saint, the conditions of its possibility, the possibilities it births and the existing relations it seizes, become a way to think through intimacy in this book.

More critical is the idea that private feeling or intimate relations with saints carry ramifications for broader regimes and critiques of power. However personal Zaheda's circumstances in the courtyard seemed to me at first and irrespective of how relations unfolded, she was, by virtue of her ties with the saint, implicated in the shrine's greater political economy. Part of this can be explained by the fact that shrines like Sehwan are public endowments (or *waqf* properties) in Pakistan, governed through bureaucratic means of the state. Authorized by a federal ordinance in 1959, saints and their places have since come under the purview of the Department of Auqaf, a subsidiary of the Ministry of Religious Affairs.[17] A move as radical as the shrine's takeover from its traditional custodians in 1960 has since served to disrupt consolidations of power among the local elite in Sehwan. These include sayyids, that is, families that claim descent from the Prophet Muhammad, and who held control over shrine revenues at least since the colonial period, as well as local Hindu patrons long associated with shrine services and ceremonies.[18] Public administration has thus also involved a straightening of the shrine's Shivaite heritage on the part of the state (see chapters 1 and 2). Given long-standing, patrilineal structures of spiritual transmission in Sehwan, fakir lines like Zaheda's are neither the norm nor exactly free of what the Pakistani state disposes or arbitrates. In fact, as part of the shrine's fractured authorities, the state's governing presence unsettles much more than just local economies and configurations of power.

February 16, 2017, at home in Berlin: I was on the phone with a journalist friend from Karachi who worked for the *Friday Times*, an English-language weekly. Just hours before, and barely meters away from where Zaheda and I had first crossed paths, a suicide bomber had struck the courtyard of Sehwan's shrine. More than eighty people were killed. It fit the tragic pattern of recent years whereby key Sufi shrines in Pakistan have periodically been targeted by hardline militants and radical Islamist networks. As I penned a commissioned response to the tragedy, it was plain to me that plural conceptions of the social and compound ideas of the divine that figures like Lal and Sehwan bear forth will always be unsettling in a Muslim-national present that rests on a severance from its polytheistic Hindu past.[19] This aside, it is also widely understood that shrines invite all manner of claim making and contest, or that Islamic saints make for immensely resourceful partners, if not also rivals. As parallel networks of social welfare, Sufi shrines provide free food, healing, and shelter to the poor in Pakistan. These are sites where devotees make vows and enter into beneficial transactions with saints and where saints return favors and generate revenue and work opportunities; where pilgrims cross religious lines, share substances and rituals, meet fakirs, and find living spiritual masters.[20] It is here that women deal with spirits; their radical desires can be publicly owned at shrines, their sorrows proverbially eaten away (Taneja 2017, 224, 266).[21]

More profound still is the underlying idea that Islamic saints as *walis* are entitled to *wilayat,* a concept that empowers their figures with territorial influence and spatial authority. In such understanding, saints are often in a relation of contest with rival forms and political sources of sovereignty. Cognates of the term *wali* encompass meanings that range from friendship to governance and guardianship and explain why, historically speaking, such figures' authority was "considered as having a direct influence on the political events and material destiny of the realm over which it was exercised" (Digby 1990, 71).[22] It is no coincidence that saints' shrines, as seats of *wilayat,* are commonly regarded as durbars in South Asia, that is, royal courts or courts of law (Bellamy 2011).[23] Saints, intimate lovers as they are in this book, are also known to act as judges who arbitrate conflicts and pronounce verdicts. Their meddling roles and reputations are part of the reason why "shrines break the order of straight lines" (Mittermaier 2008, 48) or explain, for that matter, how shrines can run parallel to projects of the nation-state, why saints are a worry to the political, or, in the interest of this book, what informs the Pakistani state's motivations to govern *with* saints (see chapters 1 and 2). These are also cues for what exasperates saints' and the state's respective and joint counterpublics in Pakistan. One could argue that at stake in recent violent confrontations is a contest of mediation, not interpretation of religion, as everyday disagreements within my family would have us surmise. Emilio Spadola has noted that in order to successfully destroy saintly authority, militants or antishrine actors are faced with the challenge of effectively destroying "shrines' literal *appeal*—the call of the shrine" (2019, 224, emphasis in original). In a historical and transcultural account of shrine destruction, Ali Azfar Moin (2015) has argued that confrontational acts of violence and desecration of religious sites are better read as enactments of sovereignty: to the extent that the attack at Sehwan by antistate actors and networks is an assertion of rival sovereignty through an act of shrine desecration, it also perversely confirms the enshrined saint as mediator and sovereign, the one who acts and calls, if not in place of, then in tandem with, powers of the Pakistani state. In Lal's durbar at Sehwan, pilgrims continue to return the saint's call in great numbers (see fig. I.3). Devotees petition as much as they await decisions, seek refuge at his shrine, or simply partake of his presence.

Folding a horrific episode of violence with a woman's labor of intimacy in the saint's courtyard—same place, different times—is not to give voice to the easy discourse of Sufis-under-threat or, for that matter, to pitch good Islam versus bad. Rather, it here serves to establish the idea that fakir relations

FIGURE I.3
In the durbar of Lal: women
by the saint's tomb, 2018.

with Lal are in fact inscribed in a greater set of radical affordances, good or otherwise, coincident or not, that Sehwan and its saint bring to bear in Pakistani society. As much as the Pakistani state regulates shrine lifeworlds, administers their manifold revenues, I argue that it also serves to advance people's material and affective access to saints. Zaheda's vexing departure from the domestic and her access to a public life at the shrine involve possibilities that dis/close by virtue of her coming close to the saint. Such affordances, I contend, are cofigured through multiple scales and relations, and fold out as part of a greater historical process. Thus, attendant to my deliberations on saintly intimacies is the idea that intimacy is a public genre: in coming close to saintly objects, as inwardly moving as such process is, individuals do not withdraw, rather draw near to public economies and historical ecologies of affect. After all, saintly relations, even at their yielding best, routinely feature moments of disorientation or occasions when such orientations fail, become knotty or obstinate, or particularly when saints no longer afford what they might once have promised.

Zaheda's story of being in the line—and also those of others in this book—serves as a perfect illustration of orientations that involve and introduce affective pathways to more-than-given histories and futures. The rendering of affective ties with saints in terms of orientations, to draw from Sara Ahmed (2006, 21), can be a way to understand how turning affections toward saintly objects is a turning away such that it threatens to take us off a certain line, displace given objects, exasperate existing social relations, and support the pursuit of less-ordinary lifelines. My view that turning toward saintly objects, or in Ahmed's (2006, 56) terms, facing some ways more than others, affords queer prospects hangs on the understanding that what is straight, properly linear, or unmarked is not a matter of a single norm but refers to a more pervasive notion of guidelines. Tim Ingold uses the example of rules and margins in school exercise books to show how such lines "present no physical barrier to movement, but nevertheless entail consequences—more or less dire—should they be crossed" (2016, 160). Fakir pursuits are famously arduous and likewise never without consequence, also for the simple fact that they betray inherited lines or extend outside commonplace logics of reproduction.

Ascribing lines to fakirs, as Zaheda did, isn't entirely novel, especially if one is to attend to the common Urdu expression *lakir ka fakir*, literally, "fakir of the line." In everyday terms, the expression conveys a lack of originality, blind faith in one's way of life, a sense of predictability in predetermined patterns of action in that to be a *lakir ka fakir* is to tread the beaten path. In short, to be unquestioning of oneself is to be like a fakir; to be uninventive in affairs of life is also fakir-like. But fakir lines, as the many life stories in this book attest, involved a fundamental questioning of their paths, an altering condition of being affectively drawn, a carrying on with relations never entirely knowable or routinely secure. What is seldom appreciated of the proverb in question is how the fakir also stands for intimacy with an object, attachment to a different course of action toward that object, such that to follow a line like a fakir is to stay the course. It is to be committed to its linearity whatever its form, to tarry with what a line in bloom offers or seizes—in other words, to remain dedicated to where a path may take us. Fakir lives in this book reveal what it means to abide by, draw closer to, expect, or await a thing, just as such committing to a line of futurity, being aligned, so to speak, can lead to a being out of line.

Coming close to saints expands one's field of social and ethical relations in the present. Growing affections also texture what being historical or futural means. The public blooms of intimacy I read in and across individual life stories are long "temporal accounts of affectivity" in Jan Slaby's (2020, 173) terms: inclinations, prospects, postures that proceed as much from the present as these are drawn from what has been going on. Slaby's rumination hangs on Christina Sharpe's (2016) notion of "the wake," which is specifically concerned with unfolding and unresolved conditions of Black non/being within the contemporary.[24] The context notwithstanding, he articulates a foundational relationship between affect and what has been. It informs the book's view that intimacy is a space of bloom. Or that, though happening in the now, intimacy is also that prevailing affective texture through which the past filters into the future or "remains operative within the sensual fabric that enables and stages, prefigures and disfigures the present" (2020, 174).

The book's notion of unstraight affordances makes it possible to discuss dis/closures of intimacy, that is, how saintly bonds in bloom reveal or foreclose historically operative prospects in the present. The ecological psychologist James Gibson (1979, 127) coined the term *affordance* to name "the complementarity of the animal and the environment" or what a historical environment, for good or ill, offers, provides, or furnishes. Unlike mine, Gibson's primary concern is visual perception. Detailing how an observer might relate to substances, surfaces, objects, and animals, he notes that "affordance cuts across the dichotomy of subjective-objective and helps us to understand its inadequacy. It is equally a fact of the environment and a fact of behavior. It is both physical and psychical, yet neither" (129). Affordance, a concept more widely adopted in design, materiality studies, and human-computer interactions, refers to "the perceived or actual properties" of an object "that determine just how the thing could possibly be used" (Norman 1988, 9).[25] For instance, one might ordinarily remark that a chair intuitively affords a sitting on, a standing on too, possibly even throwing, whereas balls afford throwing and bouncing, and only when large enough can be sat on. Similarly, knobs are for turning, and a particular design interface on a digital screen might allow users to swipe left and right. Unstraight affordances then, no matter explicitly given, implied, or hidden, are queer inclinations specified by a relationship, whether dis/closed within a given interaction or tied to a historical ecology. This said, to be afforded a thing, for good or worse, does not reduce the fakirs of this book to passive or reactive agents in relation to the saint. In fact, affordance is better understood as a reciprocal notion: "behavior affords behavior," in Gibson's (1979, 135) terms.[26] It would follow that saints are not doing the affording on their own, *suo moto*; rather, these are historical figurations of intimacy either prompted or in need of requiting, leaving fakirs, also scholars, to parse a coauthored reality that takes shape through a complex interplay of mutual affordances. Viewed another way, such companionship is about how individuals turn perceptive with saints—"a gangly accrual of slow or sudden accretions" by which saintly historical agencies reach a level of expressivity in fakir ways of being (Stewart 2010, 339)—and equally, how saints in turn find their bearings in the world as the more-than-living. Affordance in this book, as that which intimacy dis/closes, unstraight or otherwise, hangs on how each companion perceives and attends to the qualities of the other. It is therefore critical that intimate partners appreciate the limited opportunities for action, or simply recognize where in a given interaction such opportunities may lie (Taylor 2012, 8). It also means that a failure to recognize an affordance or not heeding it does not take away from the opportunity intimacy presents or its capacity to unstraighten ordinary futures. As a notion that operates in the company of queer, unstraight in this book adds conceptual capacity for theorizing social prospects that evolve against due or expected course.[27] It is also that figure of historical inclination by which our relation to the past is altered just as we can appreciate how a for-granted continuity between inheritance and reproduction is disrupted or made askew in the present. This said, what is at work here is not so much a neat, singular, or paramount history, but rather the multiple, unresolved, even sparse notions of the past and the present that are mobilized through felt and enfleshed modes of saintly bonds. Thus, unstraight affordances give name to a whole set of ideas and inclinations, feelings and knowings, figures and futures that (saintly) intimacies draw and dis/close, or simply those prospects of the social that would otherwise have remained remote or discreet, out of public path or capture, or that ordinarily hang aslant to straight, secular, or dominant histories.

Part of what this book must confront is how what ostensibly betrays the straight—"straight" being also the righteous path in Islamic terms (Najmabadi 2014, 172)—can be yielding all the same in social-spiritual terms.[28] Approaching fakir pursuits in the vocabulary of unstraight is not entirely amiss when the saint of Sehwan, after whom fakir lives are modeled and toward whose shrine fakir journeys are oriented, is associated with a thirteenth-century band of antinomian mystics, more precisely, *qalandar*s whose spiritual merit was in fact premised on their deviance and departure from established religious lines and social norms. Katherine P. Ewing has observed how the prototypical *qalandar* in its contemporary iterations in urban Pakistan "confronts the proper Muslim" and "challenges the naturalness of the prevailing social order from within" (2006, 202, 217).[29] It ought to be said that fakir quests in the postcolonial present are shaped by conditions distinct from those of their predecessors. *Qalandar*s were part of an anarchistic ethos specific to cultures of the Persian world, and who resisted the institutionalization and elite formations of Sufi brotherhoods of the time.[30] Liberated from social custom and often regarded as *be-shar* (without shariah/law), a defining characteristic of *qalandar*s, as Ahmet Karamustafa (2006) notes, was their "persistent cultural and social iconoclasticism and unconventionalism." Such figures were notorious for transgressive bodily acts, extreme isolation, perpetual wandering, and an ostentatious rejection of social-religious institutions and authorities. Reading historical sources on the symbolism of hair among Persian *qalandar*s, Lloyd Ridgeon (2010) makes the case that antinomian practice or betraying proper or standard Islamic religious code, even if designed to shock public sensibility, is not an argument for such figures' lack of attachment to Quranic and religious referents insofar as their deviant performances served to uphold an ethical relation to the divine. In fact, the *qalandar* topos, in its literary iterations, stood for the idea that deliberate and open disregard for social convention was an undertaking "in the cause of 'true' religious love" (Karamustafa 2006, 33). Similarly, Shahab Ahmed (2016) offers the fascinating case of *madhhab-i ʿishq*, a love-centered "mode of being with God where love is [equally] a way of going about being Muslim" (38). Prevalent among its aficionados—across the vast geography of what he has identified as the Balkans-to-Bengal complex in a period enduring from the fourteenth to the late nineteenth centuries—was the cultural practice of wearing one's hat crooked, *kajkulahi*. He suggests that to wear the hat thus was "an act of social bravado" and "a statement, made deliberately by the individual hat-wearer, and read consciously as such by society, that the person was not concerned to be seen to be conforming to the prescribed appearance of moral uprightness and public propriety." Yet for the wearer, he suggests, its crookedness connoted an inclination toward the divine and therefore a distinct mode of making meaning, which was located not in legalistic but precisely in aesthetic—and might I add affective—models (Ahmed 2016, 202–3). What Shahab Ahmed is arguing here is that such crooked orientation toward divine love—"loving being risky business" as he reminds the reader—does not ferry the individual beyond or outside Islam; "rather, by constituting crooked-hattedness in terms of Islam," the wearer constitutes "Islam in terms of crooked-hattedness" (204).

The reading I am, however, inclined to pursue is that fakir ways of being in the present are enfleshed and affective endurances of social deviance, religious protest, and disguised mystical excellence. These tropes have varyingly prevailed in Sufi con/texts, practices, and bodies at least since the eleventh century.[31] In other words, these are *sustained affective textures* that carry over and extend historically given possibilities of living an otherwise life. Thus, intimacy with saintly figures and the public histories they bear afford fakir individuals a situatedness to act from, a posture, so to speak, not so much outside or beyond but beside Islamic norms.[32] *Beside* makes for an interesting proposition to think along unstraight, which, in Eve Sedgwick's terms, "permits a spacious agnosticism about several of the linear logics that enforce dualistic thinking" (2003, 8) or whose "defining relationality is internal as much as it is directed toward the norms it may challenge" (9). Fakir orientation toward a thirteenth-century *qalandar* is not exactly a straightforward relation to begin with, especially when such mystics' itinerant lives and extreme isolation make them perfectly evading figures in the historical record. This is true for the saint of Sehwan too, whose hard-to-locate, mixed, and fractured heritage, as I parse in chapters 1 and 2, makes him a figure of mystery and multiplicity. Fakir lines to Lal are made up of tilting, diverging, or broken-up orientations that refract through dense legends or sparse historical record and resist orderly figurations of the saint. Consider simply the detail that Lal bears at least three genealogies—Sufi, Shi'i, and Shivaite—or that his followers cannot quite agree on his doctrinal persuasion, Sufi affiliations, not even his actual name, Sayyid Usman Marwandi. The saint is better known by the three-part epithet Lal Shahbaz Qalandar.[33] Lal's Shi'i descent through the Isma'ili line is well established; however, he is also claimed through Suhrawardi and Qadiri Sufi registers.[34] His site of burial, the present-day shrine at Sehwan, is thought to replace an ancient Shiva sanctuary.[35] Sources remain incredibly scarce, but in addition to Shi'i-Isma'ili influence in the region, Boivin (2012b, 40) notes that Shivaism and Daryapanth were two principal forms of Hinduism rooted in Sehwan at the time of Lal's arrival. Archaeological findings as well as continuing

Hindu pilgrimage in and around the region confirm a greater pattern of Sufi sites, which at times have coincided with places of Shivaite veneration in the region.[36] Jhule Lal, the modern chant directed at the saint, was once a call to the river deity of the Indus worshipped by the Hindu Daryapanthis.[37] The name Sehwan is itself a remnant of the older Shivvahan (the village of Shiva).[38] And the shrine, whether formerly a temple or not, evidences a rich history of Hindu association and patronage.[39] Lal's unresolved history explains why his shrine, along with its relics, revenues, services, and ceremonies, has remained riddled by different claims. It has historically attracted long-drawn-out disputes of authority involving fakirs, princely patrons, sayyid elite, traditional custodians, and, more recently, the Pakistani state.[40]

Whether plurally sacred or religiously risqué, Sehwan demands as much as it exhausts comprehensibility. Religious complexity, however, doesn't always warrant that we explain one tradition through the other.[41] In fact, to read Sehwan as ambiguously Islamic, as Carla Bellamy would have it, underestimates, in my view, believers' capacity to find clearings amid sacred density.[42] The ambition of this book either way lies not in how or in what terms Sehwan is an Islamic place, rather what its plural orientations, abundant histories, fractured heritage, and compound sense of the divine do to prevailing relations, economies, and processes of affect in the context of a postcolonial, Muslim national present. By the same token, it is not squarely in transgressing but in asserting otherwise, being beside Islamic precepts, distilling meaning through religion's oblique historical models, aesthetic and affective, wherein I inscribe its queer-political value.

Critical to the conceptual ecologies of this book is the notion of public intimacy. The book's deliberations follow in light of Lauren Berlant's statement, "Intimacy builds worlds." If indeed intimacy not only creates anew but also "usurps places meant for other kinds of relation" (Berlant 1998, 281), I point to the political stakes and futural bearings of saintly intimacy, which is to consider all that intimacy frustrates as it thrives, the ordinary relations it threatens to replace but also the plural possibilities of relating it births in the process of its bloom—for individuals, society, and the state in Pakistan. I explore not only what intimacy is or means in the context of individual fakir lives but also how intimacy endures or what it does in and to a particular field of power relations as it unravels, unfolds over time. The book's stance that fakirs develop intimate bonds with saints or that saints have a way of exhausting other social relations is, however, not an argument for one dyadic relationship replacing another; rather, it points to a radical copresence of polyvalent relations. In fact, saintly intimacy, even when it involves a single or dominant figure of bonding, is always already embroiled in a historical field of diverse, mediating, or hierarchical relations, which means that for such intimacy to endure, fakirs must work with the complex ethical-political demands their plural attachments bring forth in the present. To the extent that "intimacy emphasizes relationality" (Wilson 2012, 27), it must also tackle the difference between forms of coming close and conditions of being intimate, not least the ways in which these are affectively sutured. Across its manifold forms, intimacy is a way of extending into the world in close companionship, be it through forms and orders of ritual, language, time, or sex. In a different project on queer intimacies and migrant feeling, I have noted how "intimacy is always pointing us, orienting us to certain kinds of becomings, beings, temporalities, not only in the moment it plays out but also how it impinges on us and the world afterwards, takes various afterlives so to speak" (Kasmani 2019b). Intimacy is futural insofar as it precludes certain ways of going forward, or illuminates the future's distinct potentials and possibilities, howsoever they are carried in the present or even if they are unrealized or eventually lost.

In a Sufi constellation, ideas of intimacy transact with notions of *suhbet* and *uns*. In literary terms, *uns* refers to feelings of love and affection or the effect of witnessing God's beauty. It can be regarded as a spiritual-affective condition whereby the heart becomes permeated by God's love. *Suhbet* on the other hand denotes companionship. It can refer to a saintly meeting or an assembly, a discourse, or conversation.[43] Not only that, Sufi texts and manuals have historically employed erotic language of passionate love and sexual union to describe how intimate bonds take shape between masters and disciples as well as to understand human encounters with the divine.[44] A sensuous and affective play between bodies is also traceable beyond the discursive. Pilgrims kissing Lal's tomb, women singing to the saint, men's shirtless torsos in flagellation, sick and seemingly possessed bodies, screaming, losing composure, and then regaining it—all of these are daily occurrences in Sehwan. Making offerings, ingesting substances, touching relics, dealing spirits, such *erotics of piety*, to lean on Finbarr B. Flood (2014), are in this book's view tied to the ordinary formation of saintly bonds. Intimacy, then, no matter how variously conceived or distinctly experienced, is conversant with sacrality all the same.

When it comes to fakir paths, it is important to consider how intimacy endures over time, which is to critically think how those in conditions of bonding, attachment, or companionship tarry with its dis/closures, especially when relations are continually haunted by the possibility of such ties coming undone. In other words, being drawn is not enough for drawing close. In Berlant's (1998, 281) terms, for intimacy to survive, it requires a persistent activity that can secure and stabilize conditions of closeness insofar as "the unavoidable troubles, the distractions and disruptions that make things turn out in unpredicted scenarios" are facts of intimacy. With regard to Sufi corporealities in medieval Persianate societies, Shahzad Bashir (2011, 107) has likewise noted that as much as being Sufi "implied that one had come under the spell of love," such being subjected to love meant being affected by turmoil, pain, and sorrow. In a close reading of a sixteenth-century Sufi poem, he elaborates how such love, more potent than any other force, acts upon and stirs up human beings so much that "those who fall in love are urged to take the long view of the situation since they have, by virtue of being smitten, entered the most worthwhile arena of human experience" (Bashir 2011, 110).[45] To be so possessed by love, to tarry with feeling this way, and to advance in stirred-up conditions over time figures my reading of intimacy with saints as a thing that broadens one's affective horizons as well as possibilities of life that might or might not realize in its wake. To tarry, as fakirs do in intimacy's bloom, is to linger in expectation, to remain in a situation, at times, longer than intended. It enfolds ideas of delay and waiting, feeling vexed, even hindered. It is as much to abide by a thing as it is to stay with its consequences. Thus, the book also tackles the question of what saintly bonds yield in their unfolding or how these obdurately endure in forward time: the hard learnings that evolve from drawing close to saints, the not knowing which histories such intimacies precisely involve or preclude, less so where one might be headed in such relationships. Fakir efforts and anxieties around saintly bonds and conditions of intimacy substantiate the position that individuals do not become fakirs in the sense that they become a thing and stay that way.

Qurb, a term I introduced earlier in relation to Zaheda's feeling of closeness, points to an always-evolving, never-stable feeling of being close, be it in terms of time, place, or relation. The online resource Urdu Lughat describes *qurb* as closeness in its visible, interiorized, spatial, and temporal dimensions.[46] So long as to be close is as much to be within reach (of understanding or conception) as it is to be on the verge (of happening or completion), intimacy is the name I give to what blooms in that indistinct yet critical interstice between being near a thing and being nearly that thing. *Qurb* helps appreciate how and why fakir pursuits are not so much targeted at becoming the object itself, what Sufis would call *fana*, annihilation into the Truth, but rather at the cluster of promises such being critically intimate brings into view (Berlant 2011). Intimacy hangs on critical distance here. *Qurb* also denotes access, relation, and rank. And al-Qarib (the Near One in Arabic) is one of the many qualities by which God is known to Muslims: Allah is near by virtue of knowledge and awareness. To be close or *qarib* thus names a number of conditions: to be on the verge, to be distinct from others, to be within earshot of who one is intimate with, to be privy to exclusive knowledge and secrets. That love can be "a mode of being with God" (Ahmed 2016, 38) follows that affect refracted through intimacy in this work is not simply a structure of being physically near a saintly object; rather, it is by virtue of being-with, a felt mode of knowing, however slow, speculative, or indistinct such disclosures might be. Just as to be orientated around something "is not so much to take up that thing, as to be taken up by something" (Ahmed 2006, 116), *qurb* in saintly affective terms is a condition of slow revelation or refers to becoming progressively conscious in the wake of intimacy—wake also includes being awake (Sharpe 2016, 21). Though still distinct from saints, it is such being affectively sharp and perceptive that gives fakirs a reputation as guides who know better. What is however particularly queer about such affordances—something that emerges across life stories—is the not-fully-knowing the more-than-living object one commits to, is intimate with, or agrees to become embroiled with. Affective troubles are drawn not only from what fakirs abandon or turn away from but also, if not more so, because fakir relations with saintly figures are built upon uncertain communication, wound-up bonds, partial knowledge, the constant fear of the line being cut, as Zaheda once put it. More particularly in the case of Sehwan and given the abundant histories of Lal, some of which I recount in chapters 1 and 5, one might ask how such relations and intimacies are to endure when the saintly figure around which fakir desires are clustered is itself a slippery object in historical terms, knowable if at all through imaginal realms and felt registers? In fact, I take the position that in the different affective attachments of the fakirs to the figure of Lal, the saint is dynamically enacted not as one stable figure, but as multiple fragments and figurations. And yet, none of this is a case against intimacy but proof of its mystical worth and value. Impeding as these are, partial histories, multiple narrations, dreams that require retelling and consultation, imprecise signals of sound or vision, bodily pain and cohabiting spirits, signs that must be read and interpreted are all felt ways in which fakirs know and do not know, remain hooked or are on the edge, become embroiled or tie themselves up in relations of affect with their mystical companions.

In an affective rendering of saintly ecologies of Delhi, Anand Taneja notes that kin-making with djinns, deities, saints, spirits, and talking animals highlight "the self's embeddedness in and constitution through a network of ties to the world" (2017, 115). He describes this as intimacy with the invisible (107–15). Rather fitting that *qarib* in its plural iteration *aqriba'* means relatives, that is, those near ones that we make kin with. Taneja's work draws keenly on Amira Mittermaier's notion of an *Elsewhere*. Tempering the emphasis on self-cultivation in the anthropology of Islam, Mittermaier proposes an ethics of relationality that "recognizes that humans are always embedded in webs of relationships" (2012, 249), more precisely, that the sphere of social relations also includes "the possibility of having personal relationships with (deceased) saints" (2008, 63).[47] In proceeding, I take the position that the very intimacy that winds up fakirs with saints in complex ethical-political relations ensures also that saints can have an affective stake in the world.[48] This means that we ought to account for, as part of a quotidian economy of affect, human-nonhuman knots, sacred enmeshments and historical affordances through which such relations are inclined to prosper in otherwise, off-the-cuff, and less-ordinary mobilizations (Stewart 2014, 121). This, what we might call *worlding with saints*, to lean on Kathleen Stewart, underscores not just the relational, allied, and interdependent character of fakir pursuits and saintly objects, but gestures also at how they make worlds out of such ties.[49] It helps figure the felt and enfleshed ways through which Sehwan's disguised histories and diversely sacred heritage is intimately mobilized into folds of a postcolonial Muslim present—a historical bloom, so to speak. For the most part, worlding with saints is a diffused notion in this book—taken up only in chapter 5—but it brings home the greater point that such queer companionships, risqué or troubling as these might be, are in fact also ordinary mobilizations conversant with the everyday ubiquity of saints and shrines in Pakistan.

An emphasis on fakir corporeality in this research recognizes that the ethics of intimacy and politics of orientation also endure in the materiality of the body, which is to say that for intimacy to matter, its inwardness must take outward and public forms.[50] It follows that fakirs, like *qalandar*s or

FIGURE I.4
A fakir woman passing by a street shrine in Sehwan, 2010.

those crooked-hat-wearing adherents of *madhhab-i 'ishq*, must be recognizable in order for them to validate a being beside norms. To live a fakir life is to undertake "a sustained and repeated corporeal project" (Butler 1988, 522). Fakir guises in Sehwan, abundantly detailed through the middle chapters, are coded through forms of costume, color, accessories, social behavior, and habitat (see fig. I.4). Furthermore, insofar as to be fakir is to reorient the body to conform to a script or historical idea of ascetic poverty, one that is disproportionately if not exclusively male, structures and conditions of feeling close to saints are always already gendered. Even if fewer than men, women fakirs were never hard to come by in Sehwan. Also, some of my fakir interlocutors have in fact been gender-variant persons, whether intersex or transgender.[51]

On the radical possibilities of unmaking and remaking with saints, Anand Taneja (2017) has noted that a saint's shrine is a "place of becoming estranged from one's social identity." When it comes to fakirs of this book, such lines of *strange(r)ness*, to stay with Taneja's metaphor, solitary as these might first seem, are in fact public paths of companionship. Saints make for queer companions not so much because they dislodge social relations or make them strange, but more so because they escort an abundance of relational possibilities that persevere so long as conditions of intimacy persist across affect-rich trails of yearning, seeking, dreaming, finding, and losing saints. In tarrying with saintly bonds, fakir relations to inherited objects are altered, whether these are objects of thought, feeling, and desire or involve life objectives, aims, and aspirations. Intimacy, thus, serves as "a conduit to understanding concrete force of abstract fields of power" (Wilson 2016, 248) when I describe how personal dreams and saintly visions become inseparable from desirous projections and infrastructures of the state, pulling dreamers away from domestic worlds to public shrines (chapter 1). It takes a precariously corporeal turn when women cohabit with spirits to partially remedy their historical exclusion from local systems of patrilineal charisma, or when fakir guises that signal, secure, and sustain conditions of saintly relations are thwarted by rival objects of love and desire (chapters 2 and 4). Fakir doubts and dilemmas, hopes and fears offer a sense of the affective terrain that *qurb* with saintly figures affords in emotional terms but also how fakirs continue with or in spite of it (chapter 3). Similarly, fakir inhabitation of saintly grounds brings them closer not only to rival beings—living, dead, or more-than-human—but also into intimate contact with alternate histories, imaginations, and futures of place (chapter 5). Together, these reaffirm the idea that intimacy has outward skins: its affordances texture inward feeling, public life, and historical being.

CON / TEXTS

In *Religious Affects*, Donovan Schaefer rewrites parameters for understanding religion. "Because affect constitutes the links between bodies and power," affect theory, he argues, is critical to mapping religion (Schaefer 2015, 9). At the same time, he notes that inheritances of religious studies can be vital to the exploration of affect (207). Unlike Schaefer's, my mandate is not as interceptive as "what gets called religion" or as poetic as "a way of feeling out religion" (Schaefer 2015, 207). Still, to some extent, this book, like Schaefer's, is driven by the will to excite a conversation where little exists. Queer, religious, and affect studies whose fields, texts, and contexts I am here attempting to suture are new companions. Islamic lifeworlds I read and parse in this book, far less so. I am also aware that places like Sehwan, while emblematic of a particular kind of Islam in anthropology, do not strike us as sites of queer thinking. On the one hand, inheritances, crossings, borrowings, not least departures, shape the many contexts in which this book arrives. On the other, it informs the book's critical relation, a being *beside* with conversations in the anthropology of Islam, which remain largely if not comfortably oblivious to queer epistemologies. Such omissions are informed and maintained by the narrow view that queer is relevant only when researching sexualities in the Muslim world, if not also reduced to a minority hermeneutic reserved for LGBTQIA+ Muslims. A good case of such besideness is the book's companionship with Naveeda Khan's (2012) deliberation on Muslim becoming in Pakistan. Her thorough ethnographic work remains of broader contextual relevance to this project and her sophisticated argument on the dual dynamics of aspiration and skepticism mirror in a sense the open futures fakir lines are confronted with.[52] However, in limiting what she calls "scenes of striving" to theological disputations and mosque-related struggles, Khan relegates religious becoming to very straight settings that, despite their intra-Islamic diversity, eventually serve to exemplify and uphold a dominant if not weary narrative: Islam as the primary episteme for imagining Pakistan. Places like saints' shrines, ever-present in the Pakistani landscape, find no prominence in the scenes she describes; women and transgender individuals are effectively left outside concerns of futurity. In a limited sense, this work on saintly intimacy can be imagined as a queer companion to Khan's expansive project insofar as it brings fakir protagonists to the fore that are least likely to be read as futural or aspirational: An unchaperoned mother of eight who traverses a cross-country geography of shrines (chapter 3); an intersex child who abandons home on the inextricably entangled promise of dreams and the state (chapter 1); an ascetic who gives up celibacy for a girl he loves (chapter 4); a woman contesting place among tombs in a graveyard (chapter 5) or one holding audience in the men's prayer space at the shrine (chapter 2).

The importance of studying Sehwan is given precisely in its impetus to exhaust our categories of knowing. In the book's view, it is that place where Shi'i figures, events, and temporalities are not exceptions or minor figurations but rather constitute an ordinary mobilization. To that extent, this book doesn't sit straight with the Sunni-centering drive of the anthropology of Islam, whose epistemologies are predominantly served by, if they have not also produced, an active minoritization of Islam's other histories and lifeworlds. Even an erudite scholar such as Shahab Ahmed (2016) chooses to make no space for Shi'i aesthetic and affective forms in an otherwise stunning work that covers five centuries of Islamic cultures between Bengal and the Balkans. While Sufi worlds are engaged, he grossly undervalues Shi'i historical and cultural sources by dismissing them as "demographically minor" (Ahmed 2016, 104).[53] As a result, Karbala, an event pivotal to broader Islamic history and imagination as well as the aesthetic and affective forms that derive from it, is astonishingly left out of his argument on the importance of being Islamic. In the same measure, writings on saints' places in South Asia too often fail to accord Shi'i histories, beyond the descriptive, their rightful place in the analysis of shrine lifeworlds—Carla Bellamy's (2011) otherwise insightful book is a case in point. In such instances, the category Sufi serves to straighten, subsume, even silence irregular, antinormative, largely non-Sunni pasts through academic writing (Kasmani 2017a).

Whether Shi'i or Shivaite, Sunni or Sufi, Sehwan, despite its prominence, has only haltingly attracted the interest of studies on Pakistan.[54] Michel Boivin's (2011) long-standing scholarship comes to remedy such paucity. His study of relics and devotional artifacts attributed to Lal and his reading of shrine layouts, inscriptions, and ritual networks are particularly illuminating. He points to plural relations that objects build between realities, mundane and mystical, no less than the complex social and historical processes these attract and set into motion in the present. It has informed my stance that attachment to saints and their tombs, otherwise emblematic of ascetic self-mortification or unworlding, is complexly conversant with material realities so much that it is a means for becoming worldly in Sehwan.[55] Queer analytics of intimacy and futurity help bring the point home that fidelity to saints and their places is not always a recoiling from the worldly; instead, fakir labors in Sehwan constitute a purposeful coming close to saints. To the extent that fakir aspirations exceed mystical projects, the intimate scenes of striving I engage do not traffic in grand arguments around Islam or speculate on its place in the nation.[56] Moreover, the book's view that less-ordinary prospects of the public and the political are tied to forms of intimacy is aslant to dominant scholarly ways in which the relationship between Islam and the state has been imagined in the context of Pakistan.[57]

Though set in a pilgrimage town, the book's epistemic thrust extends beyond Islam or Pakistan insofar as it ruminates on how and why relations with saints or commitment to an ostensibly religious object are of value to queer forms of thinking and world making. This also means that it must navigate a capacious zone between disinclined disciplines, a theme I take up in the coda to this book. If the anthropology of Islam is yet to open itself up to queer knowledge, methods, and sensibilities, queer and affect theory's by-and-large disregard for Islamic-religious fields and objects is comparable. The glaring absence of religion proper in work on public feelings or, for that matter, affect studies' geopolitical constitution within post-Fordist American cultural and political spheres speaks volumes for what areas and objects of study accrue value in relation to certain others.[58] As part of their critique of queer studies' geopolitics and analytical habits, its contemporary resolution and US-centering drive—true also for the canon of affect theory—Anjali Arondekar and Geeta Patel (2016, 152) indicate that non-Euro-American sources, settings, and epistemes, if and when invoked, appear only as exemplars, never as sites of theory making. At the same time, scholarship that takes intersections of Islam and same-sex desire seriously is relatively new.[59] The mandate of this book, however, is distinct from its forerunners in that it is set beside sexuality. It also ventures beyond the metropole and engages queer hermeneutics, not in a reparative spirit, neither as tools for queering Islam. Its intellectual labors are rather concerned with engaging diversely sacred aesthetics, Islamic-spiritual inheritances, and religious affect, which is one way of seeking other histories of queer and a mode I here regard as reading queer religiously. This doesn't entail a frenzy of finding one in the other—Islamizing queer or queering Islam—but involves the intricate task of exploring a companionship such that scholars' categories, religion and queer, can remain in creative suspense or question at least their historical disinclination (see coda). Such reading incites a troubling of religion as a nondefinable, Eurocentric, and colonialist category in much the same vein as it imagines queerness in more-than-rights-based, nonmetropolitan, extrasecular, and beside Euro-American cultural terms. It follows that fakir lives in this book are not confirmations of queer presence elsewhere but orientations in and of themselves. Their stories in this book stretch defined and habituated figurations of religion, while remaining oblique to the genealogies and inheritances of queer itself. Sehwan likewise is not mere exemplar for queer theory nor simply discursive context. It is also a critical geography, a meeting ground where fakir lives cross and epistemological paths emerge.

Queer Companions pairs its protagonists, person and place. Every chapter is tied to a particular location in town, underscoring the importance of lived context and local ecologies. The various settings I introduce in sequence—grove, shrine, courtyard, lodge, and graveyard—constitute a geography of intimacy that unfolds through the pages (see map I.1). The book's journey takes us from affinities in image to dis/affection of saints of the state, from intimacies that take hold in song and dream to close cohabiting with spirits and the dead. Such material is diversely collected, organized as life stories, interwoven through various settings, and sequenced into chapters as a way to illustrate the situated ways in which fakirs make worlds out of saintly relations in Sehwan. Thus, what also worlds through the various life stories I present in this book is an unstraight telling, evoking feeling and knowing, always inflected, continually affected.

"Take with you what you can and leave the rest," a fakir once reprimanded me for having suggested that I record our conversation using a mechanical device. He looked visibly upset. I knew from my experience with other fakirs that the use of the recorder often reduced the quality of conversations and affected their styles of narrating. Similarly, Murad, a fakir at a local lodge whose company I used to regularly seek, thought I asked too many questions. He had rather poetically suggested an alternative: "Make it a habit to sit by the sea and it shall itself reveal the secrets unto you." I had taken such advice, though I strived as I learned to adjust to a different kind of method of being around fakirs, one that was not interrogative yet still engaging, less urgent while more oriented toward open outcomes. Interviews did not always yield explicit information. There was hardly ever a clear answer, I worried. Fakirs spoke in very complex and abstract ways. Some even refused to talk about intimate matters, either because they feared a sense of pride might get in the way or because certain secrets were best not disclosed to the uninitiated. Over time and in the company of fakirs, the default method shifted to impromptu conversations and sessions of exchange that transpired unrecorded. Hanging out with fakirs while being skillfully observant demanded more than just being present in a given context or situation (Geertz 1998, 69). As I moved from interviews to conversations, from inquiry to sharing space and time, from recording devices to reflexive processes, I was able to gain a sense of how fakirs pulled together their orientation to extraordinary realms in continuity with the mundane and the everyday. I was equally exposed to moments of tension and enjoyment, privy to everyday gossip and pranks.

This book is based on fifteen months of fieldwork. Three early field visits took me to Sehwan in 2009 and 2010, each lasting around four weeks.[60] However, more concentrated long-term fieldwork was carried out in two

Chapter 5
Graveyard

Chapter 4
Lodge

Old Fortress

Shrine of Bodlo

Chapter 3
Courtyard

Shrine of Lal

Chapter 2
Shrine

Indus River

Chapter 1
Grove

Lal-bagh

N

0   0.15   0.3   0.6   0.9   1.2
                                                    Km

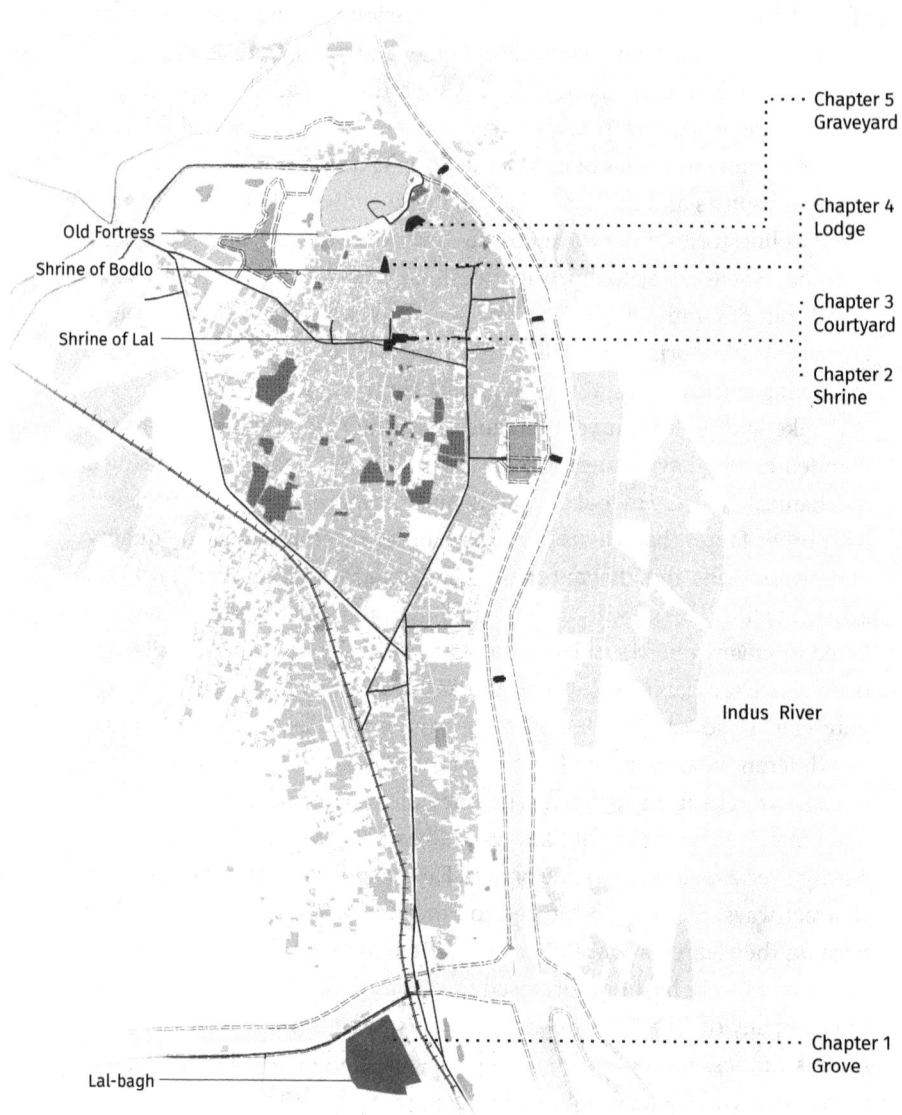

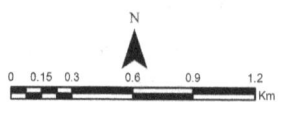

Chapter Settings
Built up Area
Graveyards & Cemeteries
Roads
Railway Tracks

Cultivated Land
Uncultivated Land
Wasteland
Canals

phases. One lasted six months, from September 2011 to February 2012; the other was of three months' duration, between June and August 2012. I returned for a month in November 2013 and finally for three weeks in February 2018.[61] I thought it important to document the changes, especially relevant in light of the suicide bomb attack at the shrine a year earlier. The fact that our interactions spread over nine years and across several field stays of varying durations has made it possible to think of fakir lives not only as they unfolded in the present or in my presence but in relation to what had been left behind and what was to subsequently unfold. The working out of a single life narrative from different points in their lives but also the changing life of the town captures the varying and time-inflected ways in which fakirs bring meaning to their life choices, circumstances, and experiences or to particular events and processes. Women fakirs, in my experience, were especially skilled at recounting their lives and struggles in the presence of others, perhaps also because narrativizing was integral to the gendered making of spiritual authority (see Pechilis 2012; Flueckiger 2003; see also chapter 2). While fakir accounts of the present were rich in content and dense with metaphor, many found it arduous to speak of their distant pasts in any great detail. The telling or the withholding of stories, their different iterations over the years, and the narrative strategies with which such pasts were made accessible to me were equally important material to consider because "composing stories about oneself," even when it involves significant erasures, is a creative act, and "oral testimonies are, in the end, stories that people tell about themselves" (Sarkar 2012, 593). Challenges around accessing histories have also meant, wherever necessary, an assembling of accounts, anecdotes, field notes, and vignettes to form biographical semblances requiring both time and repeated, consistent engagements with my interlocutors.

The main language of research in the field has been Urdu. An advanced access to Sindhi, Seraiki, and Punjabi has helped me gain a sense beyond the scope of interviews and one-on-one conversations while improving my chances for participating in group interactions. The language of the field diary was, however, predominantly English. While my first report of interactions and interviews is already an account in translation, I exercised care so as to record significant statements, direct quotations, or concepts in the original. Carefully assembled oral fakir accounts, even if not recorded as one coherent biographical interview on a mechanical device, form the basis of each of the chapters in this book. While fakirs are primary protagonists, they are not the only interlocutors in this research.[62] Interactions in the field have included interviews, conversations, and participant observation with pilgrims and residents, shrine officials and contract workers, local intellectuals and sayyid custodians, ritual specialists and shopkeepers, gurus and their disciples, and, when possible, spouses and family members of fakirs. Wherever beneficial, sources such as print literature, newspaper reports, devotional songs, images, and legends are also incorporated as well as a limited number of colonial historical records, which help situate and read the contemporary conflicts around questions of change, the arbitration of authorities, and everyday management of the shrine and its resources. Fieldwork involved a brief stint at the Sindh Archives in Karachi as well as short visits to various shrines and holy sites associated with Lal and other prominent saints in Sindh and Punjab.

As a cis-male researcher, I had access to most public spaces as well as fakir lodges and sayyid households. At times, it limited my interactions in settings associated with female publics. The privilege I drew by virtue of my social class and urban disposition, not least the saint's favor and the serious intellectual purpose ascribed to me in the field, sometimes remedied gendered anxieties around my contact with women fakirs and pilgrims, especially in the shrine premises.[63] I have, in many instances, benefited from my knowledge of local customs and languages, puns, metaphors, and references. That said, urban-rural disparities, difference in discourse and education, and class-determined character of social experience mean that I am complexly and multiply located vis-à-vis the field and my interlocutors—possibly a *halfie* anthropologist.[64] While I may not be termed a complete stranger—"scholarly participants ... who while remaining of the faith and sharing in the benefits of an insider's knowledge of the beliefs and practices of the community" (Knott 2005, 247)—the kind of religious emotion I have encountered in Sehwan is quite distinct from my own experience of the same faith, an affective distance that I have already described in some detail. It is also true that for the earlier part of the fieldwork, I remained estranged from the most quotidian aspects of Sehwan's ritual life. For instance, I did not at first partake of offerings made to the saint and was slow to fully observe ritual customs related to the shrine. Or that despite many adjustments and learnings over the years, I did not once participate in performances like *dhamal* and *matam* (drumming and ritual flagellation). Similarly, I chose not to consume any intoxicants, which is a common feature of fakir life in Sehwan, especially when fakirs gather in small groups and share a joint or *bhang*, a freshly prepared beverage made from cannabis leaves. In withholding, I was clearly marking myself, but I was also already distinguished in other ways, especially by virtue of class-based markers like dress, diction, and the very practice of academic research. The thing is that insider-ness is not necessarily more beneficial than nor superior to other positions and conditions of access; it also requires methodological work, especially to ensure that one is not doubly impeded by the assumptions a researcher may make of shared meanings or by those that are made about the researcher (Armitage and Gluck 2002, 79). In short, limitations of scope, access, and method present the contingencies and conditions under which this ethnography is written and lays out the intersubjective processes at play rather than claiming positions of (better) knowledge and objectivity.

The book's analytical choice of reading fakir life stories as they unfold in close correspondence with their places of dwelling helps bolster the idea that unstraight affordances of intimacy are individually inflected, locally shaped, and historically conversant. The opening chapter, which is set in a grove outside town, centers on the life-altering journey of an intersex fakir. Weaving the state in and out of a single life story, the chapter takes the provocative position that saintly intimacies occurring in dream are contoured by material-affective measures of the state, a framework I describe as infrastructures of the imaginal. It also reflects on the changing life and times of the shrine itself as well as the history of the saint. Chapter 2 takes the reader from the seclusion of a grove to the center of action. Situated in the audience hall (durbar) of the shrine of Sehwan, "Her Stories in His Durbar" revolves around the questionable authority of a woman fakir in a men's prayer space. Drawing on the intersecting politics of local sayyid authority and shrine administration, it explores how publicly governed shrines serve as intimate settings for women, whose extradomestic forays and less-normative spiritual careers are arbitrated in the company of the saint and the state. It also illustrates how an embodiment of motherhood comes to partially remedy women's exclusion from patrilineal charisma in Sehwan or how it hinges on the affective narrativization of mystical endurance. As a pair, the first two chapters weave in the history and political economy of the shrine. These establish how desires of the state are implicated in saintly projects or the greater conditions of governing with saints under which saintly intimacies are fostered or impaired.

The succeeding two chapters turn to the work of becoming intimate or bodily labor that is required to sustain place alongside saints, especially the emotional crises that loom about such exceptional decisions and situations. Centering on the spiritual career of a woman in the shrine courtyard, chapter 3 traces the gendered and affective troubles she faces in a time of impending failure. "In Other Guises, Other Futures" draws on the fakir concept of dis/guise to argue how being close to saints perseveres in bodied ways, tarries through feeling, and warrants a contingent publicness. It is a moving account that ties affordance with endurance in altering conditions of intimacy. It ruminates on the durational passage of intimacy as well as the affective labors it takes to continue with or without saintly relations. Going further, "Love in a Time of Celibacy" follows in the aftermath of a scandal in a men's-only fakir lodge. Reading across saintly and sexual intimacy, the chapter illustrates how being in the service of saints takes specific corporeal forms. It contends that saintly bonds, however secure in ritual terms, can come undone or show signs of disaffection, especially when saintly fields are thwarted by rival objects of desire. Chapter 5 is set in a graveyard. Through a twin account of contesting place, "Worlding Fakirs, Fairies, and the Dead" takes the position that fakir worlds are heterotemporal imbrications that alongside the saint feature the dead and the more-than-living, mythic creatures and spiritual beings. This, the chapter argues, leans into a worlding whereby fakirs, by virtue of their intimacy with saints, mobilize the place's multiple, contested, or unresolved histories into the present and, at the same time, embed themselves in long-standing affective textures of place. Finally, in the coda to this book, I take up the epistemological prospects that underlie a possible companionship between the study of religion and queer theory. I enfold the various findings that are brought to bear across all five chapters while folding out the politics that underlie my reading of the material. "Queer Forward Slash Religion" reflects on what we might do to gainfully read religious lifeworlds, not with the purpose of queering or queer-jacketing them, but rather with the sensibilities and skills to read queer religiously.

This book, like its fakir protagonists, arrives through forms of coming close and crossing far. A few months ahead of the summer of 2009, in a long-distance phone call from London, I shared with my mother plans for a research stay in Sehwan as part of a master's degree program in Muslim

Cultures. In the fraction of silence that stretched between my telling and her response, "What do shrines have to do with Islam?" was a geography of distance. Whether the saint embraced me or I embraced Sehwan, the photograph my mother would object to many years later is after all witness to labors of coming close, crossing far. In a sense, this writing captures an entire decade of arriving and departing, staying, coming to know and not knowing enough. Questions of intimacy I center in this research are somewhere, somehow also inflected by my own coming to terms with distance, physical and emotional. Or the queer affects I identify in relation to fakir lives are in part to make sense of all that I might have stirred, upended, or given up in the wake of coming close to Sehwan. Theoretical labors put aside, all scholarly citations taken away, what remains at the heart of this book are stories of coming close, ways of worlding shared with me over the years, some also as parting gifts. Through the labor of writing lives and piecing together biographical fragments, I am constantly reminded of the limitations I face in terms of access and material: the temporal character of life itself as well as the constructed-ness of the ethnography as a genre. Like the biographer, to borrow Benjamin Moser's (2014) words, the anthropologist too, "in the face of the sprawling chaos of an entire life," brings coherence where little might exist and must remain all the more aware that whatever gets told is but a small selection, one that fits a particular construction and serves a specific intellectual logic. Murad, the same fakir who suggested I ask less questions, also told me that he wants to be like me, "an explorer who travels to new locations," not to record stories of others, as he described my work to be, but to write his own story. Somewhere between crossing far and coming close, along labors of finding, accessing, composing, and telling fakir stories in, across, and between these pages, I hope to have found a story of my own to tell.

1

Infrastructures of the Imaginal

By July 2012, when a photograph with my arms around a cardboard cutout of Veena Malik was taken by Rémy Delage, Veena was already a sex symbol. In the wake of a topless photo shoot across the border in India, so widespread was her appeal in Pakistan that one could find her cardboard cutout even at a saint's fair (*mela*).[1] In this makeshift photo studio at a circus catering to pilgrims in Sehwan, a large digitized image of the shrine stood as backdrop. A handful of other cutout figures, mostly of contemporary Bollywood actresses, offered alternatives for intimate foregrounding. In being photographed with Veena, one was inadvertently also caught posing with the saint. Lal watched from behind, as it were, hovering on the backdrop in his iconic falcon-like form (see fig. 1.1). As a single most defining image of the saint, the flight of Lal that the icon represents— preserved in textual accounts and transmitted in oral legends—is more than a record of a one-time miraculous event.[2] It can be read as *historial,* a term I borrow from Hans-Jörg Rheinberger (1994) to trace not just the historical, but rather how the image of the flying saint recurs variably over

FIGURE 1.1
Lal, Veena, and myself.
Photograph by
Rémy Delage, 2012.

time, engenders intimacies despite being remote, and perseveres through a kind of stickiness in that it is actively reimaginable with every iteration and differently recorded in myriad inscriptions in and across structured forms: photographs, chants, songs, films, shrine architecture, dream space.

Digitally manipulated intimacies with the saint are all too common when it comes to pilgrim photographs in Sehwan, a point made plain in the introduction to this book. Infinitely more intriguing, however, are the saint's appearances that traverse genres, that is to say, instances when the visual turns visionary, reckoning material consequences that push limits of the imaginal. Here, imaginal is not something unreal, imaginary, or concocted; rather, as scholars of Islam have illustrated, it is an order of reality that for Sufis is a distinct and betwixt realm of perception, as reliable as it can be deceptive.[3] As a significant mode of perception, key to Sufi cosmologies, and drawn particularly from the works of Ibn al-'Arabi (d. 1240), the imaginal correlates forms of seeing and varieties of perception across wakefulness and dreaming. It involves both the eye of sense perception and the eye of imagination and requires the dreamer to also be an unveiler, in other words, to discern between imaginal and sensory objects (Chittick 1993, 8). Illustrating precisely the affective crossovers of such imaginal realms into material worlds, the central thrust of this chapter builds on the winged creature's appearances in the early dreams of Baba-Akram, a fakir, who at the time was a nine-year-old child with an intersex condition living far away from the shrine in a village in Punjab. Two years into their recurrence, they (Baba-Akram) would respond to the visions, abandon home, and venture out in search of the enigmatic saint-in-flight.[4] Decades on, when the dream was recounted to me in Sehwan, Baba-Akram (henceforth Baba) was a fifty-year-old fakir who had eventually come to settle in a grove on the outskirts of town. The chapter traces the physical and imaginal journeys the dream sets into motion, the objects it carries forth from dream to waking life, and the interpretive efforts this requires of the dreamer-as-unveiler over time.

As an afterlife of dreams as it were, Baba's fakir story illustrates how orientations to an antinomian saint upend orders of future and disrupt normative formations of the social. In his reputation as a qalandar, Lal mobilizes a thirteenth-century mystical ethos in present-day Pakistan, which, as I describe in the introduction, was premised on the rejection of social-religious norms, institutions, and authorities of the time. Only fitting that through its profoundly imaginal registers, saintly socialities involving such figures, illuminate for persons like Baba horizons that are otherwise unlikely or unimaginable. New orientations bring into view lineations and objects hitherto unseen and trigger futurities divergent from ones that are expected or commonplace. Fakir pursuits, as this book illustrates, are invariably in dispute with inherited lines and familiar objects of the social. Impaired by discord, attendant with dysfunction yet lined with fragile hope, conditions of intimacy that I identify with regard to Baba are futural nonetheless. The other point is this: saintly-imaginal intimacies mappable in the shared field of the dream, like the photograph, also point outwardly. This means that intimate interactions that occur in the dream as well as its potentialities for orienting dreamers, a point Amira Mittermaier (2011) has made compellingly in her work on Islamic shrines in Egypt, exceed the dialogical frame of the saint and the devotee.[5] On the ethical and political dimensions of dreaming, she notes how dreams and visions come from outside the dreaming subject and involve transformative encounters that place dreamers in social relationships with particular saints, the Prophet, and more generally the space of the divine, what she calls "an Elsewhere" (Mittermaier 2011, 3).[6] Such interrelationality in her terms and active intimacies with saintly figures in mine are orienting forces in fakir futures and thus of interest to the greater argument of this book. Proceeding from her statement, "dreams are never about the dreamer" (Mittermaier 2011, 3), this chapter illustrates how saintly visions and the intimacies they advance and make real are implicated in wider social and coconstitutive processes and relate to a framework that I describe as stately infrastructures of the imaginal.

Following Ara Wilson, I take infrastructure as a rubric to identify not a priori structures but the facilitation of existing systems composed of physical and immaterial elements. In other words, recognizing "the concrete force of abstract fields of power" (Wilson 2016, 248), we appreciate how saintly intimacies find ground and take hold, are enabled but also hindered. This is tied to the book's position that saintly vitality in Pakistan thrives on orders of the state; that it is sustained by the material-affective infrastructures of governance whose original or official intent might well be to curb forms of saintly intimacy or regulate transgressive and hard-to-discipline shrine worlds. Such outcomes, whether inadvertent or repurposed, point to a form of queering, which in Wilson's terms is a potentiality embedded in the very life and logic of infrastructure. Furthermore, to the extent that infrastructure remains in the background, embedded, sunk into other structures, or aims to be invisible, I point to its luminous, differently corporeal and imaginal iterations, calling out instances of return or when the presence of the state shines through or takes effect without being physically or immediately present.[7] This follows that ideology is integral to smooth workings of infrastructure, "operating in ways that obscure the labor and politics involved in that functioning" (Wilson 2016, 24). In this sense, the loitering saint in the photograph at the circus, easily disregarded as cheap graphics, is a critical citation of the state in an otherwise ordinary scene of leisure. My reading of the photograph invokes the premise that the paradoxical desires and malleable affinities that haunt such an image also haunt infrastructures that dispose the saintly in Pakistan. The saintly refers not to a distinct realm where saints dwell or act from; rather it names the historically evolving affective textures that make saintly figures relevant to the present. Thus, by attending to traces, absences, or submerged narratives, we can gain a sense how displaced saintly actors and agencies register profoundly and affectively in the contemporary (Blackman 2015, 26; Gordon 2008). In a broader sense, what I am also saying is that the saint's recurrence in and across forms, be it religious-iconic posters, films, photo templates, songs, or dreams, exceeds the present moment, hints at settings beyond the shrine, and ties up scales of the individual, the local, and the national. Rare as it is for an anthropologist, a film actress, and a saint to share an intimate scene in a photograph, its fourth and most unlikely protagonist is still the Pakistani state, I contend, evading the image yet present as a most potent ghost.

Attributing dreams to mechanisms of the state involves a measure of conjecture yet it isn't exactly far-fetched since Baba's childhood coincides with the first decade of public administration of religious sites in Pakistan. It is one step to making the assertion that the saint's appearances in photographs and films, songs and dreams, speak to far-reaching implications of governance. That the Pakistani state has engaged with shrines in ideological, legal, political, and administrative terms is well established (Ibad 2019). Infrastructures of the imaginal point to the symbolic stakes, affective means, and imaginal scopes of such an enterprise. Speaking from the quiet seclusion of a grove and weaving the state in and out of a single life story, I discuss how individual dreams might acquire a vitality beyond questions of the personal or the spiritual as these come to be propped up and intervened in by desirous projections of the state. In the process, a greater story of the contemporary life and times of Sehwan's shrine and its saint is told. The iconic falcon form of Lal, a saint in flight, emerges as a metaphor for unordinary futures and unstraight affordances that saintly intimacies dis/close, prospects that, as I illustrate in this chapter, soar on wings of the state.[8]

Of Songs, Dreams, and a Saint in Flight

Just weeks ahead of the annual fair, on a scorching summer afternoon in 2012, two women offered a lyrical tribute to the saint of Sehwan: "The flying Shahbaz knows secrets of the heart," they sang in Punjabi. The women had found some respite at a fakir dwelling on the outskirts of town. Leading the duo was Mai Dhadli, a Hindu folk singer from the deserts of southern Punjab and a regular visitor to Sehwan. "Included in the being of Allah is the ecstasy of Shahbaz," they then sang in Urdu, "Muhammad in one place, Ali in another, and yet elsewhere, Qalandar is Ram." True to Mai's lyrics, Lal Shahbaz Qalandar is a plurivocal figure and a ubiquity hard to miss. He embodies a historical continuum and bridges multiple and oftentimes contradicting genealogies attributed to him. By virtue of being a *qalandar*, he is the paramount ascetic. As a descendant of Ali, he especially attracts Pakistan's Shi'a. In the guise of a Shiva incarnate, the Hindus revere him. Muhammad, Ali, or Ram, his memory spans religious divides, extends far out from the town of his burial, and is traceable all over Pakistan— a reference locked as much in sacred geography as it lingers free in everyday forms. Song after song, Mai picked from what was a popular repertoire of saintly devotional numbers across several languages, most of which were offerings to the saint of Sehwan. Besides Delphine, a fellow anthropologist, and myself, there wasn't much of an audience really. We were sitting in the outer yard of a fakir dwelling with Baba, our fakir host, while the handful of family members who accompanied the women were inside, taking a bit of rest. As we sipped tea, Baba continued speaking of their love for the saint, and Mai tempered the afternoon with some more songs of devotion in Sindhi, Punjabi, and Seraiki. Of all the lyrical offerings Mai would sing that afternoon, none was more fitting to the place than the verses describing the falcon-saint in flight. Every so often, Baba interlaced this very song with an account of their childhood visions, which had led them to this spot in the grove. The fakir dwelling where we had gathered was anything but ordinary. It was, as Baba's story will establish, a material manifestation of their childhood dreams. The place was equally special for the fabled environs in which it was embedded. Legends had it that the saint himself had camped in these woods prior to his arrival in the city proper, thus earning the grove its name, Lal-bagh, the garden of Lal. Revered trees in the grove and natural springs in the area bespoke the saint's miracles and formed part of a whole constellation of sacred sites in and around Sehwan that pilgrims were sure to visit. Its measured distance from Sehwan made it ideal for fakir seclusion except at the time of the annual fair, when a temporary bazaar would sprawl over. Visiting bands of fakirs and large groups of pilgrims would camp on its grounds. Baba's dwelling, though modest, was spacious; a beautiful tree stood in the middle of the yard that led to two rooms at the back. Its walls were painted with the portrait of a fakir and the names Lal and Ali (see fig. 1.2). Baba had installed a tall and elaborate 'alam right at the entrance, a commemorative structure that marks the Battle of Karbala, an event foundational to Shi'i religious history and identity. 'Alams act as primary markers of fakir presence in space and, in this instance, also conveyed Baba's claim to the site. The other feature associated with fakirs was the machh, a fireplace used for both cooking and gathering around. Baba was a gracious host. Those who passed through the grove found temporary comfort in the folds of the dwelling. Like Mai, many were regulars and supported the place with donations in cash and kind. On most days, however, there wasn't much going on. Baba's spot in the grove was tranquil, a perfect respite from the crazy rush of pilgrims. It was also ideal for someone like myself, especially on days when researching in Sehwan felt all too much.

FIGURE 1.2
A view of Baba's dwelling in Lal-bagh, 2012.

Over the years I would spend many an evening in the grove partaking of Baba's hospitality. And of these, I cannot recall a single occasion when Baba didn't bring up the matter of dreams. Whether it was Baba's gesture of giving to an anthropologist or it served the benefit of guests who would invariably be present at the dwelling, there was always a story of arrival to take away. More remarkable, the story's narrative structure and style were almost consistent across the many tellings. Also, without fail, in every iteration of a long and detailed account, the contents of the dream were meaningfully interwoven with lyrical interludes from the song, allowing for imaginative and dialogic confluences of the visual and the lyrical to take hold in these tellings.[9] The fact was that Baba's childhood memory of the dreams was inseparable from the song. "At night we used to play a cassette [audio]; the people of the village would play [a song]: 'The flying Shahbaz knows secrets of the heart.' I would listen to it a lot at night and while listening I would fall asleep. In the morning, when the imam would call for prayer, in the early hours, a *khayal* [dream, lit. thought] would come to me."

This dream that in Baba's terms would come to them was more of a dream sequence. Its recurrence meant that it would bring a young Baba into sustained contact with richly structured settings and saintly figures, a world they weren't able to make sense of at the time. After all, Baba was a mere nine-year-old when the visions started appearing. Of the flying falcon traversing song and dream, Baba would routinely wonder, "What saint is this who knows well the secrets of the heart?" Then retiring for the night, to themselves, they would longingly remark, "I wish to serve that person, that saint to whom the secrets of the heart are known!" On the scholarly demands of working with saintly visions, Anand Taneja (2017, 85) rather poetically poses the question, "what do we do with a tradition that is encountered not as authoritative discourse but, as it were, out of the corner's eye, in dreams and waking visions, in stories told by neighbors and strangers, in snatches of song playing on the radio?" That Baba would rely on the lyrics of the song to decipher the figure in the dream speaks to such confluences. In such narrating, affective continuities were articulated between lyrical figures, dream space, and waking life. At a time when Baba didn't even know the place existed, the song and its imagery were already pointing to Sehwan. Such lyrical-affective pull of saints, though easily relegated to the realm of imagination, is interlocked with the physical realities of saints' places. Amira Mittermaier (2008, 53) directs our attention to the dialogical relationship between shrine space and dream space, especially to the ways in which saintly visions incur material consequences; people move between shrines and shrines too are moved as a result of dreams, she notes. Similarly, of saintly geographies, Nile Green (2006, 35) has described the instrumental role of literary texts whose recording of miraculous attributes of a saint is of little practical use to readers if not tethered to an actual site where such saintliness is physically anchored and made tangible to pilgrims.[10] No less instrumental is the circulation of photographic relics and other media, which along with state recognition serves to amplify the force of the call ascribed to saints' shrines in the age of mass media and publics (Spadola 2019, 234). Dreaming the saint, though central to this chapter, is not what is remarkable in Baba's story. Neither is the affective power of dreams my key concern here. Instead, I point to the material conditions and organizational means that prop and sustain the affective pull of such dreams, cohering across a variety of imaginal and material registers. Baba's dream, its precise imagery as well as its material echoes in song and space, are conversant with the contemporary rise of Sehwan's shrine.

The shrine of Sehwan, according to one report, was taken over by the state of Pakistan on June 24, 1960.[11] Almost a decade into its public administration and pretty much around the same time as Baba was dreaming the saint, songs of the saint were gaining country-wide traction. In the summer of 1969, a folk-devotional number, "O Lal meri," customarily performed by female pilgrims, was adopted from the shrine itself to be musically arranged for a Punjabi film. It was composed by legendary music director Ashiq Hussain, and Noor Jahan, Pakistan's most iconic singer, was asked to lend her voice to its new rendition. Soon enough the country was abuzz with its chorus, "dam-a-dam mast Qalandar," meaning, "every breath is intoxicated with Qalandar" (Lal). Across countless versions and covers as folk, film, pop, and rock numbers, it is to this day one of the widest known tributes to the saint. The song, which featured twice in the same film, sparked a short but impactful trend in Punjabi cinema of the time.[12] Lal would make a number of appearances in several films. Each time he was projected in his unique capacity to fly and was shown to rescue the female protagonist in distress. This would effectively turn one of his minor miracles into a most persevering image: a falcon-saint in flight. "The Flying Shahbaz" or the song from Baba's dream account, also sung by Noor Jahan, belongs to this trend. The winged creature in the recurring dreams as well as the one on the backdrop at the circus are citations of this pictorial and lyrical life of Sehwan's saint.

In the very years Baba was growing up in the village, the profile of Sehwan's mausoleum was being circulated in print, its saint reproduced on film, and his miracles circulated through images and devotional songs. Notwithstanding the fact that the imaginal scope of the songs and films in question wasn't exactly conceived nor directly sponsored by the state, and in that strict sense not officially authoritative, yet the draw of such interest in the shrine as well as of new pilgrims to Sehwan wasn't entirely independent of the shrine's reformed status as a public institution. The Bukhari brothers, the director-producer duo responsible for the film number, were newly drawn to Sehwan. Successful in their film careers at the time, the two would go on to organize pilgrimages from Lahore to Sehwan, reserving entire trains for their annual journeys. Private patronage such as theirs greatly complemented the state's project in Sehwan as much as it was motivated by it. Improved means of access and investment in facilities meant that pilgrims were able to flock to the shrine just as the falcon-saint was well poised to travel far and wide on wings of the state. A direct and steady investment in hard infrastructure such as the organization of saints' fairs, the upkeep of mausoleums and their facilities, and road and rail networks to sites of pilgrimage served to enhance the vitality of devotional centers like Sehwan by encouraging people's physical as well as affective access to saints.

What also makes Lal accessible to many, so readily available to multiple figurations in dream and waking life, better disposed to imaginal and sensory modes of perception, is the fact that he evades hagiographical hold and historical record. Mystery suits him better than history. As noted in the introduction, matters like the saint's origin or real name, his spiritual and Sufi affiliations, and sites and relics attributed to him are actively debated in Sehwan, and of particular consequence to local politics is the question of his precise doctrinal persuasion. Also unsettled is the year of his arrival in Sehwan, of which 1272 CE is considered to be more reliable (Boivin 2012b, 83).[13] A few sacred sites in Balochistan and Sindh are the only traces that help picture the route his journey might have taken to Multan where he was first headed.[14] He later settled in Sehwan for the last year or two of his life, and yet Lal is a figure incredibly well embedded in local religious constellations. Besides his confluences with divinities of the Indus, Hindus consider him to be a Shivaite ascetic who epitomizes a particular ideal of ascetic renunciation.[15] In terms of his Islamic histories, he is most likely to have been born in Marwand, near Tabriz (in present-day Iran), and his lineage through Jafar al-Sadiq's son Isma'il makes him an important figure of the Isma'ili line of the Shi'i faith (Boivin 2011, 15–16).[16] This also means that he is a descendant of Ali and thus related to the Family of the Prophet (ahl-e bayt). In Sufi terms, Lal is claimed by both Suhrawardi and Qadiri orders and is popularly regarded as one of a quartet of mystics, chahar-yar or "four friends."[17] For many fakirs in Sehwan, Lal is an original thirteenth-century qalandar, who they believe was initiated at the hands of the order's founding figure, Jamal al-Din Savi of Damascus.[18] Multiple spiritual affiliations are in fact possible and do not always cause a contradiction in Boivin's view; however, he also cautions that historical sources do not confirm that Lal observed chahar-zarb or the fourfold shave typical of the early qalandars (Boivin 2012b, 97).[19] Adding to an abundance of origin stories is the state's own narrativizing that often seeks to harness a plural, if not also an unstraight, tradition.[20] Multiple claims work because historical references to Lal are few and far between, a patchwork at best of brief mentions found in other saints' biographical texts. For instance, sources mention a rare scene in Multan, whereby Lal is found in an ecstatic performance in the company of other Sufi figures (Boivin 2011, 18). Such tentative presence in the historical record is a function of his itinerant life insofar as the *qalandar* "who succeeds in the goal of escaping signification also escapes from history" (Ewing 2006, 250). Though Lal, I would argue, is a figure of historial abundance, evading as often as he recurs in Shi'i, Sufi, or Hindu guises. Mai's song in the grove had it right all along: "Muhammad in one place, Ali in another, and yet elsewhere, Qalandar is Ram."

A saint in flight indeed, Lal is hard to pin down. He is a multiplicity, whether in the divergent ways the saint is historically recorded or the multitudinous forms in which he returns to the present. Miracles and feats associated with Lal are told and retold in Sehwan: by fakirs to their juniors, by spiritual masters in the company of their followers, some performed in lyric and verse at shrines across the city, others circulated through private and official publications in the form of booklets, newspaper features, and special supplements. They also survive through image: saints' posters, murals, and pilgrim photographs. My assertion that a distant saint, historically evasive and previously lesser known, who begins to make lyrical-imaginal appearances in a small village through a mediating state warrants a greater story, one that situates the crisscrossing motivations of the saintly and the stately. To suture such threads, I turn to a detailed account of Baba's dreams before returning to the story of the shrine and the state.

A Garden of Dreams

Baba's dream tellings in the grove were particularly sequenced and marked by tremendous detail; always interlaced with their memory of the flying falcon. In such a sequence, just at the point when Baba would mention the song, listening to which they would fall asleep, the following episode of the dream would ensue:

> There is a garden and in it I would go. The fruits that are unripe and green, those I would pick and place them in my *jholi* [pouch-like folds of a long shirt]. As I would put it in the *jholi*, a gardener would come to me three times. As the gardener approaches, he asks, "What is it in your *jholi*?" He asks me thrice. The first time he asks what is there in my *jholi*, I remain quiet. Then a second time he inquires, "Child, what is it?" I know I have stolen it. I have plucked the unripe fruit. And in his hand is a stick. I am afraid that he might just hit me, do you understand? I'm scared that he would beat me; what can I tell him, that I have

stealthily picked the fruits? He asked me once, and then again, when he asked me the third time, I lay open like this and there ... it had turned red! Oh! I picked the fruit while it was green—how did it turn red?[21]

Remember that when the dreams first started to appear, Baba was still a child living in a village in Punjab. Baffled by the vision, the young Baba would share the contents of the dream with their mother. "Nothing is really the matter," she would comfort the child, dismissing its recurrence as an ordinary nightmare. But Baba wasn't to be comforted. The lucid and recurring dream would serve to incrementally heighten their affection for a saintly figure they did not fully recognize at the time. In Baba's words, "How is it that the green fruit I picked has turned red, I would wonder?!" Unbeknownst to Baba at the time was the symbolism of the fruit turning red. Only years later would Baba arrive at the understanding that red was the color associated with Lal, whose variant La'l means ruby, or that Shahbaz (or royal falcon) referred to a miracle attributed to the saint. After a whole year of its recurrence, Baba went up to their mother again, this time more perturbed than before. On this occasion, however, she had a different explanation. She told Baba that certain offerings were due at shrines in the child's name, and since she had forgotten to make those in time, the incessant dream was only a reminder. The dream of the garden would eventually stop. In its final sequence, Baba would encounter the same gardener once again, the one who had questioned them on the matter of the fruit. This time, as Baba described, the gardener would make a new offer:

The same gardener, the one from the first dream, he said, on the last day [of the dream], "Child, do you wish to do *ziyarat* [pilgrimage; viewing a holy site or object]?" I said, "Yes, *baba*, I would like to do *ziyarat*." He says, "Just take the straight road." We go ahead to do *ziyarat* and on the way we find a vessel of water. I drink water from the vessel; having drunk from it, I go further to perform *ziyarat*. As I go for *ziyarat*, I enter a door, then another. As I walk through the third one, I see a man sitting; two men are sitting. ... Him on this side, and him on the other—in the center is the fireplace [*machh*]. He rises and speaks to me, the one who has this much of a beard, white in color. Such is the light of his beard, and what of his face can I tell you! He came for me, and said, "Child." I said, "Yes, *baba*." He said, "Do you wish to do *ziyarat*?" I said, "Yes, I wish to do so." And what *ziyarat* he made me do! Then I performed the *ziyarat* like this: as I see, my sight falls first on his rosary, the one that is turning. It gives off a great light. Then my sight moves toward his face. Then I see the clouds. Half of it lies behind me, half ahead of me. In the middle is the image. . . . I wonder who this saint is—who is this man? I must find him. In my heart is this: the flying Shahbaz knows secrets of the heart. I want to be a *murid* [disciple] of the one, I want to serve the one who knows the secrets of the heart.[22]

It becomes clear in Baba's accounts how the contents of the dream were more demanding than the matter of simply figuring out who the flying creature was. There is a precise geography to Baba's dream, a setting in which it takes place; there are objects, concepts, places, and persons it cites as much as there are instances and occurrences, situations and compositions that call for interpretation. Also noteworthy is Baba's reference of the dream in terms of *khayal*, literally a thought. The dream thus is not a form of false consciousness but a mode of thinking that requires a tending to, demands comprehension, a way of becoming awake in the wake of visions. Affected, Baba grew emotionally perturbed, so much that they could no longer imagine staying put in the village. "As I described this to my mother, the dream was forgotten. When the dream was lost, my head started to turn such that I cannot tell you. I stepped out of my home and told my mother, 'The flying Shahbaz knows secrets of the heart; we shall meet if we live; try and forget me if I die! My soul has become such, my mother, that I cannot stay home for five more minutes!'"

Two years had passed since that first dream. At the time Baba left home, the veiled messages of the dream would have offered little direction to an eleven-year-old. Baba somehow arrived at a saint's fair in Faisalabad, the city closest to their village. Then, once the fair was over, Baba decided to board a bus, arriving at Data Darbar, Lahore's most prominent shrine complex. It was here that, according to Baba, they first found mentorship under the tutelage of a fakir. Another year would pass and even though the dreams from the village weren't really forgotten, the visions had stopped. Baba hadn't given up on the flying saint of their dreams. They clearly recounted a day from that year in Lahore. It was the time of the saint's festival, and countless other fakirs had gathered in the city. On that day, Baba's fakir-mentor had suddenly revealed his plans to travel farther, advising them to return home instead. As Baba recalls, a bus had already been arranged to take a party of fakirs to another saint's fair in a distant place in Sindh Province. As luck would have it, right at the moment when their mentor was speaking of his plans to travel, Baba heard an audiocassette play in the background. This was the very song Baba would listen to back in the village, and which on this occasion had caused the entire party of fakirs to rise and chant slogans in the name of the falcon saint. Baba was moved to tears.

Where is Lal, I wondered; if indeed Shahbaz flies and known to him are the secrets of the heart, where are you [Lal] then, and why don't you know the secrets of my heart? As I cried, the fakir asked me, "Child, what has happened to you?" I asked him, "Where are you going?" The fakir said, "Have you heard this cassette?" To which I said, "Yes!" The fakir told me that he had received an invitation to this saint's wedding [shadi]. An invitation? And to the saint's wedding he was going? ... I must go there then, come what may! I did a courageous thing and with the fakir I arrived [in Sehwan].[23]

As the party of fakirs arrived in Sehwan, they camped in Lal-bagh, the very grove where Baba now dwelled. It was in this setting that Baba came across yet another fakir, a resident of the garden itself who had made it his duty to tend to the trees of the saint's grove. Slowly and steadily, it was in Lal-bagh that figures of the dream would turn real. Back in the village, Baba had struggled to make meaning of the winged creature; they didn't know what to make of the green fruit that would turn red in the dream sequence of the garden; and who in fact was the gardener who had led Baba to the encounter with the luminous persons in the dream? It was here in the grove that Baba would meet the gardener. It was from him that they would learn of the miracles of the saint. By the time the annual fair of Sehwan had drawn to a close and fakir bands prepared for their onward journeys, Baba had won the gardener's favor. Pledging never to return, Baba decided to settle down in the garden of their dreams.

I told him [the fakir mentor], "I have arrived where I was meant to come. May Allah keep you and make you happy; I wish to remain here. You may go if you like." He asked me why. I said to him that this place has been approved for me. I had seen a garden [bagh] in my dream, so the garden came in front of me. And the baba that I had seen in the image between the skies, the same baba is here. And so, my child, I came from there to here.

It is interesting to note how Baba had come to understand and interpret their childhood visions. In one instance, they described the precise features of the fakir dwelling in accordance with images of the dream. The picking of the fruits in the garden was in fact an early premonition that they would eventually find a place in the garden of the saint. Or the very setting in which they encountered the holy figures in the dream was the blueprint for the layout of the dwelling: the three thresholds, the spot where the water-dispensing vessel would be placed, as well as the arrangement of space around a fireplace were material echoes of the dream. The dwelling was no ordinary place. It was an imaginal setting revealed in dreams and one that had to be unveiled, found, and established materially over the years on the basis of those visions. As Baba would remark, "The dream that had come there [in the village], I had found. My dream had come true; my dream was now in front of me!"

At the time Baba narrated the events of the dream to me (2011–13), they were about fifty years of age. The garden dwelling of many years was material proof of Baba's long attachment to the saint, a spiritual status additionally confirmed by Baba's fakir disposition when it came to appearance. For instance, Baba never took off the long drape around their head in my presence, yet one could gather that they had completely shaved off their hair, including the eyebrows, which lent them a distinct appearance, the fourfold shave (*chahar-zarb*) associated with *qalandar* ideals. Dressed in predominantly female attire, marked especially by the covering of the head, they were nonetheless regarded as Baba, meaning father, a title customarily used to refer to male spiritual figures. As was custom for *khwaja-sara* or gender-variant persons in the country, Baba would switch between female and male registers when referring to themselves even though the first name they were known by was clearly male.[24] At the same time, Baba was averse to fancy garments and the use of makeup, sartorial markers associated with gender-nonconforming communities in the country. Baba selectively drew from, while also tweaking, both fakir and *khwaja-sara* ideals with regard to self-presentation and performance in public. Such repurposing and departures from the norm were validated through others' perceptions of Baba as someone who was close to the saint and whose place in the garden had been approved by the saint himself. Over the years Baba had become an integral part of the grove's life, an established figure in the garden who was regarded with reverence and respect.

Saintly Enterprises of the State

To read the story of Baba and Sehwan in tandem is to take the position that behind the contemporary soar of the falcon-saint are also wings of the Pakistani state. Its administrative means and material interventions in Sehwan have shaped the saint's imaginal and affective outreach. A rubric of infrastructure in the patronage of saints and pilgrimages in Pakistan helps identify the specific modalities of such transference in the framework of what Nile Green (2006, 51) calls the "architecture of sainthood." It is to say that the matrix of enshrining the holy through creating linkages between the image of the Sufi, the body of the saint, and the sites where it can be accessed is held in place by means, modes, and facilities that run and sustain an enterprise of saints of the state in Pakistan. More importantly, while the state finds itself a place in this architecture, the power it exercises in enabling linkages, establishing forms of enshrinement, and disciplining access to saints is often disguised if not completely out of view.

A sustained line of argument has placed the Pakistani state's motivation for governing saints' shrines predominantly in national-political or economic terms. In this narrative, the newly formed state of Pakistan comes to grips with the varied resources of the many shrines that dotted its territory as early as the 1950s. A countrywide survey of religious endowments (*waqf* properties) was already under way at the time. However, it would take another decade before these shrines would formally come to be institutions of the state, eventually organized under the Department of Auqaf and governed via the Ministry of Religious Affairs.[25] The nationalization of shrines is also in part attributed to the state's interest in determining the proper place of religion in society. The creation of a new nation demanded a disciplining of the religious sensibilities of its subjects (Philippon 2016). Tied to this logic is the fact that shrine holdings and saints' places had long enabled a routinization of power for groups and individuals, mainly from sayyid lineages, whose claims to these shrines as rightful inheritors, caretakers, and custodians were more or less upheld. Displacing such authority and gaining possession of shrine resources promised not only new financial means for the state but also guaranteed curbing the influence of local powerhouses. If one objective was indeed to harness the political reach and religious authority of shrine holders and in effect replace it with that of the state, its financial bounty couldn't have been any less appealing. In fact, according to Malik (1990), only the endowments that were profitable were nationalized.[26] Understandably then, shrine takeovers were not without conflict. Some involved long legal battles with groups and families affected by nationalization, and a few such court appeals lasted well into the 1980s. Such counteractions, however, were not strong enough to stall the process. It was through a federal ordinance in 1959 that the Pakistani state finally began to implement its writ broadly by assuming custodianship of sites that were considered *waqf* (pl. *auqaf*), an inalienable endowment. While it offered a provision for the maintenance of inherited shrines and ancestral tomb-sites, the ordinance made it possible for all nonprivate endowments that were not solely charitable to be taken legally into the hands of the state (Strothmann 2012, 55). More recently, Umber bin Ibad (2019) has illustrated how the Department of Auqaf's role has unfolded during and since the colonial period. Though focusing only on central Punjab, Ibad notes that in the colonial period, "the state did not try to control shrines directly through its bureaucracy"; however, the postcolonial state has gone further, especially by virtue of implementing a unique politico-religious ideology. This has involved, in his view, the state's desire to harness the pluralistic traditions of shrines in favor of "representing a Singular Islam" (Ibad 2019, introduction). A secularizing line of argument, however, makes a different point. It suggests that in order to be modern, "it was necessary to play down the shrine or at least represent it as a worldly institution and thus to take away its religious character" (Malik 1990, 76). The coupling of modern hospitals and dispensaries with religious sites of healing or as attachments to a shrine complex can also be read in such terms (Ewing 2006, 73). By similar logic, annual saints' fairs as public holidays and the listing of shrines in state-sponsored tourism booklets served to open up shrines to a differently motivated public, like tourists and cultural enthusiasts. As Ewing notes, public projects such as libraries as part of shrine complexes encouraged "a scholarly rather than a magical approach to shrines and Sufism," while similar infrastructural investment came with the assurance that in replacing traditional authorities, the state "was not out to destroy the shrines themselves" (2006, 74, 75). As events of the state, saints' annual fairs were systematically expanded and turned into elaborate settings. Here, in full public view of the gathered pilgrims, the state was able to stage its new symbolic role. It could now place itself where a traditional custodian once stood, an intermediary of sorts, facilitating contact between the saint and the pilgrim, and in so doing acquiring a kind of legitimacy for its own authority.[27]

Whatever the motivations, the governance of saints' places in Pakistan cannot be read independently of the state's efforts to popularize them. This is an important feature in Sehwan's story. For most of Pakistan's early years, and especially prior to the arrival of Auqaf-led administration, the shrine at Sehwan had enjoyed a largely regional appeal. It drew mostly Sindhi and Baloch pilgrims from around the region. Such a view is confirmed by senior locals and also individuals and families who had an association with Sehwan's shrine long before it started to attract more diverse publics from across the country. Also interesting is my observation that Sindhi publications of the state hardly mention the saint or the shrine of Sehwan until the late 1960s, a change observable only in the wake of its public administration.[28] The prior absence of Sehwan and its saint appears more curious when other saints of Sindh (especially Shah Abdul Latif Bhittai, Sachal Sarmast, and Shah Inayat) were regularly featured during this time, and their annual fairs were marked by special editions. Only from the 1960s onward do Urdu and Sindhi newspapers offer detailed reportage on the annual fair of Sehwan. These texts describe not only its annual rites and ceremonies but include dedicated features that record the various legends and feats associated with the saint.[29] Within a decade of public administration, things seem to have gotten moving. Among hundreds of shrines in Sindh, the *Herald* reported in 1972, the shrine of Sehwan earned the most revenues and its annual fair drew bigger crowds than any other shrine (Alam 1972, 29). What also worked in the shrine's favor at the time was Zulfiqar Ali Bhutto's (d. 1979) rise to power. As a follower of the saint, the Sindhi politician's private association with the shrine ensured a personal interest in the development of the town. It was during his term as prime minister that Sehwan Developmental Authority was established. Prospects of economic growth and promises of development attracted new migration to Sehwan, especially from the less urban and impoverished parts of the country. The new settlers had very material and observable impacts on the urban and social character of the city and over the years have lent Sehwan a cosmopolitan character unlike other towns of its size in Sindh.[30] Similarly, improved rail and road networks meant that the falcon-saint of earlier Punjabi films was increasingly within reach. Sehwan would soon begin to attract urban visitors from afar, especially with the construction of the superhighway in the early 1980s connecting major towns and cities across the length of the country. It was also during this period that special trains like the Jhule Lal Express were initiated to facilitate the annual journey of pilgrims connecting Sehwan with Lahore, the capital of Punjab.[31]

If new administrators encouraged new publics, they also brought architectural modifications, extensions, and expansions to the old shrine structure. Plans for the construction of the new mausoleum were eventually executed during the early 1990s during the premiership of Benazir Bhutto. Like her father's, her personal interest in the site as well as the official patronage it accompanied over the years meant that a much larger structure would replace the old Sindhi mausoleum. The new architectural

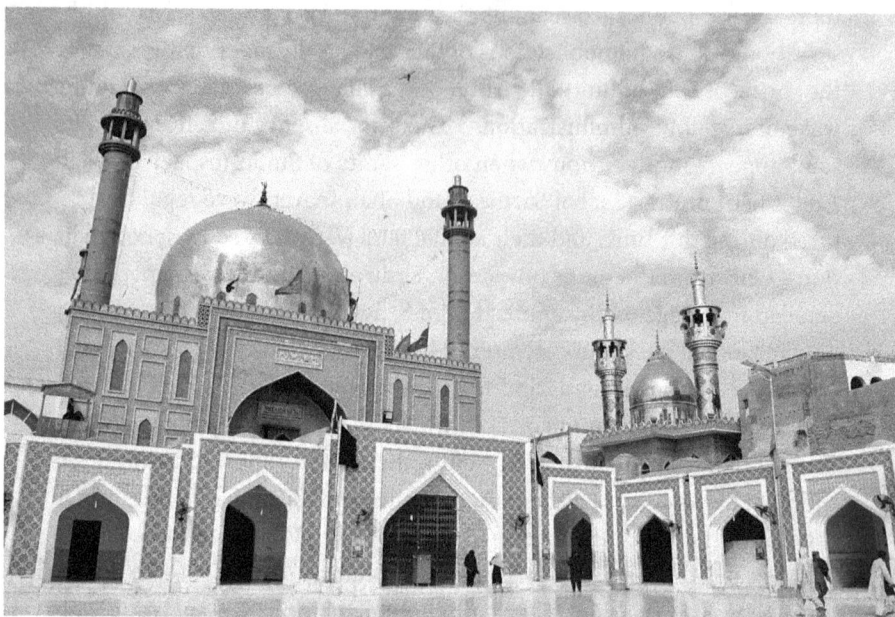

FIGURE 1.3
The remodeled facade of Sehwan's shrine complex, 2018.

vocabulary and its endorsement of Shiʻi symbolism in built form is a curious development, especially when it comes at the hands of a predominantly Sunni state. The shape of the shrine's golden dome and the form of its minarets replicate those of the mausoleums of Shiʻi imams in Iran and Iraq (see fig. 1.3). It might well have been influenced by the Shiʻi devotion of the Bhuttos since both father and daughter were personally involved in architectural and development plans. All the more interesting is that such symbolic recontouring of the shrine has coincided with a growing interest and traffic of Shiʻi mourners and pilgrims to Sehwan. It is not exactly surprising that Sehwan came to be adopted as a site of communal identification and resistance politics for the Pakistani Shiʻa during the 1990s, a decade synonymous with an intensification of sectarian violence and political division in the country.[32]

As much as the architectural shift from the vernacular to the "truly Islamic"—as the shrine's construction report describes it—is aimed at broadening the shrine's appeal, the choices that determine what of the old is retained and what is not are tied to politics of patronage and governance.[33] The reorganization of shrine space under offices of the state is a means to prioritize certain claims to the site over others, marginalizing some as a result. For instance, when, in a 2013 redesign of the tomb hall, the customary five lamps of the saint were not accommodated, it disenfranchised a local Hindu spiritual figure. His twice daily service of lighting lamps, which I had observed in years prior to the renovations, was no longer possible at the shrine. This forms part of a gradual but systematic fading away of the shrine's Hindu character at the hands of the department. Similar administrative measures have included the removal of the doorbells and, more importantly, what some locals have described as a Shiva lingam-like object from the shrine during early repairs in the 1970s.[34] Such regulating of the shrine's unstraight heritage through architectural design continues to this day.[35] Whether such decisions were premeditated or taken arbitrarily is hard to tell. The constant and highly elaborate remodeling of Sehwan's shrine from the 1990s until its latest and ongoing expansion in 2018 is proof of its increasing importance. It also reveals the faith of the state in its economic worth and value or how the Department of Auqaf participates in a larger project of reauthoring the saint through a remodeling of the place of the saint.[36]

Saints and the state are not exactly strange bedfellows. The vitality of their partnership in the present has historical precedents. As scholars argue, elite and imperial patronage of Sufis has taken varied forms and met various ends.[37] It has pushed saintly geographies into conflict with political territory as much as it has brought Sufi activity in line with worldly authority and power. It is also how sometimes living Sufis become posthumous saints, enshrined materially and symbolically as friends of Allah. As Omid Safi has noted, systems of patronage aimed at Sufi persons, places, networks, institutions, and pilgrimages have regularly secured, for both Sufis and sultans, political legitimacy and popular support, a binding process of exchange he calls "bargaining of baraka" (2000, 265). When it comes to Pakistani shrines, such exchanges are increasingly marked by unintended outcomes of governance (Philippon 2016). What makes the modern story of governing shrines infinitely more intriguing in the case of Sehwan is how, despite the explicitly Sunni-Islamic disposition and agenda of the state, its infrastructures have systematically furthered a historically Shivaite and an ascendant Shiʿi site of devotion. Furthermore, in practical terms, the presence of the state at shrines like Sehwan has afforded, even if inadvertently so, women and gender-variant persons an advanced access to saintly futures. It has enabled new and unconventional publics to lay claim, embody, and instrumentalize saints' spiritual power through fakir and other less-customary forms of religious careers. As fakirs dispense with ordinary futures, stir up crises of inheritance, and betray what is in hope for what might come, they do so on wings of the saint and the state. Fakir pursuits that I describe in this book, though ostensibly summoned by saints, are also propelled by state-sponsored infrastructures of the imaginal.

Affordances of the Dream

"Love ['ishq] had taken over me! *Shahbaz flies and knows ...* and see where I have arrived. The master [*murshid*] brought me here"—Baba's fakir story is a story of intimacy that begins with a song in the village, entails pilgrimages and encounters in dream space, traverses Sufi shrines across the Punjab, and finally locates its object in a grove outside Sehwan. This story of Baba that I heard many a time over the years would often end with the line, "and so, my child, I came from there to here." The *here* in Baba's narrative is both the garden and the fakir being. To be here is to be not at the village, to turn away from structures of home and family; to not be what could have been but to be in perpetual pursuit of what ought to be. It is a critical reminder that fakir pursuits and the saintly orientations that hold such pursuits in place come to fruition only at the expense of competing objects, other futures. "I abandoned my parents. I left behind my siblings, my relations, my family," were words I heard from Baba on a few occasions. "I came here having left behind everything, you understand? Whether they [parents] were alive or dead, I did not turn around to see. The only thing I kept in sight was my love for him [Lal]. His ... love ['ishq] is all what I considered!"

The interest of this chapter has been to illustrate how saintly intimacies prosper alongside and at times through desires of the state such that its projections come to intervene in life through felt modes and imaginal forms. The relationship of the imaginal to the question of futures is an important one to raise in Baba's story. Being a child in a poor rural family in central Punjab, one who is regarded as intersex means being given to particular bodily horizons, oriented to certain futures more than others. For instance, a most likely trajectory for a child such as Baba would have eventually involved a life with the *khwaja-sara*.[38] Given male names at birth and in most cases also registered as sons, intersex sons do not extend the social promise of family lines that cisgender sons are expected to offer. If not given up by their parents, such children, once older, seek gurus and masters themselves and are known to leave family in favor of *khwaja-sara* households (Kasmani 2021). Such departures are in line with what Sara Ahmed describes as the "normative" or "an effect of the repetition of bodily actions over time, which produces what we can call the bodily horizon, a space for action, *which puts some objects and not others in reach*" (2006, 66, emphasis original). Baba's story, however, is a perfect example of stretching, or an opening up of that collective and social bodily horizon. Moved by the affective pull of song and dream, drawn in search of a saint and heeding forceful calls of the shrine carried forth by the state, Baba abandons inheritances of family while also interrupting expectations of futures with adoptive kin and community. A willful, albeit open-ended, orientating toward a different space of action, toward a different object and location of desire, qualifies as a significant divergence from the expected course of things. In turning toward the saint, Baba turns away from a life with the *khwaja-sara* and thus from socially prescribed, communally rooted, and economically secure gender-variant futures. To the extent that saintly affects are entangled with desires of the state, Baba, by coming close to the saint, invariably draws near to the state. What is worth taking forward to other chapters, other life stories, is the understanding that prospects of life that open up or are foreclosed by virtue of one's intimacy with saintly places, objects, and figures are in some measure also a queer surplus of governance.

In March 2018, I returned to Sehwan after a break of many years. As I drove into the grove and arrived at the spot where I recalled Baba's dwelling stood, I was unable to find it. I traced my way back to the main street. Then, in a second attempt, I seemed to have driven to the same spot again. There was no sign of Baba or the dwelling. Even if I were a little off the mark, I would have been able to spot the tall '*alam* from a distance. The grove wasn't that big or populated to begin with. The tea seller at a roadside joint was quick to spot my cluelessness and asked whether I was indeed looking for Baba. To my utter disbelief, he revealed to me what had come to pass in the grove just months before. Baba had been evicted from their dwelling of forty years by the Department of Auqaf. As a site associated with the saint, this piece of land was public property, and the department, it now seemed, was taking a renewed interest in the upkeep of the grove, ridding it of what it considered encroachments. Where the beautiful dwelling once stood was now a characterless park, the department's shabby attempt at literally re-creating the garden of Lal. Once again, I thought, the state's infrastructural measures had intervened in a dream, this time to its affective and material detriment. The dwelling of Baba's dreams was real no more, the 'alam now dismantled to fit the new layout, and a fakir left to cope with a future, impaired.

The man from the roadside joint led me to a place outside the grove, along the highway, where I was to meet Baba. It seemed Baba had quickly come to terms with what had happened. In the few interactions we had over the next days, Baba came across as resolute. The actions of the department in Baba's view weren't independent of the saint's will, as if the state and the saint could only act in tandem—partly reflective of the line of argument I have here pursued. It was after all the saint who had allowed Baba to tend to the garden in the first place. Since their eviction, a local landowner had come to the rescue, offering a temporary place of refuge in a vacant and walled compound. This was a much bigger plot of land for which Baba had to pay monthly rent. Without the open publicness of the garden, Baba could no longer perform a fakir persona or host passing pilgrims. Baba was now more than ever dependent on the generosity of others.

One evening, Baba took me to the banks of the drainage canal on the other side of the grove. The landlord had plans to encroach on this newly reclaimed strip of land and had offered to allow Baba to settle there. Baba spoke of their plans to build a new dwelling; they described the layout to me on this empty piece of land, pointing to where the entrance could be, where they would install a new 'alam, and so on and so forth. But there was no history that sacralized the setting; no saintly vision that validated an arrival; no scenography of a dream that served as a blueprint for its layout. As I listened to Baba, it was clear that what had been lost was far greater than a piece of land. I also wondered how a fakir would manage the large sum of money necessary for construction. And even if a generous donor were to be found, Baba knew well that a new dwelling would not be in the grove; that the one of their dreams, like the dream itself, was now lost. Once more, Baba had been compelled to leave the comfort of home, once again by the crisscrossing will of the saint and the state. Despite altered conditions, Baba's feeling of closeness with the saint hadn't frayed one bit. The question of the future, however, was now more pressing than in the eight years we had known each other. My parting memory of Baba is of them standing by the road just when we said our goodbyes, with the usual blessings they would shower upon me. As I drove away from Baba, I could see them in the rearview mirror of the car, waving at me. The farther I drove, the smaller Baba appeared. That diminishing perspective is an image lingering in my mind. Insofar as it lasts, I am left to wonder: how must one live with futures of intimacy that are impaired by the loss of dreams?

In the footsteps of Lal, who once camped in the grove before approaching the town, with chapter 2 this book arrives in Sehwan proper. I turn to the shrine and to the story of a woman fakir contesting place in the men's prayer area. I do so to illustrate how fakir futures play out in close intimacy with the saint's tomb and in constant negotiation with public offices of shrine administration. As a singular scene of striving, her story echoes a whole range of struggles: the state's imaginal infrastructures and macro dispositions that I have illustrated in this chapter must confront the shrine's many claimants as well as its contested histories and heritage.

2

Her Stories
in His
Durbar

"One ought to not sleep in the presence of the King of kings, my son!"
Amma reprimanded me as she interrupted an afternoon nap. It was
during the first spell of fieldwork in Sehwan, when taking respite from the
heat and the crowds, I had found myself some quiet in a corner of a prayer
space. The summer heat in 2009 was unforgiving, and crowds from across
the country were pouring into Sehwan. With the annual fair of the saint
fast approaching, the excitement at the shrine was palpable. Benefiting
from the lull between the noon and the afternoon prayers, I had hoped to
get some rest. In no time, I had fallen asleep and in no time, awoken. As
I gathered my wits, I could hear Amma detailing the etiquette I ought to
have observed in the saint's durbar (lit. royal court). She was referring to
the magnificent hall that this corner space overlooked. At its center stood
Lal's tomb-shrine lined with silver, bedecked with silks and rose petals,
and from where the saint as emperor (*shahanshah* or the King of kings)
was said to hold court and grant audience.

How could I possibly have come across a woman in the one spot at the shrine reserved only for men? The question kept returning in my head. I knew that saints' places in Pakistan were particularly relaxed when it came to the mixing of genders. At Sehwan's shrine, too, one could find women, *khwaja-sara*, and men crossing paths in many places and on most occasions. Yet there were exceptions. For instance, the evening performance of *dhamal* (ritual drumming) was carefully segregated, and so were these two corners of the durbar where women and men could temporarily part ways to read the five daily prayers. For women, it additionally offered greater privacy within the public hall where they could hang out on their own. The spaces' relative elevation from the ground meant that many would sit by their arches and gaze upon the shrine, since they offered an uninterrupted view of the saint's tomb. These weren't really mosques but semiprivate sections reserved for ritual prayer, peripheral spaces of the shrine durbar located in the architectural excess resulting from an octagonal layout in a square plan.

Less than a fortnight into this first encounter with Amma, a pilgrim would formally introduce her to me as his spiritual guide. It all started to make sense. Her all-black dress and distinct demeanor were signs that she was no ordinary pilgrim, rather a woman unlike women, as I would in later years come to describe fakir women (Kasmani 2016a). Her unusual place among men was an added marker of her charismatic authority, which, although largely respected, was hard earned and never entirely beyond question. In fact, keeping this place required constant negotiating, be it with shrine officials or men who frequented the space. Centered around Amma, this chapter details a fakir life in the dual company of the saint and the state. "Her Stories in His Durbar" is about the ways in which women fakirs' authority is tied to local intimacies with male saintly figures and enabled by an interceding state. It is also about how an embodiment of motherhood comes to partially remedy women's exclusion from patrilineal charisma in Sehwan. Amma's story in this book illustrates how the prospects that saintly intimacy affords women are contingently derived. Or that these need to be effortfully secured over time through an effective exteriorization of inward mystical experience and the affective narrativization of ordinary endurance. Attendant themes of misfortune and hardship point to ways in which women's less-ordinary pursuits of the saint were bound for affective disturbance, characterized by dual crises of inheritance and extension.

Like futures of the dream that Baba (in chapter 1) was left to deal with, women's pursuits of saintly objects were uncertain life projects, contingent on the saint's will and deficient in social sanction. In testing the norm and at the same time being undermined by it, women's self-brokered fakir careers in Sehwan were lone and stubborn pursuits, carried out with little or no patronage, and though accommodated at state-run shrines were invariably affected by the politics of place making and gatekeeping. Alongside a fakir life story, this chapter advances our understanding of the ways in which the state's administrative presence pushes forward a limited democratization of shrine space, proliferating further the shrine's historical orders of authority. To this end, the chapter describes how the authority of women fakirs is exercised alongside that of other authorities, be they the officials of the state or local sayyids, Sehwan's traditional households that trace their descent from the first disciples of the saint, also Prophet Muhammad, and whose control over the shrine was replaced by the state in June 1960. We also acquire a sense of why fakir futurities can be twice as impaired when it comes to women, or the ways in which the saint's durbar, the greater setting of Amma's story, is host to manifold contestations that the state provokes, but also arbitrates.

Fakirs of an Interceding State

Amma—a title meaning mother—as she was reverently known to the shrine public, is a Balochi-speaking woman from Jacobabad. A fakir for over two decades, she lived with her husband and three children in a rented house just minutes' walk from the shrine. As chance an encounter as ours had seemed, I would eventually come to realize that Amma hadn't simply sauntered into a space reserved for men. It was where she would be found every day, year after year. Upon closer observation, one could find a little grave in a cove-like corner of the space, which had been rather oddly incorporated since the redesign of the tomb-hall sometime in the 1990s. In fact, she viewed herself as the lone guardian of a forgotten grave, a duty central to her own understanding of her fakir objects. Dark and stout, she would unfailingly be dressed in an all-black *shalwar-kamiz* offset by the *hal-vaslah* she carried: a studded necklace, fetter-like anklets, and the many brightly colored rings that she wore on her fingers. She spent her days sitting in a corner guarding one grave and overlooking another, that is to say, the saint's tomb, never out of her sight. Also, given

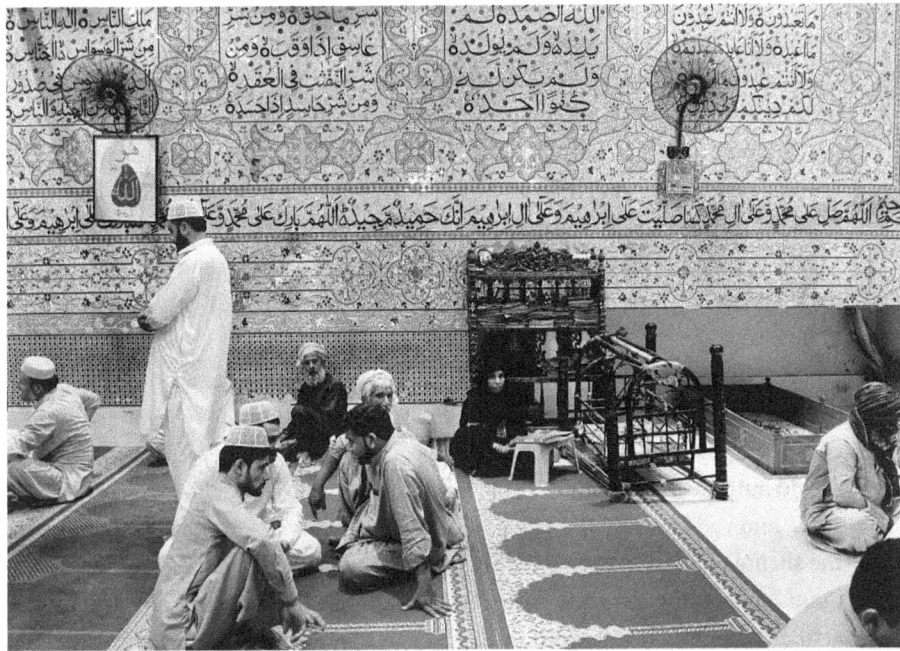

FIGURE 2.1
Amma among men at the shrine, 2018.

her unusual circumstances in the prayer space, invariably, all of Amma's followers were men.

Sitting in a corner did not mean that Amma was peripheral to what went on at the shrine. In fact she was implicated in the shrine's affective economies and impacted by the greater politics of administration, whether it meant newly appointed managers or architectural changes in the shrine layout over the years. Similarly, Amma's quiet but invasive presence in a corner of the durbar had far-reaching ramifications. The space in which Amma was to be found, and where I was caught sleeping, was where Sunni worshippers were expected to gather (see fig. 2.1). A separate room was designated for Shi'i prayer in an adjacent part of the shrine. When I was awoken by Amma, though I had immediately caught on to her gendered presence, I was unaware of her Shi'i persuasion. While men at the shrine sought her out for spiritual consultations, many also knew that she handed out *sajdah-gah*, a small tablet of clay used by Shi'i Muslims for ritual prostration. By enabling the Shi'a to pray within the durbar and in an otherwise Sunni place, Amma's quiet work in a corner of the shrine was messing with expected and established orders of place and performance.[1]

One view to take of Amma's place in the durbar is to say that the Pakistani state offers saints' places as grounds for women and other less-customary publics to lay claim to a saintly figure and develop their reputations as spiritually capable bodies. This is relevant especially since fakir pursuits of the likes of Amma's are at variance with local systems of elite sayyid authority, where proper access to the saint can work only through male sanction and on the basis of patrilineal transmission and spiritual inheritance. As significant an outcome as this is of the state's administrative role at shrines, the emancipatory tenors it might suggest on the part of the state are unintended, inadvertent at best (Philippon 2016). Equally compelling is the idea that through a patronage of nonhereditary, non-sayyid authorities, the state is able to proliferate the field of claims so as to serve and validate its own function at shrines (Kasmani 2019a). Insofar as the shrine of Sehwan is also the core of its material and spatial relations, a point Michel Boivin (2011, 89–125) makes in his discussion of devotional artifacts attributed to Lal, Amma's place in the durbar is part of a greater arrangement of the saint's heritage and its disposal, whether material or otherwise.

In order to make this plain, a brief historical sketch of Sehwan's shrine and its various patrons is in order. We know that the earliest mention of the saint's grave occurs in a fourteenth-century account of the North African traveler Ibn Battuta (d. 1369). If one is to follow Boivin's (2011, 30) stage-wise process of the shrine's historical transformation, a first mausoleum was in place as early as 1357 and another was built around 1585. Such developments suggest how the shrine grew from a nondescript grave site to a center of public pilgrimage. The shrine's rise in prominence during the Mughal period and especially its architectural development would have been concurrent with its ascending material prospects. It is therefore plausible that a sustained interest of princely figures and elite patrons in the site would have eventually pushed out its first ascetic and possibly also Shivaite caretakers, or accommodated more organized and privileged social groups, the Muslim sayyids for instance.[2] In tracing their lineage to the Prophet, a predisposition to patrilineal structures of inheritance not only empowers sayyids but also equips them with charismatic systems to reproduce and consolidate their claim on the shrine and its resources over time.[3] In the period following the eighteenth century, British colonial records document duties and services at the shrine being shared between

Hindu and Muslim groups. More prominent in such records are lengthy court disputes regarding its revenues, especially the issue of the shrine's custodianship involving two notable sayyid lineages of Sehwan, the Lakkiyari and the Sabzwari. These families continue to hold a significant influence in the town, though their claims on the shrine and its revenues, both immediate and ancillary, can be documented only as far back as the colonial period.[4]

What makes claims to the saint's inheritance all the more troubled in the contemporary, whether it is the matter of material assets or spiritual transmission, is the fact that as an antinomian mystic, Lal was a celibate figure and thus without issue. A shrine without legal heirs could not be deemed familial inheritance, which in fact was a key line of argument in the modern state's takeover of the shrine from its traditional sayyid custodians. Sehwan's former custodian families, however, trace their lineage back to the first heirs of the saint. Their ancestors, as the Sabzwari claim, were select disciples who accompanied Lal on his journey from Iran; the Lakkiyari, from the neighboring hills of Lakki, assert that they descend from the saint's primary followers who received the journeying ascetic on the outskirts of Sehwan.[5] Rivalries endure in Sehwan to this day, and a speculative claim making around the figure of the saint flourishes under the state. The shrine complex too has consistently grown in size and grandeur. While the present-day structure was built in the early 1990s, several rounds of repairs prior to and since have been undertaken by the Department of Auqaf. By installing a bureaucratic structure, expanding access to the saint and viewing itself as the latest in a series of Muslim rulers who have acted as the shrine's patrons, the Pakistani state is able to lay claim to the shrine's symbolic reserves as well its manifold revenues, which it can disperse and dispose of as it wills, often in alliance with the local sayyid elite or the shrine's former custodians (Kasmani 2019a; Ewing 2006, 75). To observe how the state exercises its authority alongside the shrine's traditional power structures, let me turn to a daily ceremony at the shrine. Ahead of Amma's life story, it sets up the greater context that circumscribes her access to the saint, however invasive or interwoven her place might be in the daily fabric of the durbar.

It was around 3:30 a.m. on a Friday morning in November 2011. The streets of Sehwan were gradually recovering from the Thursday night frenzy characteristic of saints' shrines in Pakistan; and even though Sehwan felt quieter than usual at this hour, in the half-slumber of its vendors and teahouses one could sense a lingering bustle of its day pilgrims and weekend visitors. Despite the early hour, people were gathering in small numbers at the main gate of the shrine to witness the daily ceremony of *ghusl* or the ritual bathing of the saint's tomb.[6] For a few hours now, the tall and heavily carved wooden doors of the durbar had remained closed. A metallic lock was in place, wrapped in a red silken cloth. The ones gathering in the white marbled forecourt were Department of Auqaf employees, contract workers and cleaners, a handful of fakirs, visitors, and pilgrims. A policeman tried to keep things in order. The junior manager of the shrine arrived with keys to the shrine. Also present were *khadim*s, some state-employed, and other workers on contract whose duty is to serve the saint and his shrine. A fakir from a prominent lodge of the Lakkiyaris walked in with a large bundle wrapped in red cloth. Another one, representing a secondary shrine in the town, carried a big basket filled with rose petals. The mood, as always at this hour, was somber and quiet. People stood with hands folded, heads lowered. A soft whisper of prayer could be heard. Sharply penetrating the reverent mood of the courtyard were the intermittent but regular chants of a fakir, his sharp and distinct voice a regular feature at the opening of the shrine doors as well as its closing at midnight. The other sound was that of the drum and the metal disc placed just where the entrance portal gives way to the open courtyard. Its periodic striking signaled the approaching time for the opening of the shrine doors.

This gathering, though small and routine, was by no means ordinary. There were policemen and officials of the Department of Auqaf that stand in for the state; objects and materials that connect the shrine with the sayyid households of the town; histories of exchange and service that can be traced in the contributions to the ceremony. A custodian of a fakir lodge was present, as were locals whose families have long been associated with devotional duties at the shrine, whether cleaning, drumming, or lighting lamps at the shrine. Most striking, however, is the arbitrating role that the Pakistani state assumes in the orchestration of this daily ritual. That it is performed by a junior manager of the department who possesses the keys to the shrine is an everyday staging of state power, a reminder that the shrine of Sehwan is no longer familial inheritance but public asset. A figure like Amma, though present daily at the shrine, couldn't be part of such a service. The few fakirs involved are disciples of local sayyids and part of their fakir lodges.[7] Not only is Amma without the protection of a sayyid master, women's participation in traditional routines at the shrine is often restricted by local customs, many of which are also upheld under state administration.[8] State control and interest have also effectively disenfranchised local Hindu families who once enjoyed a greater role in similar services at the shrine.

As the high doors were flung open that morning, the policeman on duty tried hard to contain the fervor of the gathered crowd; only those men assigned the task of washing are allowed to enter at this time. One by one the two side entrances of the durbar were also flung open, the large donation boxes slid away, and the lights switched on. Workers brought in wipers as buckets full of soapy water were splashed across its marble floors. The manager stepped into the tomb enclosure. The large red bundle was undone. Inside was the *dastar*, headgear for the saint's tomb. New sheets, fresh rose petals, and the newly prepared *dastar* would eventually replace the old one. It is the Lakkiyaris, the more influential of the two custodian families in town, who provide this most important item for the tomb's dressing. It is prepared with fresh leaves at one of their *kafis* (fakir lodges) located just outside the shrine premises. A representative is present every morning to deliver the *dastar* and to collect the old one, which is then taken back to the lodge and placed at a minor shrine therein.[9] This changing of the *dastar* is one example of a greater system of exchange of favors that continues between the state and the sayyid elite of Sehwan. Ornamented jewels, decorative flowers, and peacock feathers add the final touch to the dressing of the crown of the saint, finished by the use of perfumed oils and sprays.[10] Occasionally, wealthy pilgrims also contribute gifts of ornamental value for the dressing of the tomb. Their participation is often made possible through government contacts or the intervention of local sayyid families who use their influence to confer favor on their disciples, thus broadening their share by indirect participation in the ceremony. This is also true for work allocations and income opportunities at the shrine. Many of the contract workers seen washing the shrine floor would have found entry into the town's most important economic network through an exchange of favors between the Auqaf and the sayyids. The stakes of the department's working relationship with Sehwan's elite figures extend far beyond the morning ritual and remain crucial to the state's success in organizing the more important and elaborate events in the year. These include the shrine's major ceremonies and the town's annual ritual processions during the time of the saint's fair as well as in the holy month of Muharram.

The washing continued in the durbar. Outside, women and men sat by the threshold observing the auspicious and solemn ceremony. The mood was quiet, although the echoing song of a devotee standing by the door

FIGURE 2.2
A state official dresses the saint's tomb during the morning ritual, 2013.

rendered it suitably lyrical. As the cleaning drew to a close, the Auqaf manager walked over to the three doors of the durbar and sprinkled rose water on those witnessing the ritual from outside. Now sharing the substance of the ceremony, his primary role in the ritual lent his otherwise civil office a quasi-spiritual character. There was a loud wave of chants as people flocked to the tomb to touch and kiss the freshly dressed tomb of the saint. They brought new covers and fresh petals and offered sweets and money to the saint.[11]

Every day, in bathing and dressing the saint anew, the state, through its functionaries, renews and reaffirms its authority (see fig. 2.2). It stages itself as the figure that officiates access to the holy. Its interceding role is not without an awareness that public administration of a shrine like Sehwan is a complex undertaking, which involves, among other things, the upholding of some its traditions and the successful and amicable management of its multiple contestations. In placing a state official next to the saint, right where the sayyid custodian once stood, by collecting donations in his name, and through patronage of new or nonhereditary claimants, the state disrupts an already existing order of authority at the shrine. This speaks in part to what I have argued in chapter 1, that the Pakistani state's interest in governing shrines includes its affective registers and symbolic stakes. Or that it intervenes as much in its material orders as it shapes its immaterial figurations. Drastic as state measures have been, its interventions at the shrine have not dismantled operative logics of hierarchy and power in Sehwan. Instead, the state disrupts only to accommodate itself. Sayyid influence and social authority are locally respected, and Auqaf's strategic operation of shrine administration in alliance with the town's elite is an acknowledgment of that. Such teaming up of resources and authorities mean that saintly pursuits like Amma's are twice as affected. Her life story in this book reveals how her relations to the saint and the shrine are subject to the will and actions of the state as much as these are undermined by customary models and local systems of authority. From the elevated corner where Amma sits, the view of the saint's tomb is uninterrupted. However, her access to saintly objects and futures is not as direct. Her stories in the durbar reflect an acute awareness of the obstinacies and obstacles that Amma faces as a woman and a fakir.

Inside Out: Women, Spirits, and Patrilineal Authority

Amma had turned to a fakir pursuit at a time of immense economic hardship. The constant ill health of her husband had meant an erratic income with little or no security. When he finally gave up his job as a truck driver in Jacobabad, they decided to come to Sehwan, along with their two children, taking refuge as many do in the shrine arcades. At the time of our first meeting in 2009, Amma had already been a fakir for over a decade. She had had a third child while in Sehwan and, through her reputation and daily practice as a spiritual guide and healer at the shrine, was the sole breadwinner for a family of five. A few months into their arrival in Sehwan, while they were still camping in the shrine arcades, Amma had begun to experience a cohabiting spirit. This, as she explained to me, was accompanied by a series of signs and visions that confirmed for her the idea that Lal had chosen her to remain in his service. During this early period, a spirit or fakir-of-the-inside, *andar ka fakir* in her words, would make itself present each evening, a pattern that lasted for months at a stretch. On such occasions, when Amma would lose her bodily composure and in states of the spirit's withdrawal, Abba, Amma's husband, would sit next to her, comforting her as she returned to full composure. Over the years, Amma has had to learn to master the cohabiting spirit. What such management entails is gaining an objectified knowledge of spirits (Lambek 1993), which in the case of fakirs is mediated on a number of levels, involves complex registers of gender, and exceeds the dual sphere of the host and the spirit. For example, Amma's communication with her male cohabiting spirit serves as a bridge to the (male) saint; the demands of the possessing spirit are both demands of the saint and conditions for enabling the link between Amma and the saint. Equally notable is that messages from the saint are rendered intelligible via the mediating spirit, made manifest in the utterances that Amma-as-host performs.[12] These can be recovered only after the performance is over through the explanations of her husband, present on the occasion. As Carla Bellamy has noted, proclamations made during such performances "are only meaningful if witnessed and rearticulated by someone other than the possessed individual and the possessing spirits" (2008, 40). Not only does a public performance and its subsequent interpretation matter, it is a fakir spirit, always male, that furnishes women like Amma's outward claims to be fakirs themselves.

Amma's description of the scene matches a regular sight at the shrine. Each evening in the white marble courtyard of the shrine, women from across the country experience *haziri* (lit. presence; see fig. 2.3). Responding to the sounds of drum and reed, cohabiting spirits are believed to become present during a ritual performance, leaving hundreds of women in bouts of exhilaration. Once the performance of *dhamal* concludes, family members help loved ones recover from the exhausting experience of *haziri*. One can also observe how visitors at the shrine approach them to seek divination from spirit hosts who are making these passages, already attributing a possible line of futurity to such women. But as Amma explained, not all possessions lead to fakir futures. A distinction comes to be drawn between ill-meaning possessions that are demonic and commonplace and those which involve cohabiting with noble and enabling spirits. Willed by the saint himself, fakirs-of-the-inside are few and far between. Also, one receives or meets a fakir spirit, in contrast to djinns and malevolent spirits that mount persons.[13] It is also for their abilities to discern good from bad spirits that fakirs are often summoned to watch over women's passages during *haziri*.

Mastani is one such figure at the shrine who claims she can force djinns and spirits into submission. Her matted, henna-dyed dreadlocks signal her fakir status. Unique as she is in terms of her appearance, she isn't the only one to make such claims, either at the shrine or beyond it. Mastani must share the field with other healers, Amma being one of them. That said, what women like Amma and Mastani are set against is not one another

FIGURE 2.3
A woman during *haziri* in the shrine courtyard, 2010.

but the femaleness ascribed to their bodies and the commonly held notion
that spiritual authority isn't a thing to acquire but to inherit, reproduced
in acts of exclusive transmission between men. Only meters away from
the marble court, in a glamorously bedecked pink healing room, sat Shah,
one of Sehwan's most renowned spirit healers (*pir*). The room has since
been demolished to make way for the ever-extending shrine. Even without it, the *pir* in question remains an important figure because enshrined
in his sayyid status is his relation to the Prophet Muhammad.[14] Shah has
a double claim to make. Like Mastani, he has the power to tame malevolent spirits, but in contradistinction to her, his practice is a function of his
patrilineal descent. The gift of healing, as his brother explained to me, was
divinely bestowed upon their family. It has been transmitted over gen-
erations and, as was characteristic of local sayyids, was transferred from
father to son by means of a ceremony that involves symbolically drinking
spirituality from a cup (*pyala*). However great their efforts, fakir healers,
as he told me, could never equal historically secured volumes of charisma.
In a sense, he was on point. Fakir claims of intercessory virtuosity in Seh-

wan were fragile and revocable, their positions invariably undermined by the social, economic, and historical privileges that hereditary masters like Shah enjoyed in Sehwan. In fact, fakirs knew that even in instances where their capacities were distinct, their influence couldn't supersede that of a sayyid *pir*.

Sayyid power in Sehwan wasn't simply a spiritual matter. Like Shah, most sayyids in town traced their descent to the primary disciples of the saint. A long history of attachment to the shrine and its revenues, social privilege, and official favors spanning centuries have enabled these lineages to prosper in both economic and political terms. Their social positions as *pir*s but also adjudicators and patrons are deeply grounded in Sehwani life. And while the nationalization of shrines has dramatically reduced their roles at the shrine, limiting it to the ceremonial, former custodian families continue to hold considerable leverage through other forms of participation—the description of the morning ritual above serves as elaboration. The sway they hold over the ancillary resources of the shrine, its related market and economy, for instance, can hardly be overstated.[15] Former custodians (*sajjadah-nashin*) regularly seek some measure of say in the upkeep of the shrine by offering advice to the state and its functionaries, being part of shrine committees and the organization of annual ceremonies. Not least, they have secured a place of influence through their claims to and management of the greater spiritual and material heritage of the saint. This is particularly true of their patronage and control of the fourteen-*kafi* system, a network of the town's primary and ancient fakir lodges believed to have been established by the saint himself.

As exclusively male institutions, *kafi*s offer the most common access to a fakir life in Sehwan. These are fakir fraternities, which are headed either by the *sajjadah-nashin* himself or through one of his affiliates.[16] With the shrine out of their hands, Sehwan's sayyids and custodian families are able to retain part of their historically principal roles by virtue of their positions as patrons and masters of fakirs at such lodges. It is also the most routine way through which a fakir initiate from outside Sehwan is accommodated in local constellations of power, recruited to serve the interests of Sehwan's spiritual economies (see chapter 4). Women and *khwaja-sara* individuals are systemically excluded from such networks, rarely accommodated at fakir lodges in Sehwan, and must therefore find other, mostly independent, ways to pursue fakir lives.

Neither male nor sayyid, figures like Amma and Mastani are therefore doubly disadvantaged. In Sehwani logic, notions of inherited 'ata, the charismatic gift available to men like Shah, and 'amal, the acts and exercise of (women) fakirs, are not the same. The sayyid of the pink healing room is unlike Amma by virtue of the difference in the respective lines of spiritual power and sources of authority they each have at their disposal. As Shah's brother continued explaining to me, fakir performance is fundamentally different from the gift that the sayyid enjoys: 'ata, once bestowed, cannot be revoked; it can only be transmitted down. As outsiders to both systems of inheritance and structures of patronage, women must strive to acquire their capacities through a tenuous process that involves individual exercise and sustained action (*riyazat*). Failure to secure its conditions could result in such powers being lost or, worse still, revoked.

An exclusion from dominant tradition means that women must innovate with what is available to them. According to Karen Pechilis, a prominent and also distinguishing characteristic of women spiritual masters "is personal experience both in the sense of independent spiritual realization outside of initiation in a lineage (many female gurus are self-initiated), as well as a pragmatic orientation that relates experience of the world to spiritual knowledge" (2012, 114). Baba-Akram's journey to Sehwan on the basis of dreams and waking visions, detailed in chapter 1, is equally a pragmatism borne out of the gendered limitations that Baba faces, and so is self-initiation that works through a masterful cohabitation of spirits. Figures like Amma have neither access to fakir lodges in Sehwan nor recourse to patrilineal structures of sayyid-ness, a social distinction that revels not only in transmitted inheritance but equally in intimacy, that is, such a figure's closeness to the Prophet through lines of descent (Gautier and Levesque 2020, 2).[17] With meager institutional support or sanction, for many women fakirs the key to and the proof of their fakir credentials lies in their embodied experiences and accounts of dealing with spirits from the saint. Such bodied and affective entanglements with noncorporeal beings means that Sufi spiritual transformation, which typically depends on dyadic relationships of authority and dependence between men (Malamud 1996, 90), can take multitiered forms when it comes to women. To the extent that fakirs-of-the-inside help establish a link between the fakir woman and the saint, such cohabiting with male spirits is a complex mode of intimacy. Affording bodied, affective, and emotional disturbances attendant to such coming close to saints, women are able to secure an unstraight or gender-distinct route to spiritual authority and transformation. While such women are able to circumvent the need for a sayyid spiritual master or the dependencies that come with life at a fakir commune, their progress is all the same affected by their life-long relationship with mediating spirits, not least their husbands or family members who assist, accompany, and help make meaning of women's passages in the shrine courtyard.

Amma regularly spoke of the long-term strain that accompanied fakir goals or how dealing with spirits affected her physical condition as well as her mental well-being. Such stories of hardship were also tales of intimacy refracted through accounts of fakir mastery. Maintaining her capacities and her effectiveness as a fakir meant fulfilling demands that the saint or the fakir-of-the-inside made of her. On a visit to her home, back in November 2009, Amma had shown me an elaborate set of iron chains and shackles. She had been instructed to wear it in remembrance of Sajjad, a Shi'i figure who survived the tragedy of Karbala (680 CE).[18] In a few months, despite the saint's orders, Amma had discontinued the practice as she could no longer endure the physical hardship that it entailed. Four years later, during the holy commemoration of Muharram, when Amma appeared at the shrine with the same chains and shackles, she elaborated on her reasons for resuming the elaborate guise. This time she was additionally instructed not to bathe during this period, nor was she allowed a change of clothes.

> My son, it has been seventeen or eighteen years since I was instructed by the saint [sarkar] to wear this. I did not wear it for a year. I wore it for six months. After six months, I took it off. I would give it a wash, do everything to it, but I wouldn't wear it. I have seen and suffered through many difficulties. It was in the durbar that the saint said, "I will bend your foot!" My foot got sprained for the first time in the durbar. It became so turned that I could not walk or do anything. I would keep sitting in one place; I suffered a great deal. Then a second time, a third time, and then my foot got burned. I said to myself, the saint will not spare me now. . . . It was 'urs of the saint [lit. wedding; saint's fair] and I was instructed to wear it. I did not do so. As the 'urs passed, my condition got serious. I was finished. For two months, I could not perform my duty, neither would I be able come to the durbar, nothing! Then I came and sought his forgiveness: give me health and respect in the name of Sajjad and the pious women. I will be your prisoner once again! So, I was supposed to wear it on the first day of Muharram.... But I did not wear them. I kept pushing it, an oversight. Then I faced hardship. I felt the rigor. Last night I faced difficulty; it also affected my eyesight. ... Then I took these out yesterday. I got these washed by

Waqar [her son]. I got them placed at the 'alam, applied fragrances to them. ... I woke up very early, remembered Allah, the *panjatan*, Qalandar, and Sajjad, and I wore the chains of Sajjad. Wearing these, I came to the feet of the saint and said, "I will take these off on the fortieth day." I was suffering so much, my son, that I thought I would breathe my last.[19]

Failures to observe saintly commands involved consequences. The demands of a fakir life, as I had learned from other women, were bound to affect their well-being in the home, especially fakir women's relations with family. So often did Amma's pursuit take the shape of illnesses and physical suffering that its public performance in the durbar had become an integral part of her fakir repertoire. Out of countless conversations, I cannot remember a single occasion when Amma didn't bring up her dealing with illnesses, her struggles with economic hardship, or the physical and emotional endurance that fakir life demanded. Suffering, as Kaveri Harriss (2010, 170) notes, can be a powerful feminine ideal. Writing on the gendered dimension of chronic ill health among British Pakistani women, she illustrates how narrativizing illness can offer certain rewards. A reputation for endurance, she argues, is the very leverage that women use to sanction release from everyday roles or increased control and in so doing are able meet pragmatic ends within the household (179–80).[20] Equally emotive performances of enduring hardship and misfortune are characteristic of Pashtun women's lives in northern Pakistan (Grima 2004). What such studies also show is that inasmuch as a performance of suffering can be strategic, it is premised on other people's knowledge of one's endurance. Without masterful and gendered self-representation, these women would not have the leverage within local contexts of power through which they seek to negotiate change in their interpersonal worlds. Amma's description of her hardships, of the initial challenges of dealing with and domesticating the fakir-of-the-inside and subsequently of its long-term corporeal consequences can be situated in such poetics of suffering. However, unlike Harriss's and Grima's cases, the extent and viability of her performance are not limited to the familial or interpersonal sphere. Her suffering navigates more public worlds. Amma's performance and narrativizing in the shrine-field to her followers and listeners is part of the healing rhetoric that female healers must employ in order to highlight their chosenness for, and to sustain their right to, positions of spiritual authority, which in the case of their male counterparts is culturally assumed (Flueckiger 2003, 267).

In all instances, where pursuits of saintly intimacy are self-brokered, fakirs must rely on their embodied and inward experiences while also making it outwardly manifest, whether through a performance of distinct bodiliness or in a pendant narrativizing of their affective experiences. Seated among men and between graves, Amma's performance additionally stood out by virtue of her guise. Her dress and demeanor were neither random nor of her own making. During her first months at the shrine, an unknown woman had approached her with black clothes, adding how in a dream she was instructed to deliver the garments to her. Amma viewed this as an injunction from the saint. The colors, clothes, gems, and accessories all came to be customized over time as per the saint's will. In the public eye, it referenced her chosen status, singled her out from other women, and in a sense legitimated her access beyond the domestic. Her doing of place in a space reserved for Sunni men was already a performance in and of itself. Yet when Amma appeared at the durbar in chains, her narrations of illness, suffering, and hardships took a spectacular form in an undeniably Shi'i aesthetic. The customization of fakir guise staged afresh her claim to a life of saintly service. It established in the eyes of the public the legitimizing knowledge that her fakir body was a capable and enduring body, and more, that Amma was no ordinary woman who simply sat in physical vicinity to the saint's tomb but one who was critically close to the saint in affective terms.

Women Un/Like Women: The Authority of Mothers

"He chose me out of so many women here and gave me the guardianship of this mosque; I am the first woman to have been given such a duty"—this is a statement from our earliest recorded interview. It wasn't the last time that Amma would bring up the distinctiveness of her place in the durbar. It was in fact tied to Amma's view on women's spiritual authority. In one of our subsequent conversations, she used the word *bechari* (one who is helpless) to describe a woman, though in so doing she had effectively turned a notion of vulnerability into a valuable trait. She argued that given the subordinate status of a woman in society and her inferior condition, it was almost impossible for the saint to refuse a plea when forwarded by a woman fakir. Also, Lal knew well that in order to be a fakir, a woman had to overcome many more obstacles than a man, especially when it came to ties with the family, and for this reason alone, she said, the status of a woman fakir was indeed great and her capacities more effective. Abba, who was also present on the occasion, had his own two cents to add to the conversation. Evoking the concept of *niyani*, or little sister in Sindhi society, Amma's husband explained how among locals, the greatest of conflicts can be resolved if one of the feuding parties is able get a *niyani* to intervene on their behalf. Women fakirs were therefore perfect instruments for intercession in his opinion. Amma, by herself, was clearly aware of the extraordinariness of her situation. When she brought up the matter of her chosenness, she also in the same sitting reaffirmed the cultural notion that women are frequently unclean. "After my third child, I sat outside the durbar as I was *na-pak* [lit. impure; unclean]; I begged Lal to rid me of this monthly cycle of impurity. What kind of *fakiri* would that be, if one had to stay away from him [the saint] for a week every month?"[21]

This did not strike me as surprising. In South Asia, menstruating and postpartum women can be considered to be in an active state of pollution, attributed with a capacity to defile, which prevents them from full participation in many ritual practices across various faiths. On the bodied dimensions of dirt and gender in India, Sarah Lamb has noted that women are believed to be "more open anatomically: things (such as menstrual blood, sexual fluids, and children) flow into and out of women's bodies in ways that men do not experience" (2005, 219–20). Conceived and described as more porous compared to men's bodies, women are thus taken to be more exposed to mixes and impurities, also more prone to possession. Women fakirs are similarly aware that their spiritual pursuits come with distinct issues, matters of the body that ought to be properly managed. Such preemptive explanations when interacting with women fakirs weren't unusual. It demonstrated a heightened self-consciousness of the critique their public roles were subject to, no less than the questionable character of women's bodies and the validity of their roles and practices beyond the domestic. "I am just like yourself," Amma told me in our first meeting, adding that even if she appeared like a woman, she wasn't one in the real sense. "I am no longer like other women," she claimed—all this without me explicitly bringing up the issue of Amma's gender.

"Just like yourself" and yet, one might notice that in being called *amma* or mother, Amma's fakir status was unmistakably borne of femininity. I have elsewhere argued that women fakirs' articulation of their gendered selves involves a double burden: they must position themselves not only in relation to masculine ideals of ascetic practice but also in contradistinction to other women (Kasmani 2015, 2016a). This relation to ordinary women isn't a performance that leans on the fakir subject's masculinization; instead, it opens itself to different, multiple, or other femininities, insofar as such claims rest on feminine ideas of saintly belonging. My point is that less customary spiritual careers require additional work: Amma's discursive self-representation as being unlike women is not an overcoming of ascribed femaleness per se; it is instead "the effortful device through which her fakir aspirations are accommodated despite her gender" (Kasmani 2016a).[22]

The commonly adopted and given title *amma* (also *ma* and *mata*), in the South Asian context, lends women in godly pursuits the postsexual authority of a mother critical to their public circumstances (Pechilis 2012, 123).[23] On the one hand, it makes public contact less suspect. The woman fakir strives to establish that she is postsexual in her capacity as a mother-guide, that she is ritually pure and beyond desire, and that any public interaction between herself and the devotee is thus free of sexual tension. On the other hand, it affirms how it is in fact the experience of actual motherhood that furnishes women with social maturity, respect, and greater affective knowledge of the world. It lends the woman an authority unlike young unmarried girls, who, as Benedicta Grima (2004, 13, 162) argues, are not considered to have begun living since they have not experienced the kind of personal depth, affect, and suffering that come with marriage and offer women certain status in society. This, in my observation, has practical implications also for women's religious prospects. Readings of Pakistani women's dependence on structures of marriage and the experience of motherhood suggest that more mature social status as wives and mothers enhances women's social potentials and elevates them within a given female social hierarchy. "Women have gradated access to the outside world," as Anjum Alvi (2013, 182) writes in the context of a Pakistani village, where "young unmarried teenage girls with no social responsibilities are the most restricted"; they also have the least access to resources in a household (Chaudhry 2010, 105).[24] Moreover, "elder girls get around more in order to look after the livestock and for other such duties," while mothers, and especially mothers-in-law, "move freely within the village ... [and] maintain relations between villages through the visits they conduct alone on ritual occasions" (Alvi 2013, 182). Marriage, and by extension motherhood, is therefore seen as a first step to social maturity as it enables a woman to start her own gift exchange with other women and enhances her social chances. Such possibilities are also furthered as they grow older; women become less constrained by the notion of bodily impurity in widowhood and after menopause.[25] Moreover, it is only women with children, predominantly through their roles as mothers, who can legitimately establish a household without a man (Chaudhry 2010, 65).

These readings corroborate what I have observed in Sehwan. Motherhood was in fact what paved the way for women's spiritual careers, a futurity disclosed once a woman had performed and demonstrated her social worth as a childbearing and child-rearing individual.[26] This is to say that spiritual enlightenment is not excluded from a woman's social (and also bodily) horizon, even if the operative norm dictates that a woman's comparative social worth lies fundamentally in procreation (Mooney 2010, 158). It is therefore important to consider the ways in which such female figures of authority are invested in the project of articulating a distinct space of femaleness, which stems from their understanding of themselves as being differently bodied, on the one hand from men and on the other from house-holding women. When Amma first told me that she was like me, in her words, clean, and thus suggesting she was rid of menstruation, she also established that she no longer maintained conjugal ties with her husband. As I grew familiar with Amma, I came to appreciate how such departures from the straight were made possible. Abba demonstrated a rare understanding in this regard and himself explained to me how ritual and corporeal purity was essential to Amma's work as a fakir.[27] Saintly instructions for women initiates to maintain bodily purity and integrity were not unheard of. In fact, the requirement to suspend sexual relations was a frequent one. Premised on ideals of purity and fidelity of the woman fakir, it was possibly also a sign of possessiveness on the part of the saint, though it was often articulated as a demand made by the cohabiting spirit. Saintly careers in the case of married women, as Ramaswamy (1996, 34) has illustrated in her work on the Virasaivite movement of twelfth-century Karnataka, involved a rejection of their worldly husbands followed by a subsequent identification of Lord Shiva as their groom.[28] Women's styling of their spiritual careers in such frameworks involves an adherence to patriarchy, she argues, and therefore in her opinion qualifies not so much as an act of defiance but as one of deviation. Karen Pechilis (2012), however, has argued that spiritual women, through their rejection of sex as a definition of marriage, wife, and woman, refuse on the one hand what it means to be a woman on society's terms, destabilizing especially the binary constitution of women in opposition to men (Butler 1990, 143–44). On the other hand, in refusing sex they refuse to sexualize their identity. Either way, refusing a substantial part of what it means to be a woman, or a wife in the conventional sense of marriage, does not come easy, and it requires tough and sometimes lengthy negotiations on the part of fakir women. What makes such moves relevant to this work on intimacy is how such coming close to a saintly figure or divine object requires that one reappraise and alter one's relationship with the social or, to paraphrase Berlant (1998, 281) to my benefit, how intimacy with Lal effectively usurps places originally reserved for other relations. Affective troubles follow, since decisions like these are not always met with support; husbands, as will become clear in Zaheda's story in chapter 3, can resist and counteract such moves, causing a slowing down of a fakir's progress. Further, with regard to the prospects that saintly ties dis/close—unstraight affordances in terms of this book—it is worth noting that as much as fakir figures were subject to cultural norms of segregation of the sexes, styles of purdah that women were expected to observe did not apply to women fakirs in equal measure. Mastani did not cover her head, and Amma interacted with men all day. In most cases, women fakirs were expected to drape their heads in public, and their interactions with unrelated men were not without scrutiny; however, their fakir roles allowed more relaxed styles of covering and eased participation in public contexts. The distinct corporeality of women fakirs, or the issue of dis/guise I take up in chapter 3, though hinging on an axis of male-female difference was aimed less at *I am like a man* and more at *I am not like other women* (Kasmani 2015). Such understandings on the part of women fakirs also curb a wholesale emancipatory reading of their religious projects.[29]

A Great Distance

"At great distance is *fakiri*" is a refrain Amma would regularly use during our countless interactions over the years. It always summed up a great deal of what it meant to be a woman and a fakir in Sehwan. She wasn't the first to evoke metaphors of distance; she wasn't the only one commenting on the impossibility of arrivals. Such relentless journeying was common to many fakir pursuits. For over twenty years Amma had strived to maintain conditions of intimacy, a public performance, which she regularly described as "strangely difficult work [okha kam]." Its arduousness was a given so long as to come close was "a contingent and always-in-the-making process of saintly orientations, which fell short of furnishing individuals with stable charismatic dispositions yet enabled their reputations for other-worldly access" (Kasmani 2017b, 81). Part of the struggle a fakir must endure in order to establish her credentials among visitors and pilgrims included the arduous and often time-taking process of finding, establishing, and maintaining a regular spot in the durbar. And hence one of the ways to also identify a fakir at the shrine of Sehwan was to pay attention to the consistency of a fakir's presence at a particular spot. It is no surprise that most of my meetings with Amma took place in the durbar and only a handful of these were planned. Whenever I was at the shrine, I knew I could depend on Amma's company, sometimes just to take respite from the busy durbar, somewhat akin to our first encounter. Each time I returned to Sehwan and its shrine, I would return to Amma as well. But when I returned after a gap of several years in 2018, I didn't find Amma at her usual spot. I first assumed that she might be sick, but, not having found her for the second day in a row, I began inquiring. A beggar woman who was usually seen cleaning the shrine floors informed me, to my utter surprise, how just weeks before Amma had been removed from the prayer space. This, as I was then told by others at the shrine, was an administrative action on the part of the new management. Worried, I tried reaching her on her son's mobile phone, but to no avail. Amma had also moved to a different house.

A lot had changed in Sehwan since my last visit. A lot had come to pass too. The administrative and security apparatuses of the shrine had been entirely revamped in the aftermath of the suicide attack of 2017. Just walking into the shrine was now an ordeal. There were numerous security checks, and police and security cameras were everywhere. Auqaf was no longer pulling all the strings at the shrine, it seemed. The state's presence was denser than ever. With the arrival of intelligence officials, the order of authorities had become more complex, and everyday decisions regarding the shrine were filtered through multiple channels. Offerings to the saint were thoroughly screened, and metal detectors were placed at all entrances. The daily bathing (*ghusl*) of the shrine that I described earlier was now a completely private affair; visitors were no longer allowed in the courtyard to witness the auspicious ceremony in the early hours. The bustle of the shrine courtyard was greatly affected; the activities in the durbar were duly monitored. The shrine now had a section of the police force dedicated to its protection. In fact, as I would later find out, the decision to remove Amma had come not from the Auqaf manager but from a senior police official who had been newly posted.

Through incessant inquiries in and around the shrine, I was finally able to locate Amma. As we sat down to catch up, I realized that the fateful night of the attack was now part of her repertoire of stories. Amma had witnessed the bombing and survived it too. During this two-week stay in Sehwan, I observed how Amma had dealt with being expelled from the durbar. Even if she wasn't able to claim her usual spot and spend the day tending to the adjacent grave, she would visit the shrine daily to pay her respects. In our meetings in her home, I noticed that she was much calmer than I expected, quite confident that she would be able to overcome the temporary setback. She had started to contact influential followers of her own, who she knew would make the right phone calls to the right authorities in her favor. Above all, she was settled in her view that her place in the durbar was willed by the saint and no authority superseded his. After a suspension lasting about three weeks, Amma was back at the shrine. When on the last day of my stay in Sehwan I eventually saw her resume her usual spot, I felt relieved. I was also reminded how Amma's stories in the durbar were her stories of fakir endurance, after all. It was as much a record of a life spent at the shrine as it was a story of the shrine itself. Years ago, when Amma had started to care for the forgotten grave, it was just an underused, leftover space in the durbar. Only in later architectural modifications of the shrine was a prayer room introduced, putting into question her original place of many years. Every time her place among men was questioned, whether by pilgrims or by newly arriving officials of the shrine, Amma had been quick to remind them how a growing shrine had overtaken her place and not the other way around.

Despite troubles, a publicly owned shrine offers fakirs like Amma opportunities for self-brokered access to the saint, to operate without hereditary masters, to establish an independent following and earn a living as healers and spiritual guides—not a given if it were still a privately held heritage in the hands of the sayyid elite. Sayyid control over fakir lodges regulates the exclusion of women from fakir ranks through retaining rights of admission and presiding over rites of initiation. In the context of the saint's durbar, however, women's gendered authority as mothers can operate alongside other authorities, no matter their disadvantaged social status. Tarrying with such saintly bonds, to be in intimacy's wake for women, involves particular obstinacies: be they intimate histories of embodiment, unfolding relations with cohabiting spirits, or the exteriorization of inner mystical experiences, women must additionally remedy their lack of access to saintly objects. Coming close to the saint in the setting of the durbar reminds us that the futurity of women's public religious careers is circumscribed in a greater contest of authorities and shaped by the state's arbitrating role at saint's places.

From the durbar and the question of the state's place at shrines, I turn to inward feeling, affective embodiment, and its unfolding in the shrine courtyard. My story of Zaheda—the woman fakir I introduced in the opening pages of this book—is a tale of endurance set in a time of impending failure. Her struggles with fakir dis/guise make plain that being in saintly company hinges on critical bodiliness, which must be successively and successfully performed in public. Zaheda's altering relations with the saint, his shrine, and her family offer a way to understand how saintly relations endure over time; what transpires when intimacy works in one's disfavor; what it takes to continue in the face of failing relations; or when saints no longer afford what they once promised.

3

In Other
Guises,
Other Futures

It was late afternoon on an autumn day in 2013. The crowds at the shrine were sparse still—not for too long, though. As the time of the evening *dhamal*, a daily ritual of drumming, drew closer, visitors would begin to claim every spot on the courtyard's white marble floor.[1] Benefiting from the still quieter atmosphere of the afternoon, I had invited Zaheda, a fakir my readers will recall from the introduction to this book, for a conversation. My friend and fellow anthropologist Delphine Ortis would join us too in our exchange. The three of us found some quiet and privacy in one of the wings, a leftover and underused space between the arcade and the busy durbar, the octagonal audience hall where hundreds circled the tomb of Lal, Sehwan's primary saint.

Only meters from this spot was where our paths had first crossed in the summer of 2009. Most often clad in a dark red chador and unfailingly surrounded by visitors at the shrine, Zaheda, who was forty years old at the time of our first meeting, was only finely discernable among women of the courtyard. Not easy to spot from afar, on closer look, the metal rings around her wrists and ankles as well as her practice of spiritual consultations in the courtyard bespoke her extraordinary public circumstances. "People recognize me to a great extent," Zaheda had confidently pointed out to me back then, "those who are able to recognize, that is, ones who have that sight, those who understand this. ... Then, if I walk two steps, they, to quite an extent, recognize that this person is walking with a purpose or is very close [qarib] to Lal." Little did she know back then that it was her closeness to the saint that would one day hang in the balance. Capturing what transpired between 2009 and 2013, this chapter pensively oscillates back and forth to cover the trails of Zaheda's endurance and fidelity amid conditions of dilemma and doubt. It assembles an account of her unordinary life from a place in time when it seemed that crisis had become ordinary.

Four years on, when Zaheda, Delphine, and I had gotten together for a chat in the same courtyard, things were not quite the same. The shrine's facade and its interior had been remodeled; the marble floor of the courtyard was newer and whiter than it was in 2009; I was wrapping up fieldwork in Sehwan; and Zaheda's changing personal circumstances, it seemed, were affecting her long-term pursuit for the worse. In fact, in the weeks preceding this meeting, I had already taken note of how significantly altered Zaheda's appearance was: the signature chador was no more; her fakir accessories were missing; and her practice of consultation in the arcades of the shrine was no longer observable. I didn't quite know why though. My efforts to reach out to her over the past weeks had proven less fruitful than I would have liked. She had not been very communicative either. Given such unease, I would not even pull out my diary in her presence. Our recent exchanges had been brief and carried out mostly on the go as we crossed paths in the town or at the shrine. On this particular day, however, Zaheda was surprisingly chatty. Upon learning it was our farewell meeting, it seemed she had finally chosen, and quite voluntarily so, to answer a number of queries I had casually brought up in the previous weeks. "Omar, aj kya jadu kar ke aye ho?"—or "What magical spell have you come with today, Omar?" she would eventually remark, surprised as if by her own disclosures. Not wanting to miss the opportunity to record, I pulled out my diary and started taking notes on our discussion. Zaheda, on the other hand, ordered some tea to go with our conversation.

As we proceeded with our exchange, I noticed a young woman walking toward us. She came and stood beside us, facing, however, Zaheda instead of me. I knew that an interview situation at the shrine could sometimes draw onlookers. I wasn't exactly paying attention when, interrupting our conversation and using gender-neutral speech, the woman remarked, "Kya yeh pir hain," meaning, is this (person) a *pir* (spiritual guide)? I was quick to assume that the question was addressed to me and that it concerned Zaheda. I chose not to answer immediately. In fact, I was keen to wait and see how Zaheda would react to the interruption—more precisely, whether Zaheda would refuse the title of *pir* in humility or perhaps acknowledge the honor of being a spiritual guide to others. Consulting fakirs and *pir*s in the shrine courtyard was commonplace. Our interactive situation, I imagined, might have given the impression to an onlooker that we were indeed involved in a spiritual consultation. It was at this point that the woman repeated her question, making clear that she had meant to ask if indeed I were a *pir* and not my woman interlocutor. Both Zaheda and I were taken by surprise.

We didn't really talk of what had just come to pass, though one could possibly conjecture that with two women, Zaheda and Delphine, in audience, the approaching woman had quickly assumed that I was the spiritual guide and not Zaheda. Such gendered bias proceeds from the common perception, however disputable, that most spiritual guides in Sehwan are men.[2] Apart from a studded fakir-like ring, there was nothing about my own appearance that could have overwritten her status. In fact, on that day, I was dressed in jeans and a shirt, clothes that a *pir* or fakir was least likely to appear in given the context of Sehwan. Spotting fakirs among others involved outward cues of performativity as well as more subtle citations of the body, a fakir grammar known as *bhes* (also *ves*). If to be a fakir, as this book contends, is to pursue saintly objects as well as to be committed to other futurities such desiring ushers in, *bhes* is the material-corporeal sign of being affectively proximal to the location of desire. Put differently, Zaheda's moment of public failure, if one might call it that, where a fakir of eleven years appeared to be only an ordinary pilgrim, is in large part a failure of her *bhes*. Through reading Zaheda's struggles in the framework of *bhes*, a key notion of this book comes to mature in this chapter: insofar as *qurb*—or intimacy with saints—names that critical distance between being near a thing and being nearly that thing, coming affectively close does not evidence the attainment of an object but refers rather to one's performative ability to sustain conditions of intimacy. Literally meaning both guise and disguise, *bhes* in this chapter reveals how a being close to saints perseveres in bodied ways, tarries through feeling, and warrants a publicness. It is a moving account of commitment and continuance in the face of altered conditions of intimacy, that is to say, the arduous affective labors it invariably takes to tarry with saintly relations, affordances, and knowings. To the extent that unstraight affordances are not only about what intimacy yields but also how what it affords finds continuance in forward time, Zaheda's life story and her struggles with *bhes* illustrate the durational passage of intimacy. It ties affordance with endurance.

Between this fateful meeting and our early encounters is a long story of meeting, losing, looking for, and finally finding Zaheda. Her candid disclosures that afternoon would make up for some of the gaps and open up a few more to collect my thoughts on what had come to be since. While my story of Zaheda delves into the unshaping of her fakir horizons, the compromised conditions of possibility, and the adjustments that were necessary in its wake, an equally yielding line of inquiry that accompanies this narrative is one that is caught somewhere between Zaheda's affected orientations to the saint and her altering *bhes* as well as the changing life and times of the place where our story was forever set: the saint's courtyard.

A Courtyard of Her Own

Barely meters from where Zaheda and I had first met in 2009, the suicide bomber had struck the shrine in 2017. This long rectangular space leading to the durbar was much more than a courtyard. It was that one place where Sehwan routinely came together, all its sundry protagonists as if perched on a stage. Host to exceptional crowds and ordinary gatherings, it was in its folds that fakir women found refuge, spirits surrendered to the sound of drums, and Hindu pilgrims brushed shoulders with Shi'a devotees, but also where locals simply hung out: tea sellers and vendors of all kinds solicited customers, and children played with little care for what generally went on. Now, in the wake of the attack, new security measures were altering its routines, affecting and limiting what was possible in the courtyard. A decade earlier, when I first arrived at the shrine, many of the visitors, especially women and poorer families, spent the night under the shaded arcades that flanked the longish courtyard. Its length was all that stood between the hustle of the bazaar and the fervor of the durbar where the saint lay buried. And it was in this space of respite that women could find a place for themselves. A great deal of what I had observed in 2009 was already changing as early as 2011. A terror attack at Lahore's most prominent shrine had led to security measures being beefed up at major Sufi sites across the country. This had direct consequences for shrine vis-

MAP 3.1 (opposite)
Plan and 3D visualization of the shrine of
Lal. Drawing courtesy Yves Ubelmann.
Illustration design by Rubab Paracha.

itors, especially affecting the poor and unaccompanied women. A little after midnight, as the high doors of the shrine would be ritually closed, people would now be asked to withdraw from the courtyard and were thus relegated to adjoining spaces outside the shrine gates. What used to be an old public square—featuring the *qadimi ʿalam*, an old structure commemorating the battle of Karbala—was now paved and enclosed with a low wall, creating an outer yard, remodeled as part of an ever-extending shrine complex (see map 3.1). Such ongoing architectural and spatial modification of the shrine, especially at the hands of its administration, was already compromising its organic relation with the bazaar and had greatly altered the place's nightlife.[3] The relative retreat of the inner courtyard was not to be found outside it. Here men were known to loiter, and musicians would perform to small audiences. There were no arcades either to protect pilgrims from the elements. More importantly, the privacy and intimacy that women visitors felt in the proximity of the saint, doubly tempered by the protection of the state, wasn't exactly available to them outside the shrine gates. This would be eventually lost in the securitized architecture of the shrine complex following the suicide bomb attack. By 2018, when I last visited Sehwan, the entrances to the shrine had been pushed further out, metal detectors and security cameras were in place, and police and intelligence officials roamed about. Meanwhile, the shrine had turned grander in scale; its facades had become more ornate than before, the dome more golden than ever. But given all that had come to pass, neither the nightlife peripheral to it nor the daily fervor of the place itself was observable any more. I had the feeling that in a courtyard where Zaheda had once flourished, it was now unimaginable for a lone woman to have a place of her own.

Back in 2009, Zaheda was firmly established among women of the courtyard. Pakistani women visit shrines for all manner of reasons: to make offerings, to sing tributes, to celebrate, to complain, to cry their hearts out, to find healing, and sometimes to simply chill on their day off—but equally to mend their circumstances, domestic or otherwise, petitioning saints as they remake their worlds, so to speak. Fakirs like Za-

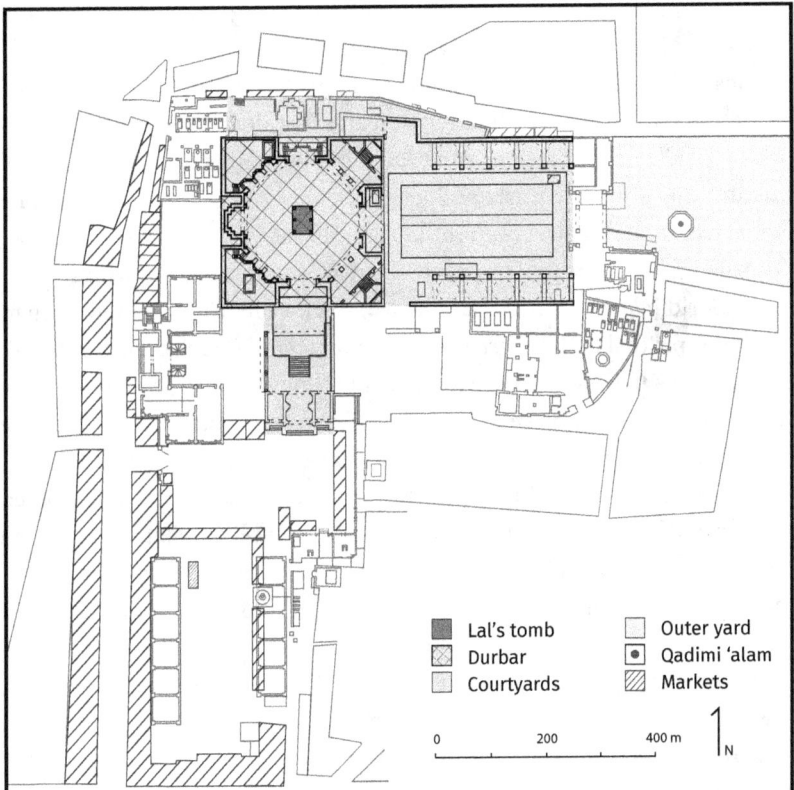

■ Lal's tomb		□ Outer yard	
▨ Durbar		◉ Qadimi 'alam	
░ Courtyards		▨ Markets	

0   200   400 m

↑ N

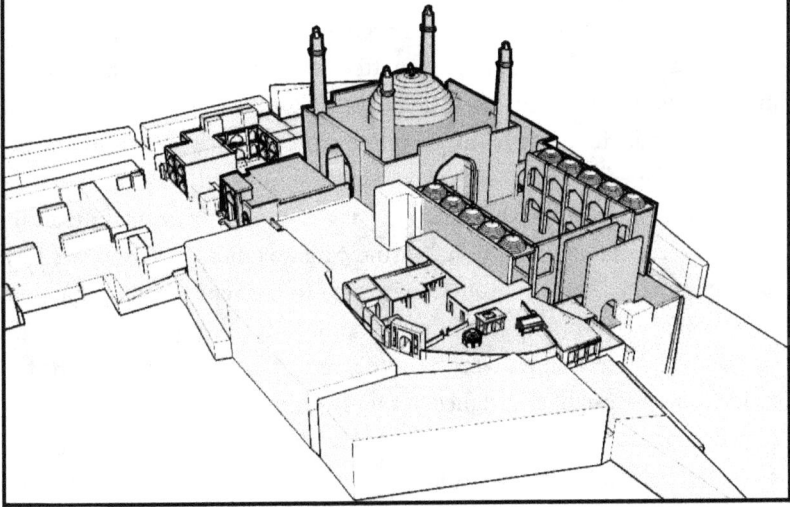

heda are perfect instruments for better conveying women's desires and wishes and for effectively forwarding their pleas to the saint. Women guides in South Asia, as Kelly Pemberton notes, conform better to an associational model of spiritual relationship that does not require an obligation of allegiance on the part of the follower nor the sanction of formal institutions of mystical Islam. Such a *pir*, she notes, is usually someone who "has acquired a reputation for sanctity" as well as "forms of 'secret' knowledge (such as how to interpret dreams, communicate with the unseen world [*ghayb*] or make amulets) and who can use this knowledge to provide spiritual and material services for others" (Pemberton 2006, 62). Zaheda was not one to write amulets but would offer spiritual guidance to shrine visitors, pray over substances like water, or bless people over the phone, and in one case had used her saliva as a healing agent. The setting of the courtyard offered a measured publicness, a place where women guides like her could interact with unrelated people in relative safety and eventually establish a following. Space is indeed key for women's religious careers, though in Pemberton's terms, "where women have the greatest scope for becoming *pir*s in practice, if not in name, is often outside of the purview of the general public" (2006, 67). Fakir women in this book are distinct in that their relations with saints afford rare prospects of a public life. In other words, what was possible at the shrine, a publicly administered institution of the state, wasn't easily imaginable outside its confines. For instance, Zaheda knew that her exchanges with a fakir mentor, a man she would regularly consult over matters of spiritual significance at the shrine, would draw a lot more suspicion if it were to take place outside the courtyard. Hence when in 2011, following the change in administrative rules, Zaheda, who spent her days in the courtyard, was forced to stay the nights at a guest house nearby, it was a move that proved difficult for her in both social and emotional terms. She was increasingly aware how staying the night in town brought new risks to her reputation or that conducting herself in public meant opening herself to heightened scrutiny. As much as fakir women were able to conduct a public life at state-run shrines, an unstraight affordance of saintly intimacy so to speak, their unordinary circumstances also meant that such women bore an additional burden of convincingly and durationally citing their spiritual dispositions via their *bhes* in the very places they inhabited. This is exactly what had betrayed Zaheda on that fateful afternoon in 2013, when she passed as an ordinary pilgrim in the courtyard.

FIGURE 3.1
Mastani, a fakir at the shrine of Lal.

To be read as a fakir is an important target in the life and practice of fakir individuals, where heightened visibility of *bhes* is seen as conversant with charismatic effectiveness (Kasmani 2012). It turns critical especially in the case of women, because without their *bhes* they would not be able to explain their purpose beyond the domestic sphere of the family nor validate less-ordinary ways of appearing in public. For instance, Mastani, a fakir described in chapter 2, was made recognizable at the shrine by her matted, henna-dyed hair. In a context where all women loosely draped their heads, her unusual choice of exposing hers was not questioned but regarded as part of her fakir guise (see fig. 3.1). *Bhes* can be worn, received, or, in its most frequent fakir usage, one is in *bhes*. It refers to a collectivity of attributes that include but are not limited to styles of dressing, bodily adornment, and social behavior, spatial practice and place-based relation-ships, codes of diet and sexual conduct, and manners of sitting and walk-ing as well as styles of speech. *Bhes* is codified to the extent that it is a citational practice that can be customized—a dynamic and always-in-the-making corpus in Heghnar Watenpaugh's (2005, 547–48) cross-reading with Butler—meaning that fakir doings and dispositions, unique as these are in individual instances, cross-reference performances of other fakirs, living or dead, whether received in dreams or cited in pictorial and textual representations of saints, ascetics, and mystics across Islamic histories and geographies. These serve as performative sources from which *bhes* derives a time-honored legitimacy and through which it becomes affectively intelligible in the present. For instance, in the story of the grove, Baba-Akram's full shaving of the head and the eyebrows is a citation of *qalandar* ideals as much as covering it with a long drape typical of women is Baba's way of customizing it for a gender-variant performance (see chapter 1). By virtue of such *historiality*, that is to say, a returning trace of something that repeatedly but varyingly exists over time, *bhes* refers to a dynamic, locally varied, and malleable corpus of fakir etiquette whose eventual test lies in the validation it offers to fakirs' less-than-normative or otherwise ways of being in the world.[4]

In Zaheda's own words, "the one who is *qarib* [affectively close] to the saint, his or her appearance and demeanor, manner of speech, lifestyle, diet, every such thing undergoes distinct alterations. S/he will then appear different from ordinary men and women." By explaining *bhes* as well as her own public situation in terms of intimacy, its affective disturbances and distinction, Zaheda had suggested that insofar as *bhes* indexes a condition of attachment, it also accompanies the body's departures from socially inherited objects, places, roles, and situations. It offers a contemporary illustration of long-standing Islamic-mystical ways of being beside norms, a point I've raised in the introduction to this book, and confirms "the historically and culturally specific belief that deviant social behavior (however it is defined) manifests in the materiality of the body" (Terry and Urla 1995, 2). Furthermore, that *bhes* in Zaheda's case operates not only in relation to the inherently masculine fakir norm but more critically also in contradistinction to other women informs my argument about women's distinctly feminine religious careers in Sehwan (Kasmani 2015; see also chapter 2). Thus, in the case of Zaheda, it is important that we ask: How and in what ways is her physical failing to be recognized in the shrine field an affective failure of her social orientations and saintly affections? Or how, more precisely, does the loss of such dis/guise come to jeopardize her social standing as a woman and fakir? The courtyard is where Zaheda's ties with the saint were nurtured. It is also where they nearly came undone. Changing contours of the courtyard parallel Zaheda's altering feeling of *qurb* with the saint, captured to some extent in issues of dis/guise, though what Zaheda's long story best illustrates is how the loss of intimacy is also a loss of futures promised.

When, in 2009, Zaheda said that she was "in the line of *fakiri*," a statement I have discussed in the introduction, she also elaborated how her pursuit by virtue of its orientation to the saint precluded other objects, other locations. "When I catch this line, I miss that train," Zaheda said in one of those early interactions. Dilemma was a striking feature in her personal accounts. The choice of a spiritual career kept her consistently torn between family and *fakiri*—a term approximating fakirhood, if you will, or what fakirs do. The demands of a spiritual career and expectations as a caregiver at home were not easily reconciled. She was, after all, a mother to eight children and had been married for twenty-five years. In the absence of institutional patronage like that available to men across fakir lodges in Sehwan (see chapter 4), women turn to saints at publicly administered shrines. As discussed in chapter 2, fakir paths for women are advanced under the patronage of the state, but their claims of extraordinariness must be validated through personal experience and the embodiment of endurance, and, in particular, their narrativization of dreams and visions, pain and suffering, powers and capacities. Zaheda similarly spoke with a sense of achievement when referring to the aesthetics of her *dhamal* and the control she was able to exercise during its performance. This is when hundreds move to the tune of reed and drums every evening in the shrine courtyard. "I have been given *dhamal* like no other; it is just for me," she once noted. According to her account, not only would she receive praise for its aesthetic qualities, she was able to endure it without letting her chador slip from her head, making a clear separation from countless ordinary women who, every evening, are seen to lose their bodily composure and with it, propriety of dress. Zaheda was aware that she was a woman unlike women, a corporeal and discursive project detailed in chapter 2 and one that is crucial to one's reputation as a fakir.[5] Much like Amma in the saint's durbar, Zaheda was aware that fakir goals set her apart from the ordinary, though living away from home and family, her challenges were manifold. She often reflected on the difficulty of her situation but had not for once, at least until then, doubted her decision to pursue a fakir line.

On a November evening in 2009, after the daily performance of *dhamal*, I spotted Zaheda in the shrine courtyard as she exchanged notes with her mentor. She would occasionally consult him on matters new to her or those that she wished to understand better. Such guidance was not exceptional in the case of striving or junior fakirs. I watched from a short distance and joined in only once their consultation was over. Taking advantage of the situation, I put the question of women's fakir pursuits to the teacher. I was curious as to what he would say of his female junior. "They [women] are incapacitated to undertake such a thing," he told me. His response was as surprising as it was categorical, given that he had agreed to guide a woman in the first place. As I turned to Zaheda for a reaction, she sat composed, with just a smirk on her face. Going further in his response, he quoted the example of Adam's expulsion from heaven to remind us both of Eve's role therein, evoking the common woman-as-temptress motif. In his view, the presence of women's bodies in whichever shape or form beyond their socially defined domestic roles carried serious disorientating risks to public social and moral order.

In this moment, Zaheda withheld her opinion, as must a respectful junior in the presence of her mentor. But once he left, she began to reflect on the exchange of her own accord. It was precisely the limitations of being a man, she explained to me, that prevented her teacher from understanding the workings of a woman. I asked her what she thought of the Adam and Eve story that her mentor had just quoted to invalidate her life's work. According to Zaheda, Adam was led to the forbidden fruit, not by the tempting force of Eve but instead by her embodiment of God's will. I grew more curious as she spoke. The only reason for God to create the world, according to her, was God's desire to be known. Thus, in Eve's intercessory force lies the very creation of this human society; in fact, she is the instrument through which God's desire comes to be fulfilled, Zaheda argued. Then, of her own progress, she noted how "the path for men and women is the same in *fakiri*," but just as men and women perform distinct but equally important functions in society, they do so in *fakiri* as well. The proof rested in her own experience, after all. Had it not been the case, "the saint wouldn't have made it work so far," she added. If indeed the path is the same, the difference, she believed, stemmed from the manner and style in which the journey is experienced. She went on to speak of the important condition of maintaining purity of body and soul. And just when I had expected her to refer to the femaleness of her body, she pointed my attention to the limitations of a male fakir. The fakir woman is distinct, she argued, because her pursuit includes the possibility of being chosen by the saint as his spiritual wife, a potentiality that in Zaheda's view was impossible for her male counterparts. This summons what Vijaya Ramaswamy notes with regard to Virasaivite saints of the twelfth century in South India. Reading literary verses, she argues that imagery for consorting with the divine in the framework of a (heterosexual) marriage comes naturally to women saints, who unlike their male counterparts do not have to first take on femininity in relation to a male object of worship (Ramaswamy 1996, 30).

The unordinariness of Zaheda's closeness to the saint wasn't lost on her either. "Something strange has occurred to me, I tell you," Zaheda once said of her fakir disposition, then added humbly, "I am not worthy of this at all. Neither I ever was, nor I am, and I know not if I ever will be! Lal has blessed me immensely, way too much. I am very close to him!"[6] The transformations that Zaheda describes in this statement are made contingent by her linking of fakir corporeality to saintly relations, a being intimate with Lal. But the difficult work of maintaining conditions of intimacy, as she would come to realize, could also jeopardize the entire pursuit. Months later in the same courtyard, I found a rather perturbed Zaheda. She spoke in veiled metaphors but convincingly established the impression that she had been instructed to devote her body exclusively to the saint. This was neither new to me nor unexpected for fakirs; other women fakirs I knew had spoken of their struggles to keep their bodies clean and pure by refusing sex with their husbands. It is important to note here that despite having experienced reproductive cycles, Zaheda was not the postsexual mother in the field in the ways that Amma was (chapter 2). By this I mean that unlike the more common practice of addressing spiritual women as *amma* or *mother* in South Asia, she was addressed as *baji* or *sister* in the shrine-courtyard. This follows the norm of addressing strangers of the opposite sex using a term for a close relative, extending a familial frame to a public interaction (Alvi 2013, 180). In fact, cousins or related individuals who may even get married in the future are known to address each other with familial forms like *baji* (sister) or *bhai* (brother). Insofar as such terms are temporal and easily suspended, they do not desexualize the interaction as effectively as the term *amma* does. In fact, Zaheda's earlier suggestion of the possibility of being chosen as the saint's spiritual wife was not a rejection of sex as a definition of marriage, wife, and woman but, like Ramaswamy's (1996) twelfth-century women saints, an embracing of her sexuality despite being a mother and a fakir.[7]

The reason Zaheda appeared so vexed and disturbed that night was because her husband (Zafar) was not willing to cooperate on the matter. Time and again she had spoken of the difficulty she faced with her husband, who was unable to fully understand the demands of being a fakir.

She had also tempered such statements every time by adding that he eventually comes around. Her tone this time was altogether different. She had had enough of Zafar's intransigence, she told me. In a new dream from the saint, she was shown a sword, enough for her to interpret the severity of the matter and the costs it might entail. Though she had regularly spoken of the domestic pressures and demands on her time, hindering her progress, never before had she sounded so categorical. I found her to be at a decisive crossroad that evening. She would give up her husband, she told me, should push come to shove. Notwithstanding the consequences, she sounded tenacious, determined to fight her way through, as the dream suggested. That evening she told me that she could no longer suspend her fakir line, whatever the cost.

Little did I know that from that moment on, when Zaheda was venting over a heightened domestic conflict, our paths wouldn't cross for a very long period. In the years that followed, I kept returning to Sehwan and spent extended periods of time doing research in the town, but Zaheda was nowhere to be found—in a sense lost, but she wasn't exactly absent. She had become a haunting force; our long and detailed encounters would return in so many of my interactions with other fakirs, drawing me toward her and her kind. And her metaphor of the line had remained an orienting conceptual tool in my research. But most of all, she left me wondering how she had chosen to respond to the conflicts and dilemmas I had since found her facing. Zaheda in my fieldwork was unfinished business.

Toward the tail end of my long-term stay in Sehwan and days after the annual festival of 2012, her mentor finally agreed to help me get in touch with her. He provided me with a telephone number. Zaheda, as I recalled, was perhaps the only fakir I knew who at the time did not use a mobile phone. The number I was given belonged to Zafar, her husband, who lived in Sargodha. It turned out that he wasn't aware of her exact whereabouts either. For months now Zaheda had been on her routine tour of shrines, he said on the phone. I could not tell at first if this was indeed the case or if he was simply not interested in letting me speak with her. His frequent phone calls and his curiosity regarding the circumstances in which we had known each other were marked with a degree of discomfort and confirmed what Zaheda's teacher had said of Zafar's unease with his wife's male contacts. A few weeks later, Zafar called me again. In his search for Zaheda, he had now arrived in Sehwan. We decided to meet over a cup of tea not far from the shrine itself.

Zafar's account of Zaheda's fakir life was a stunning echo of what she had herself shared with me years before. I could also sense, as I had gathered from Zaheda's descriptions, that he cared, how he was bound by his love for her, as she had once described to me, and that much like his wife, he too was caught in a double bind of his own. He struggled with her constant absence from home, yet he wanted to make space for her wanderings; he found it hard to approve of her public life, but he also knew that Zaheda was deeply drawn to the saints, a pull he believed he didn't stand a chance against. There was as much a hint of resentment in his account as there was of resignation. But what troubled him the most was that he wasn't exactly sure where she was at that moment. He knew that she had been in Sehwan for the saint's annual fair, from where she had called him three weeks earlier. He had wired her some money at the time and was now worried if she had enough. Zaheda, it appeared, had disappeared in the intricate geography of countless shrines and saintly places, lost somewhere in the flow of saints' fairs and festivals that pop up on this landscape every so often. Zafar, it was clear, had to consider all such possibilities. Had Zaheda indeed proceeded to Lahut, a revered site in Balochistan, as do many fakirs upon the culmination of the three-day annual fair of Sehwan, or had she chosen not to follow the usual itinerary in favor of her favorite shrine in the Punjab? And if she was indeed in Lahut, would she trace her journey back to Sehwan or would she rather follow other fakirs and proceed to shrines in Karachi? Three weeks later, there was still no news, and I had already wrapped up a year of fieldwork in Sehwan, then returning with the knowledge that in the huge crowds at the saint's fair of 2012 our paths would have inevitably crossed, yet Zaheda and I had not found each other. Zafar would have to count days until Zaheda decided to call him; and I, as my field diary records, would have to wait until the night of November 14, 2013.

At midnight as the doors of the shrine were drawn, an elaborate prayer was held, which was led by the Auqaf manager. As I was photographing the crowd that had gathered at the end of the court, I was most pleasantly surprised to spot Zaheda. I could not believe my eyes. We were meeting exactly after four years. Our last meeting was in the courtyard in November 2009 when she had spoken about the difficult domestic situation and the conflict with her husband. Today she looked much weaker, her signature chador replaced by a black shawl and there were no signs of rings or the *bedian* [shackles] she used to wear. She appeared quiet and unsettled. She told me she had missed me, a brother to her, a lot; that she often thought of me. ... But she kept reminding me that she had nothing to tell or give me; no *khas bat* [special or extraordinary stuff], though I told her that I was after the *'am bat* [ordinary stuff]. To ease our first conversation in four years, I did not record her, I did not take out my recorder neither did I reach out for my notebook. Under the old *'alam*, Delphine and Zaheda sipped tea. She was wearing a light pink *shalwar-kamiz*, covered mostly by a big black shawl. ... Her hair was grey, with more white streaks since I had last seen her. She told me she had been ill for almost two years. ... She did not travel to shrines and neither was she in Sehwan during this period. ... Around 8 months ago she left home for Sehwan. ... She emphasized again that the two years she did not come was because she was not asked to come by the saint. And even now that she has pressure from family to return home, she argues she cannot leave without the permission of the saint.[8]

In the time that stretched between losing and finding Zaheda, I was once again reminded how it was through her dilemmas and experiences that I had first come to imagine fakir pursuit as a matter of orientation, of being pulled toward a certain object, especially in counterrelation to other objects. Four years on, the balance that Zaheda had once wished to strike seemed all the more delicate. She remained pulled in dissimilar directions. Zaheda appeared increasingly insecure. And of the effectiveness of her once-functioning line, as she had described her fakir pursuit, she was now to report, "It is indeed the line that is not to be found. The line is cut! There is no communication these days." A recurring impression in my new interactions with Zaheda was that of being lost; there was an apparent lack of directionality. She was also increasingly skeptical of the promise of destinations that might or might not be within her reach anymore: "I'm asking the saint myself that he may show me a way but I am not able to understand anything so far." With such descriptions, I was left to consider how by the time we were to meet again Zaheda had come to view her fakir line and its attendant challenges.

Of our latest interactions in 2013, I noted the following in my field diary:

> Zaheda has been elusive as expected. I don't see her for days and then suddenly she appears before me but always at the shrine. In my conversation with her last night, again, I got the impression that she is less certain of her *fakiri*; she looks less composed than 4 years ago and is not sure where she goes from here. She almost sounds depressed. In her previous account of illness her doctors had told her that there was no physical illness but it was something to do with her mind. She is trying to understand the change in her relationship with the shrine and the saint. ... So, she wonders why the saint doesn't keep her in Sehwan especially when in the past she felt more welcome here.[9]

There wasn't a single major event in Zaheda's description of the near past that I could use to reliably explain the palpable change in her condition, although she did speak of a protracted illness. She looked visibly weaker than before. I was reminded of Zafar's description of her health: "She eats very little. Her stomach has become weak due to excessive fasting," he had said, or that "two years ago she fasted for a whole year."[10] She looked weak much as she sounded low. In her words, "Neither have I peace of mind, nor is my heart at rest. I do not like anything, not even myself."[11] One thing was clear. She was less confident of her choices and her abilities than ever before. She had even stopped offering healing or consultations since we had last met. I wanted to know the reason behind the change, reflected also in her altered appearance, the lack of fakir accessories for example. In sharp contrast to her once proud statements of appearing distinct among women in the shrine field, she told me that "putting on the fakir garment makes a fakir more visible to the public eye and that is exactly what I do not want." With this in view, one could say that the event of going unrecognized at the shrine, with which I have opened this chapter, was of Zaheda's own choice and making. The accompanying sense of loss, however, was unmistakable. "People go forward; my journey has gone backwards," she told me. "I see no development that I could tell you. ... Now it seems that Lal is not even speaking to me. I don't see anymore, the thing that used to be between Lal and myself."[12]

What exactly has changed, one might ask? One hint lies in Zaheda's understanding of the change in her relationship with the shrine of

Sehwan. The Zaheda I had known years ago was firmly grounded in the shrine courtyard. She derived strength not so much from her familial ties as from her status among women of the courtyard. I have already pointed out how the character of the courtyard has changed over the years, especially due to an increase in security at shrines across Pakistan.[13] Now, displaced from the courtyard, Zaheda described how she felt unwelcome at the shrine: "I would not even step out from here but even then, I had to go away from here. Now, why did I have to leave? Only Lal would know. I don't know it!"[14] Her sense of distance, however, had to do with more than just moving away from the courtyard. As it turned out, she had recently found some peace and comfort at a small village shrine in Sindh. When not in Sehwan, she is at Gaji-Shah, she told me. This wasn't an easy move because switching between shrines, as she herself knew and feared, could cost her pursuit dearly. It is a question of loyalty to saints.

The change of site, like a change in orientations, to lean on Sara Ahmed (2006), meant discontinuing ties with a particular saint and letting go of certain orientations as well as the intimacy and futurity those lines would have potentially offered. In other terms, it meant an abandonment of certain objects and its accompanying cluster of promises (Berlant 2006). Different saints have different things to offer, Zaheda had herself told me, explaining how at one point she was quite close to getting her fakir pursuit authorized by a particular saint when she decided to divert her focus to Sehwan. In a brief moment of reflection, she wondered if this was indeed a mistake. During that time, too, as Zaheda was redirecting herself to Sehwan, she had kept her ties somewhat intact with other sites, other saints. In some ways, Zaheda was once again torn between choices. This time the tension was not between family and the saint, as she had expressed in 2009. It was instead between shrines and their competing saints, a dilemma most poetically captured in her rhetorical question: "This Medina, that Medina; which Medina to grasp, which Medina to let go?"[15]

The sense of loss that Zaheda evoked in her conversations suggested a not knowing where she was headed. She suspected a difference in the strength of her orientation to the saint and of the saint's affection toward her; less proximity to his shrine is a direct outcome of this change. In not being invited to Sehwan as often as in the past—fakirs believe that saints summon them—she had lost considerable ground, she admitted. And the smaller village shrine she now regularly visited had only added to her problems. Illness also affected her progress. Zaheda's sense of disorientation, if one might call it so, was most palpable in her altered appearance, or in the giving up of *bhes*, allowing her to go unrecognized, as she explained. But this also meant that Zaheda's motivation to be at shrines was now more suspect, as her *bhes*, or the lack thereof, no longer explained nor supported her advanced and unchaperoned presence in a public space. There was nothing about her outward appearance that convincingly established her social role as a guide, nor was her sexuality neutralized by the guise of women fakirs.

A few days later, Zaheda, Delphine, and I met in the courtyard for our farewell meeting. I found her in a reflective mood. "What is good in this world, Omar?" she rhetorically asked, adding, "I do not like anything these days." What followed was Zaheda's attempt at ordering her past and present in a meaning-making narrative. According to her description that afternoon, a part of the answer to her currently deteriorated situation lay in a dream. It was a prophecy she had received some twenty-five years ago but was revealing to me for the first time. One of three sisters and two brothers, Zaheda grew up under the influence of her paternal grandfather, also a fakir. He lived in a nearby village, and though she did not grow up with him, she spent considerable time in his company during her childhood. He would often read the poetry of his *murshid* (spiritual master) to her, and Zaheda, drawn to its message, would soon take a liking to such matters. She described her grandfather as knowledgeable, someone with necessary spiritual reach or access (*pohunch*). By this she meant that he had the spiritual capacity to influence her fakir case, effect a favorable outcome, or transfer his knowledge to her. Though she had insisted for years, she came to the realization that he did not wish for her to be a fakir. At twenty-two, Zaheda was already a mother of three and living away in a nearby city. She continued to make frequent visits to her ancestral village in the hope of winning his favor. If she wasn't one to give up, she wasn't able to change his mind either. "Whatever there is, the saint will give you. I cannot give you anything," he told her categorically, then leaving it for his own spiritual master to decide her case. "So, in a dream, he had taken me to his *murshid*," Zaheda told me. She seemed to recall the dream occasion in clear terms. "The *murshid* of my grandfather said it to my face! I was there, my grandfather and the *murshid*: We will give her nothing. Because if we were to give her something, it would cause hard times on her and sickness would come to her. You will get nothing at all whichsoever shrine you may go to!"[16]

It is obvious that Zaheda had proceeded on her path despite the warnings in the dream. It is also interesting that while she had only once before mentioned the fakir character of her grandfather in our exchanges in 2009, she had never brought up this particular dream or his hesitation on the matter. It was an explanation in retrospect of why she may have not found the desired results she had once foreseen for herself. In other words, it was her way of ordering the past, making it meaningful through her engagements with me as well as with the conditions of time and place in which this particular telling was taking place (Sarkar 2012, 585). "I did not give up. It was my love, my commitment, my *'ishq* [passion, love]. It may have been possible perhaps that someone else would give me something; that I would go to another shrine and he [that saint] would have given me something. I have wandered through numerous saints' places. I have also tried two or three times at Abdullah Shah [a shrine in Karachi]. I even broke down into tears. Having left Punjab behind me, it has been ten to fifteen years that I find myself here."[17]

Zaheda's new account was a reminder that her fakir pursuit was temporally and spatially far greater than any story captured in our encounters in the courtyard. It was in the early 2000s, when her husband found work in the army, that she had moved with her family to Karachi for a few years. It was then that she got acquainted with the shrines of the Sindh region. It was also during this period that she came to hear of Sehwan. Her first visit to the shrine was just a few hours long. She had accompanied her mother then, who wanted to petition the saint regarding a pending dispute over a family property. Zaheda felt such an immediate attachment to the place that she did not feel like leaving; of her first visit, she explained, "I held the *jali* [metal latticework around the tomb] and made him [the saint] my *murshid* [master]. I found a great deal of peace. Lal, do not ever abandon me! I would stay with you all my life, so said my mind, and Lal too, I had the feeling, loved me back."

Within a week or two, Zaheda was back at the shrine, this time by herself. She stayed four nights, and on the fifth day, Zafar, her husband, followed her to Sehwan in order to take her back. She could not leave of her own will, as she explained to him. "The *murshid* has stopped me. The saint has put a rope around me. You must go at this moment. I will follow once I get permission from the *murshid*. How could I leave now when the *murshid* hasn't given me permission; he hasn't yet given me a sign." Two days later, when she returned home, Zafar was furious. They argued a great deal on the matter, and then he hit her a few times, as was his habit, she told me. This was the first time she would ponder the conflicting domains and the contesting authorities of her *murshid* and her husband: "He who doesn't let me follow the wishes of the *murshid*, or if someone wants to belong to Allah and the person doesn't let you do so, in my opinion such a person is *jahil* [ignorant]." Just as she wept, remembering the saint, she received a *bisharat*, that is, a divine sign or inspired word, from Lal: "Leave everything and come to the shrine at this very moment!" Within hours of quarreling, as the family retired for the night, Zaheda packed her bags and proceeded to the shrine. Soon after her arrival in Sehwan, another message from the saint was to follow: "You must remain here!" In recounting these events as well as the prophetic dream, Zaheda creates a double impression. The account seeks to explain to herself more than anyone else that her fakir career was bound to have grave repercussions given the prophecy of the saint who appeared in the dream with her grandfather.[18] Not to forget that her husband's lack of support remained a problem. In her stream of reflections that afternoon, she once again brought up the domains of the husband and the *murshid*, but the crossings were a lot more conditional than conflictual in this instance. "When he [the husband] is not in agreement, then how will the *murshid* be convinced? His approval is important—in Islam, in *tariqat*, in *shari'at*. If he does not agree, then it will not work. He [the husband] is my owner in a way; I am bound. If he does not agree then my avenues will be blocked. There will be obstacles. ... I had this in my heart since the beginning, that my *murshid* would persuade him in his own way."

Zaheda's conversations were filled with a search for explanations and answers. As much as she recognized the obstinacy that the dream posed, she was also aware that notwithstanding its prophetic contents, there was once a sense of progress. However, whatever she had found, she had had to acquire by force, by stubbornly insisting on her demands, by not letting go of her goals. And it would be fair to say she hadn't given up. Zaheda revealed a kind of endurance in her object of desire that is evocative of what Berlant (2006, 22) has named "cruel optimism," that is to say, "a relation of attachment to compromised conditions of possibility" even when its presence threatens the subject's well-being or "the continuity of the subject's sense of what it means to keep on living on and to look forward to being in the world" despite an apparent loss of the object of desire. Writing on the affective lives of queer Indonesians, Ferdiansyah Thajib has noted how, in enduring the impossible, his Waria interlocutors in Aceh relied on hopefulness as a resource. Yet such engaging with hope, he argues, "does not simply mean clinging to some abstract promise of happy finality or embodying inner strength or human flourishing that is often characterized as 'resilience' but necessitates arduous affective labor" (Thajib 2019, 237). Zaheda's will to go on despite her altered relation to the saint revealed how commitment to her fakir line did not depend on certain promises, and less on knowing where she was headed, but that such endurance was "a means of continuing to continue" (Simone 2013). Writing on the urban poor and their relation to the city, AbdouMaliq Simone distinguishes endurance from survival in that the former depends on "the willingness to suspend the familiar and even the counted-upon in order to engage something unexpected." At the same time, he notes, such "engagement may sometimes simply reiterate a commitment to what already is, where the person decides that it is better to stay put with what is familiar" (Simone 2013). Zaheda's story likewise is a moving account of commitment and continuance in face of, or despite, the challenges she has had in the past or the im/possibilities that are carried over into the present. Her ties to the shrine and the saint, as well as her family, were no longer as they once used to be. Whether given through a recourse to past dreams, an ongoing domestic conflict, or a likely rivalry between saints, impasse here was a bodied form of knowing by way of feeling. Neither was continuance part of a plan in that going on or staying put did not involve a path of action or a line of futurity that Zaheda could see in its entirety. That what Amma, a woman fakir in chapter 2, had evocatively called "a great distance" was true for Zaheda too, insofar as being a fakir was not so much about the attainment of an object as it was about continuing its pursuit. With little or no progress, successful or otherwise, Zaheda was in the wake—that is, a staying with "a form of consciousness" (Sharpe 2016, 15). She tarried, as fakirs do, with affective relations, knowings, and obstinacies, unstraight affordances that continued to unfold in various ways as a result of years of coming close to saints. In our farewell conversation that afternoon, the same day when I was mistaken for a *pir* and she was not recognized as a fakir, she left me with these words from a popular film song: "I am a forgotten tale / A thought of the past / One, no one is able to comprehend / That question, I am!"

Her Line to Loneliness

Zaheda's metaphor of the line has helped articulate how to follow a line like a fakir is "to become invested in that line and also to be committed to 'where' it will take us" (Ahmed 2006, 176). The capacity of orientations to draw us in certain ways, to take us somewhere other than here, is forever courted with moments of orientations' many failures: unorientations, or instances and occasions when fakir intimacies discontinue, weaken, or are rivaled by other objects of desire, or when relations do not quite deliver the rewards they might have once promised. Thus, also through a long account of Zaheda's labor as a fakir, we are able to read how failures to maintain conditions of a specific intimate relation, that is, losing sight of the line and where that line would have taken us, involves, in Berlant's (2006) terms, a slipping away of objects that anchor us in the first place and an accompanying cluster of promises previously reachable.

Zaheda's statement in 2013, "when one becomes a fakir, one becomes lonely," had come at a time when she had tested the waters for almost eleven years. Loneliness, as she had described in this particular moment, stemmed from a social failure: the isolating experience that comes with the gradual realization that not many around her could comprehend or appreciate her reasons to pursue saintly objects, especially when progress was slow if not also unyielding. Being in the fakir line had also meant constantly being at odds with what came predetermined for her as wife, mother, and woman. Fakirs like Zaheda were regularly reminded that not only were their extradomestic pursuits questioned at home, unaccompanied women at saints' shrines were additionally subject to greater public scrutiny. They were also not welcome in the all-male circles of fakir lodges, to which I turn in chapter 4. Set in a prominent fakir lodge, the story of Murad builds on but also pairs with Zaheda's case. Like her, his story illustrates how being in the service of saints is a corporeal project sustained through *bhes* but also how saintly fields are consistently thwarted by other intimacies and rival objects. While Zaheda's feelings of loss, loneliness, and disorientation take place in the saint's courtyard, Murad's intimate crisis unsettles a close community of fakirs and puts him at odds with his own future at the lodge.

Zaheda's loss, inasmuch as it persists, also involves a loss of futurity. What prevailed in our final exchanges in 2013 was how she was dealing with her relation to an object of attachment under compromised conditions of intimacy. If her descriptions have taught me how being a fakir is being in the line of something, she has equally shown how deviating is in itself a commitment to a different line. Her struggles with *bhes* show how lines of reorienting or returning were no less arduous in emotional and affective terms. These also reveal how being in the company of saints is a material-corporeal project. In other words, saintly intimacy hinges on critical grammars of the body, whose successful performance serves to establish one's closeness with saintly objects and locations as well as to mandate one's being out of step with straight rhythms of the social. Failures of intimacy or worsening saintly relations, inwardly tormenting as these are, take very public forms.

At the time of our last meeting in November 2013, Zaheda was treading a thin and fragile line between finding recognition and losing respectability. Without her fakir *bhes*, the temporal and precarious character of her pursuit was made visible, and she had found it difficult to validate her unchaperoned presence at shrines. Whether she would in fact return to the folds of domestic life is a question that remains unanswered. What became clear, however, was that there were no lines sanctioned for her as a woman that involved destinations other than the home and saints' places. At the time of our first meeting in 2009, Zaheda was in the line, oriented and emplaced. And four years on, it was clear that to have no lines to follow was to be going nowhere, and to be without lines was to be without place. Zaheda's pursuit of intimacy as it would unfold before me would also become the raison d'être of this work. Orientations of the researcher and the researched were indeed distinct, yet lines of work and our labors toward making those lines work, of research and of fakir being, intersected in these years as much as they parted or ran parallel to each other—though it is Zaheda who has shown the path. She has illustrated how being in the wake is a form of endurance so long as it means to tarry with objects that a line may bring into view, to remain attached to the futures it may preclude or involve, more so, a means to continue in the face of intimacy's impending loss.

4.

Love in
a Time
of Celibacy

"Did you hear about ba-Murad?" I had barely exchanged greetings with a
middle-aged woman from Karachi when she voluntarily offered her two
cents on the most recent developments in the life of a fakir. Murad was
our sole point of reference, a fakir she affectionately called *ba* (short for
baba or father). It was in Murad's company that I had first met her in June
2012. Now, almost a year and a half later, when our paths crossed on my
first evening back in Sehwan, she asked me if I had been to the *kafi* (fakir
lodge). Bodlo-kafi was a prominent fakir lodge in Sehwan centered around
the shrine of Bodlo, the saint's primary disciple. "He is not there anymore!"
she exclaimed in half horror, as if aware of the controversial character
of the news she was delivering to me. In this chance meeting under the
qadimi ʿalam, the old memorial structure in the center of town, which
barely lasted a few minutes, she had revealed to me with an odd mix of
urgency, surprise, and disappointment that Murad was now married, in
her words, "to a girl half his age"; that he had developed a conflict on the
matter with his spiritual master; and that above all, when asked to choose

between the said girl and his fakir duties, he had quietly surrendered his *wardi* (lit. uniform; fakir costume).[1] She was referring to the long red tunics characteristic of fakirs of this particular lodge. Not only was Murad no longer in Sehwan, he had, to her utter disbelief, abandoned his fakir objects. Or so went the story at the time.

Stunned as I was at the details, the woman pilgrim wasn't the first one to break the news to me. The story of Murad's departure from the lodge had gradually unfolded throughout the course of the day. On our road journey from Karachi to Sehwan the same morning, my friend and fellow anthropologist Delphine Ortis had disclosed to me that Murad was no longer in Sehwan. She had had it straight from the horse's mouth, as it were, when she phoned Murad prior to our journey. We already knew that he had left the fakir lodge and had relocated to Lahore as a result of a conflict with his spiritual master (*murshid*). Or that he was currently based at Bibiyan-pak-daman, a shrine in Lahore dedicated to women saints and particularly revered by the Shi'a. However, Murad hadn't really explained why. He had left us wondering, as my notes from the day confirm. Hours of conjecturing on the road were put to rest as we reached Sehwan. Finally, at the lodge itself we met Dost, a young fakir whom Murad had been mentoring in years prior. Dost also confirmed that his teacher had contracted a civil marriage with a young woman of his choice. The two had in fact met here in Sehwan, he reported. She was a young pilgrim visiting from Lahore and Murad a fakir she had consulted at the shrine of Bodlo. They had exchanged numbers and had since been in contact. I was suddenly able to make sense of the countless occasions during my previous fieldwork when Murad would be occupied with his mobile phone, chatting for hours at a stretch, especially late at night, leaving me in the company of Dost. Now, the same fakir, barely twenty-three years old and who, a year before, I'd have best described as a shadow to Murad, was describing his version of the events with a clear sense of disapproval. Life was moving on at the lodge, it seemed. Murad was no longer an authority and Dost no more a trainee. Since we last met, he had been formally initiated into the fakir lodge during an annual ceremony.

Whatever the circumstances surrounding the scandal, the speculations and responses it generated among fakirs at the lodge were impressive. As it turned out, the events in question were fresh and hardly a few months old. "You must have heard" or a variation of the phrase was a most common refrain when I returned to the lodge in November 2013. This short three-week stint of fieldwork was planned to address gaps in my writing on fakirs. Catching up with fakir lives a year and more later, I had hoped, would effectively open possibilities to engage afresh with new and previous material. Murad's case turned out to be a perfect example of such catching up. He had been a key interlocutor in my fieldwork even if there was little biographical information that Murad ever revealed to anyone. He was perhaps around forty years of age back then, possibly even less, Punjabi-speaking one would reckon from his Urdu accent, literate with some level of formal education, and word had it that he had been living at the lodge for about twenty years. And now, in his decision to marry for love, he had become a passionate point of argument in fakir discourse at the lodge. Even in his absence, Murad was present in the controversy he had sparked; conversations and discussions among fakirs at the lodge centered around his decision to abandon the fakir ideal of celibacy. Murad, enigmatic as he had been, was now a divisive figure.

The opening vignette, I hope, provides a supple entry into two interconnected themes that run through the course of this chapter. A first and overarching interest is to illustrate how fakir bonds and fraternities are established within the homosocial framework of a lodge. The setting is distinct, especially because male fakirs like Murad and Dost at fakir lodges across town were subject to (unwritten) contracts of patronage and structures of dependence that other protagonists of this book have not had access to, mostly due to their genders. Lodges such as Bodlo-kafi are male-only fakir institutions in Sehwan, considered an integral part of the saint's heritage in that these are fraternities whose histories are tied to Lal's earliest disciples. Many of these lodges are in fact named after such figures and run by local elite, most of whom also trace their lineage to contemporaries of the saint. The other object of this chapter is Murad's scandal. In tracing its impact on the lodge, I point to linkages between sexuality and sacrality, love and marriage in fakir arguments, or the ways in which ideas around sexual intimacy inflect fakir narratives on intimacy with saints. Murad's life story in this chapter, along with tales around his departure from the lodge, accompany an important insight: unstraight affordances are queer affects that not only support otherwise ways of being in the world but can equally work against intimacy, especially when the pursuit of saintly objects is contracted on pacts of submission and the abandonment of rival intimacies. No less interesting is the insight that failures of saintly intimacy accompany one's return to economies of the heterosexual family. Insofar as Murad's love for a young woman also upset his place in the homo-sociality of the lodge, his decision to marry, to stay with the metaphor of fakir lines, afforded a restraightening of his social horizons.

Desiring Men: Life at a Fakir Lodge

There were several reasons why the story of Murad attracted the attention it did. Charismatic and also well versed in fakir etiquette, Murad was no less than a poster boy for the lodge. Among those residing at the lodge, he was known to attract young initiates, devotees, and (foreign) research-ers alike. In addition to the long years he had spent at the lodge, he drew a sense of importance from the well-known fact that he had the ear of his master, the custodian and spiritual master of the lodge. His public persona resulted in a visible air of rivalry and competition with his peers. While se-nior fakirs often made light of the crowds he drew, juniors longed for his company. Murad clearly enjoyed the attention he received. That initiates too derived a sense of importance from their mentorship with him was no secret. Known for his oration and rhetoric, he was often seen holding court at the lodge. His extended discourses on saintly service and espe-cially celibacy were routine. Murad's unlikely decision to give up his ideals in pursuit of a woman had understandably become a gravitating point of discussion among young and old at the lodge.

Celibacy wasn't a condition for residing at the lodge, though it was central to its ethos. It was common knowledge in Sehwan that Bodlo, the foundational figure of the lodge, was *jatti-satti*, a term associated with seven celibate saints of Sehwan. Following Lal's example, Bodlo too re-mained unattached to women, foregoing relations of family and matters of the household. His celibate devotion to Lal was enshrined in the many stories, legends, and miraculous accounts that circulated all across Sehwan. Even in popular visual representations, Bodlo was inseparable from Lal. In a widely circulated image, the duo is depicted in a loving embrace, just as in the photo template that had irked my mother, an episode I described in the opening pages of this book. Bodlo's head rests on the knees of his mas-ter, while the saint is shown returning his gesture by lowering his head. "Whoever comes to me must first go to Bodlo," Lal is believed to have said, or so goes the saying in Sehwan.[2] Most pilgrims therefore make their first offerings at Bodlo, making the otherwise small shrine a destination of great importance in Sehwan. Similarly, its lodge is considered founda-tional to the establishment of a system of fourteen *kafis* in Sehwan, prom-

FIGURE 4.1
Fakirs during *dhamal* in the forecourt of Bodlo's shrine, 2011.

inent lodges associated with Lal himself. Such lodges' vitality in Sehwan's devotional life and their reputation for fakir mentoring fit a historic template.[3] The exact number of secondary fakir lodges, however, is hard to determine in Sehwan. The one at Bodlo is also prominent because it has a prominent shrine attached to it, though, unlike the shrine of Lal, this one is privately run.[4] Both lodge and shrine are headed by a single custodian figure who is also the patron and spiritual master of all fakirs residing at the lodge. It is these fakirs, and not state officials, who perform ritual services at Bodlo's shrine and manage its everyday routines and revenues. The lodge in question is the largest in Sehwan, which, according to one estimate, had eighty initiates, at least twenty of whom were long-term or permanent residents (Ortis 2020, 316). The overlapping spheres of the shrine and the *kafi* are made manifest every evening when the lodge's fakirs perform the ritual of *dhamal* facing the tomb of Bodlo (see fig. 4.1).

This northern tip of Sehwan, where the shrine complex is located, is fabled, to say the least.[5] Its topography is etched with a spectacular account of Bodlo's death. Legend has it that his body was cut into pieces by the ruler of the time and thrown all across the neighborhood. Also, a furious Lal, on learning what had been done to his beloved, turned the fortress upside down.[6] Today, right under the shadow of the fabled "inverted fortress" (*ulta qila*), the sprawl of Bodlo's shrine and lodge is a material reminder of his body-in-pieces. It is a growing complex that includes several secondary units spread around the fabled hill. These include a community kitchen, a number of fireplaces associated with fakir gathering (*machh*), minor shrines and pavilions, a section of the custodian's old family home, a rest house for visiting pilgrims, and an underused mosque as well as a stable for horses.[7] Though supplementary to the lodge's main purpose, most shops in the bazaar leading to the shrine are in fact properties of the custodian, which confirm his growing influence in this part of town but also provide the economic means to run the lodge. The outreach of its fakirs is equally expansive. An entire network of satellite fakir dwellings can be found beyond Sehwan. These are reclusive settings established on the edges of towns and outside villages by journeying fakirs of the lodge, whose companies inspire a young and male following on the way. Many of these men arrive in Sehwan in pursuit of the saint or his fakirs (see fig. 4.2).[8]

Bodlo's ultimate sacrifice serves as the blueprint for fakir devotion in Sehwan and particularly so at the lodge in question, where fakirs mostly refer to themselves as *talibs*—the Urdu word (from Arabic) means seeker (of knowledge) but also denotes craving and yearning. The fakir in this sense is the one who desires the saintly and seeks the path of the mystics. Desiring-seeking at the Bodlo-kafi is not a self-brokered line exclusively involving dreams, visions, or a cohabiting spirit like those of Baba, Amma, and Zaheda of the previous chapters but takes place in the company of men and primarily through the intercession of a living spiritual master. In fact, one might say that affective formations at the lodge are premised on the exclusion of women and transgender fakirs. Explaining the dynamics of sexual difference endemic in particular Islamic religious contexts, Ali A. Mian notes that it is "neither female-male nor female-female desire, but male-male desire that is channeled into communal formation" (2019, 143). He further argues that despite the strong prohibition on anal intercourse, same-sex desire remains unencumbered and serves rather as the *affective adhesive* that pulls men together through intimate socialization and strengthens devotion to the divine.[9] Such male-to-male axis of desire in Sehwan is enshrined in the love between Lal and Bodlo and lived through fakir homosocial bonds at the lodge. While this was true for all

FIGURE 4.2
An aspiring fakir at the
Bodlo-kafi, 2013.

*kafi*s I knew and visited in Sehwan, there was a brief period of time when two female-presenting fakirs were residing at Bodlo.[10] Their status, as fakirs themselves tried to explain to me, was unclear at best, and their participation did not extend to all aspects of the lodge's daily life. They were also housed in a private section of the lodge. Their exceptional status was proof that maleness was in fact the norm at the lodge if not also a prerequisite for full membership. Fakir admission in the lodge was, however, also conditional on the custodian's approval and involved rites and ceremonies of formal initiation. New fakirs were regularly sought and recruited. Aspiring fakirs that arrive at the lodge first draw the attention of a fakir by offering their services and by being present in fakir company. In most cases, an aspiring fakir must find a fakir referee in order to be considered for initiation into the lodge. Admission doesn't equal initiation. Once admitted, fakirs are mentored by senior members and are expected to participate in the collective upkeep and maintenance of the lodge. Fakirs at the lodge are assigned different duties like the safekeeping of visitors' shoes at the entrance of the shrine, the preparation of day meals, and the daily collection of food donations from the various quarters of the city in the evenings.[11] Fakirs also serve as the labor force of the custodian; some may work his lands, and others might help construct new units of the lodge. Fakirs of a lodge are not employed but are dependent on their sayyid masters for their subsistence; they receive a daily stipend. Most duties are rotated and are held by different fakirs for different periods of time.

A key organizing principle of *kafis* in Sehwan is that they tie fakirs with their patrons in intimate bonds of dependence. This is confirmed in rites and rituals through which fakirs are initiated. The master, most often of sayyid descent, acts as their guarantor and protector, meaning that fakirs must profess full submission to his will and authority. In being initiated at the hands of a spiritual master, male fakirs are able to situate themselves in an authorized line of spiritual transmission as well as in a fraternity of desiring men. They can also depend on the material generosity of their masters, especially when faced with misfortune and illnesses. In the event of a serious dispute, the master reserves the right to revoke fakir privileges and provisions. Excommunication threatens a fakir's removal from chains of saintly access as well as from the larger social network of fakirs. Much of this is also what would have been at stake in Murad's case.

The Enigmatic Murad

Murad was the most popular of mentors at the lodge, yet his history was also surprisingly the least known. Few people knew of his beginnings and especially of his time before he turned to a fakir life. There was an air of enigma around him. No one at the lodge knew his exact age, his first or birth name, or the name of his village or any details of his family. He was known only by the name a *talib* receives from his master upon initiation into the lodge. Unlike many, when asked, he did not have a proper story of arrival in Sehwan. "I don't remember anything" would be his usual turn of phrase to questions concerning his past; or of his personal circumstances, he would say, "My identity is Bodlo. All that I have is what I found here."[12] What I did gather, however, from his meagre tellings and others' accounts of him was that he arrived in Sehwan from Punjab, as some fakirs estimated, about twenty years earlier in the first half of the 1990s. Of his arrival at the lodge, he once mentioned how just when he was about to enter the shrine of Lal, an old bearded fellow had directed him to this place, instructing him on the custom that one ought to make the first offerings to Bodlo. To this sparse description, Murad had duly added, "I had not come to go back—this much I knew!"

I had known of Murad's preeminence ever since I first set foot in Bodlo-kafi in late 2009. Back then he was assigned one of the most arduous duties at the lodge. Every evening, right after the drumming ritual (*dhamal*) was over at the shrine of Bodlo, he would perform the traditional role of Bodlo's she-camel (*dachi*). Ringing a large bell in one hand, which was hung around his neck, he would do the rounds of Sehwan for about forty-five minutes. Barefoot and completely mute, head and eyes lowered, his task as a *dachi* was to walk the streets of Sehwan, collecting milk in a bucket and food in a big pouch, carried on the shoulder and across the chest. The physically demanding nature of this daily performance brought respect among onlookers as well as the fakirs of the lodge.[13] Over a period of time, I also became aware of his appeal. His reputation for attracting the company of urban visitors, especially journalists, filmmakers, and foreign researchers, wasn't hard to confirm. He was, in my opinion, the most-interviewed fakir at the lodge. This partly explains why, despite being introduced to him, I had not actively sought to interview him. At the time, my friend Delphine would often spend time in his company, and on a few occasions I had accompanied her during interviews and conversations in the field. Just as I knew Murad from a distance, he too recognized my purpose of staying in Sehwan largely through my association with a team of French researchers that Michel Boivin was leading at the time.

Late one night in the autumn of 2011, almost two years after we were first introduced, Murad and I would properly meet. I was on my way to the rest house on the hill, the place where I used to stay in Sehwan. Walking to this northernmost edge of Sehwan always involved walking past Bodlo-kafi. I heard Murad call out my name from behind. Against my intentions of retiring for the night, he invited me for tea. He inquired how my time in Sehwan had been and complained that I had been ignoring him. An intriguing yet sparse account of himself meant that he would keep me engaged for the night. With numerous such occasions to follow, Murad was to make clear his choice as well his intention of becoming an interlocutor in my research. At the time, Murad was no longer the food-collecting *dachi*. He was now assigned the task of collecting shoes at the shrine gates. The spot also became the occasion and site of our many exchanges in the months that followed. I would sometimes assist him in his duty by the gates or would chat with him in a room by the stables. For a short period of time he was made the caretaker of Nilam, the lodge's resident horse, reserved for annual processions during the commemoration of Muharram.[14]

A striking feature that runs through all our interactions, from the scantiest of interactions in 2009 to our last detailed conversation in 2012, even the brief phone calls in 2013 and 2018, has been his refusal to talk about his past. On occasions when I tried pressing for details, he described himself as a corpse, lifeless, wrapped appropriately in a blood-soaked shroud, a symbolic reference to the red garment that fakirs of the lodge wore. "Do not remind me of what I have forgotten; even if you were to wake up the dead, you'd be terrified to see the beast inside the shroud."[15] Only in the rarest of instances would he let his guard down. And even then, there was hardly a fact or figure or a biographical vignette that would disturb the veil that he so consciously upheld over his life prior to Sehwan.

> What do you reckon, who has been taking care of me since I was a child? I have had to wash people's dishes in order to be able to study. I have not become Murad today just like that. I have seen those that have taken oath on the Quran that for them there is no one save me. I have also seen the same people fire a pistol at me. I am not scared of death because I have known it to be so close. I am not afraid of the prison or the courts. Had I not feared Bodlo, I would swallow them all up. ... I am the dirtiest of all human beings. ... You people ask me of my background, home, this, that—I have nothing of it![16]

The only consistent impression I was able to get of his past was that there was something that he did not wish to revisit; that he, like many fakirs, may have found a new beginning and a renewed sense of purpose through his association with the lodge. A break with the past, while severe in Murad's case, is not unique to his story. Fakirs are often able to find new beginnings in saintly pursuits. The initiation of fakirs into a lodge involves and celebrates such discontinuities through ceremony. Initiation marks an important transition from the death of a social subject to the birth of a new *talib*, the one who is prepared to seek and desire. The new fakir receives a *wardi* and with it he is given a new name. So strongly was the past severed in Murad's case that he would never come to reveal the name of his prefakir days because, he "remembered nothing, nothing at all," as he would so often remark with a smirk.

In a conversation on sexual abstinence in the summer of 2012, then perhaps not knowing how life would unfold for him, Murad said, "Somebody who simply wears a red *wardi* [costume or uniform], performs service, while also raising children, cannot be a fakir!" He further used the term *lung-langot* (a garment that covers the loins) to refer to maintaining sexual abstinence and celibacy among fakirs.[17] He was categorical in his position that being fakir excluded sexual intimacy with women and attachments with family. Just a month earlier, in a different but related conversation on desire, Murad had described fakirs in the following terms: "The fakir is not dead; he has the attributes of the dead." Sexual abstinence in Murad's view was an ideal that needed to be constantly guarded. The fakir garment, which Murad often described as shroud-like, was both performance and reminder that the fakir is comparable to the dead. Though not being dead per se, the fakir is susceptible to sexual desire, a thing that would come to risk Murad's own fakir credentials.

The question of celibacy and sexual abstinence among fakirs in Sehwan is a hard one to settle, especially given the history and prevalence of nonnormative sexual behavior among *qalandars* and *be-shar* mystics or Sufis-without-shariah. Historical accounts suggest that abstinence from sex was not always abstinence from sexual pleasure or that notions of celibacy were in some contexts centered around a refusal to engage in reproductive economies of family and the society.[18] Similarly, Lloyd Ridgeon has noted that even though the literature on *qalandars* does not discuss celibacy thoroughly, it specifies requirements to abandon lust and sexual gratification. Such absence, he cautions, should not mean that *qalandars* enjoyed free license to engage in sexual acts. Quoting the case of Haydari *qalandars*, he notes that "the use of iron implements around the genitals ... in addition to the general lifestyle of poverty, mendicancy and otherworldliness, militated against marriage and sexual relations" (Ridgeon 2010, 248–49). I wasn't quite able to establish whether ideas of abstinence in fakir accounts referred exclusively to marital and reproductive sex, or if they indeed excluded nonnormative forms of sexual practice, especially given the homosocial environments of fakir fraternities like the lodge. Part of the difficulty also stemmed from the fact that most fakirs in Sehwan did not directly engage with questions of sexual practice. In the case of women fakirs, such issues were brought up in their discussion of maintaining purity and ritual cleanliness. For example, speaking of discontinuing their sexual relations with their husbands, women would try to establish that their marital ties did not correlate to those of a husband and wife. When speaking of it, fakirs regardless of gender often relied on veiled metaphors and implicit references.[19] In such conversations among men at the lodge, fakirs would bring up the local notion of *jatti-satti* to refer to a person's nonsexual condition as well as unmarried status.[20] Another term was *lung-band*, literally the sealing of a man's loins, which suggests a refusal of all forms of sexual pleasure. Dost once described that his *nafs* (carnal self), here an indirect reference to his genital organ, was kept unnourished so that it no longer retained its erectile capacity.[21] On an earlier occasion, he had however expressed a desire to marry, that is, once the long fakir process was complete. Vows of abstinence, as I understood from such exchanges, were not always lifelong commitments and could also be taken for limited periods of one's life.

"Among them there is no marriage." Pointing to the shrine of Bodlo, Dost was now gesturing at the incompatibility of marriage with the saint and his like. In that moment, he was acknowledging that Murad's actions found support in *shari'at* or that he was well within his rights to marry. But he also added that the fakir who follows *tariqat* is actually in pursuit of intimacy with saintly figures like Lal and Bodlo, whose defining characteristic was their *jatti-satti* condition. Like Zaheda, he relied on the word *qurb* to refer to feelings of closeness and intimacy with saints. While there was no religious blame on Murad, Dost was adamant that his new love would adversely affect Murad's stature as a fakir. He told me that a fakir who decides to partake in the intimacy of a woman is bound to lose his grasp of the hidden aspects of the world or powers of the unrevealed (*ghaybi taqat*). A few days later, in a heated argument with his peers, he maintained the same position. An otherwise ordinary conversation steered toward the scandal. Listening to the discussions, it was becoming clear that Murad, in the eyes of Dost, was now a weaker if not lesser fakir. In his descriptions, the realm of the celibate fakir was the masculine realm, one associated with the Mawla (Ali, the primary figure of devotion among the Shi'a). It was superior to its counterpart, the worldly realm, defined by its feminine character.[22] In prioritizing his love for a woman over his duty as a fakir of Bodlo, Dost was confidently arguing that Murad had bargained for the feminine and therefore lesser world. In equating the feminine with the sexual, he was reaffirming an easy binary, which holds that spirituality, intellect, and rationality are attributes of maleness and men, or that women are enormous threats to men's spiritual progress. By such logic and perhaps reaffirmed by the homosocial community of fakirs at the lodge, sacrality is incompatible with (hetero)sexuality. Though prevailing, such views have been neither unanimous nor uncontested in Sufi con/texts. Sa'diyya Shaikh (2012, 186) takes a radical position when she identifies "a complete interpenetration of spirituality and sexuality" in the thirteenth-century writings of the Arab-Andalusian scholar Ibn 'Arabi. Parsing themes of gender and sexuality across a compendium of texts of a major Sufi thinker, she figures how "love between men and women is an inherent aspect of loving God, bringing human beings closer to God" (187).[23] Shaikh isn't referring to metaphorical love or reading desire in an abstract sense. In fact, she identifies in these writings "a celebration and affirmation of the body and sexuality as intrinsic components of human spirituality," to the extent that "sex provides the mystic with the opportunity for one of the most comprehensive experiences of servanthood and receptivity" (189). For Sufis, the experience of losing oneself in the divine can be "an incredibly erotic movement" (Mian 2019, 135).[24] Sexual intimacy thus conceived and experienced is not a hindrance but a form of affective knowing, a self-disclosing experience comparable to total annihilation in the Truth. Dost's reading of Murad's situation was neither as generous nor as reconciliatory. His peers, however, did not share his uncompromising views. An excerpt from my field diary documents an argument I witnessed among junior fakirs gathered around one of the fireplaces at the lodge. Matters were relatively fresh and emotions understandably high.

> Last night at Chhuttal-Shah [a section of the Bodlo-kafi], an argument broke out among Dost, Fez and Raja. Raja was telling me how while cleaning, he came across Murad's *hal-vaslah* [fakir accessories and objects]. He missed him then. Dost attempted to explain to us that he [Murad] had left after surrendering his *wardi* [costume]. Raja interrupted him and said that his *wardi* has not been taken from him. His status is the same and he is sure that he [Murad] is imparting the same knowledge of *tariqat* [the mystical path] to others in Lahore. There too his status is the same. There is no difference. Dost attempted again to explain that "when someone commits a *mistake*, the master, according to principle, takes the *wardi* back." Raja got very upset at Dost's mention of the word *mistake* [English in original]. He has done no wrong. His stuff is only kept here because he left it in the care of the master. His *wardi* was not taken from him, it was not stripped away! This

question whether Murad left his *wardi* or was asked to surrender it is unsettled here at the *kafi*. Raja insisted that in a year or two *baba* [Murad] would return and resume. Dost seems to disagree on the maintenance of his fakir status. While Dost also respects Murad, it is clear in his discourse, also from other occasions, that a fakir loses his powers or capacities once he opts to sleep with a woman. On some level Dost sounds a little disappointed. ... The argument got out of hand. Dost was patient but Raja was extremely upset, especially when Dost tried to explain how a policeman on duty has to surrender his gun and his *wardi* if he is suspended. For Dost, Murad's decision of marriage is clearly a mistake on the fakir path and that it will have consequences both material, i.e., the giving up of *wardi*, and spiritual, in terms of fakir capacities. ... The debate remained unresolved.[25]

The argument that evening had raised a few important points. First and foremost, what is referred to as *wardi* here is not restricted to the long red shirt that fakirs are seen wearing at the lodge. Raja mentioned that he came across Murad's *hal-vaslah*, not simply the fakir garment. This would suggest that in addition to the long shirt, common to all fakirs at the lodge, there were other items like scarf, rings, bracelets, necklaces, and earrings that were included in the material that Murad had left behind. Fakir objects customarily include items like the begging bowl and the baton, material objects and wearables that a fakir possesses. The important point this raises is the relationship of this set of items and wearables to the status of a fakir.[26] When Dost compared the event to the policeman's surrendering of his uniform, it was not the first time that fakirs described *wardi* in the light of duty and privilege. More important, as per Dost's view, conferred privileges could also be withdrawn. Put in the argumentative framework of the *pir* of the pink healing room (in chapter 2), Murad's wrong act had impacted the progress of his fakir work for the worse. Fakir spiritual prowess had to be acquired through practice and action (*'amal*) and not bestowed as an irrevocable gift (*'ata*) of the sayyid *pir*. Moreover, for Dost, the presence of Murad's fakir objects in Sehwan indicated that there was something fundamental that Murad had lost, surrendered, or left behind. In other words, the question fakirs were arguing over that evening was whether or not minus his fakir objects Murad was indeed the same fakir. Also, the debate among the junior fakirs rested primarily on their positions regarding the relationship of marriage with fakir life. It is clear that Dost saw Murad's decision as a mistake and the loss of fakir privileges as an understandable cost that follows this mistake. Other fakirs remained convinced of Murad's return to favor as well as into the folds of the *kafi*.

In a sense, what was equally at stake in these discussions were questions of saintly intimacy and fidelity. I was reminded how Zaheda had once remarked that a fakir woman, owing to her gender, had the distinct potential to be close to the saint in a way that would not be possible for male fakirs. While a continuing struggle for herself, it was in Zaheda's opinion an unsurmountable barrier for male fakirs. At the lodge, however, gender wasn't a hindrance to establishing intimacy with the saint. On one occasion, Murad had in fact quite literally spoken of the possibility of contracting a marriage with Lal, describing it as the distinguishing character that sets apart formally initiated fakirs of a lodge from ordinary ones that hang out on their own at shrines: "[Those] fakirs only have a fling; they do not have a ladder, because a *nikah* [Muslim marriage] is not contracted. When Lal [the saint] contracts a *nikah* with someone, that someone is then his wife."[27] Seen in this light, Murad's decision to marry is more than a transgression of ideals of celibacy. It involves infidelity, a shift in his object of desire, a taking up of intimacy with someone other than the saint. It is a decision that puts his love of the woman above his love for and fidelity to the saint. Once again, intimacy is that veering force that takes a fakir off the straight path of *fakiri*—or at least that's how Dost put it to me. I would however add that so long as desiring saints in terms of this book involves and issues unstraight affordances, the abandonment of such intimacies, as we find in Murad's case, constitutes at the same time a return to straight paths, projects, and economies of the social.

A World without Murad

In one of our conversations in November 2013, Dost described how actions like those of Murad jeopardize the promise of a fakir's intimacy with the saint:

> The ones who have seen the saint, who have received his audience [*didar*], they remain *straight* [*seedhay*; emphasis added]. The ones that have seen the saint in a dream are celibate [*jatti-satti*] fakirs. If they sleep [*soye*] with a woman they will not be able to sleep with the saint [*murshid*]; they will not be able to enjoy the comfort of the saint. Because the Ism-e a'zam [the greatest but secret name of Allah] is such

that it is lost by being in bed with a woman; this is the issue! Because he [the saint] did not marry either, he had cast it [his loins] in iron. The ones who have met the saint or are joined with him [*mile huey*] lead such lives. From them emits the fragrance of the saint.[28]

In making this statement, Dost was casting doubt on his mentor's accomplishments as a fakir. In a way, he wondered if Murad ever was as close to the saint as he implied. For those who have indeed received the saint's audience, in his opinion, ones who have enjoyed his company and his presence, who have tasted intimacy with him, would not even dream of looking elsewhere, of facing another direction, of taking an object of desire other than the saint. In the moment, Dost was speaking in such confident terms that I could only marvel at the distance that he had covered since we last spoke. Dost had come to be rather secure and assertive in his opinions, which wasn't really the case in our conversations just a year or so before. One such chat was recorded during our routine nighttime hangouts at Bodlo. Things would usually get calmer at the lodge after midnight; the doors of the shrine were closed and fakirs had the chance to chill until duties resumed in the early hours of the morning. Many a time, Murad, Dost, and I would hang out together. Both shy and out of reverence, Dost wouldn't speak much in Murad's presence. But on this particular summer night in 2012, Murad had busied himself on the phone. In hindsight, one might conjecture that he was speaking to the young woman he eventually married. Retiring for the night, Murad had left Dost and me to hang out on our own. To an earlier statement of his that to be a fakir is to be cut off from the world, I then asked him how it was affecting his life.

> It makes a difference. What matters is that what the fakir leaves behind, the deeds he turns away from, the desires he foregoes, they keep returning to him. They don't let go of you, you know! One remembers only what one has done, not what is yet to happen. Okay! This is what doesn't go away. … It is a strange feeling. One doesn't really know if it is the right thing. But the ones who understand the saints, who maintain a bond with them, who remember them in their thoughts, they are the ones who find a way into their spiritual-ness, they find peace therein. … The ones who do not have their spiritual-ness, theirs is useless. But we do not have his [the saint's] spirituality! Things may turn around anytime. One doesn't know to where one would drift in a matter of seconds or what one would do, right? Because he [the saint] hasn't given his *qurb* [being close, intimacy], he has only given his duties. He has

given everything else; also respect. All day people kiss my hands, some even kiss my feet, okay, he has given me respect. I also recognize that whatever is happening is actually happening to him, not to me. He is making it happen. But he is not giving his *qurb*, his *didar* [audience, viewing], he is not giving his sign, he is not meeting me in a dream so that life may have an assurance, or I may have faith in my life, in my way, that there is a destination after all, that I really belong to my *murshid*, right? That faith is not there! For so long as his *qurb* is not there, his *didar*, or his miracles [*karamat*], or some progress, there cannot be *didar*, there cannot be certainty [*yaqin*]. There is certainty, but I don't know what kind of certainty that is. It is such that it could break any moment. If he gives his *qurb*, if he gives his *didar*, if such a thing would happen with us, we too would believe that the saint meets us and that we are now his. Even now we live as if we are his but it would be more comforting. Life will have a purpose, it will have a direction; we shall be on one side. On one side we shall be, right! At the moment, we sometimes go here, sometimes there, you know? We also think of other [options], because we don't have his spirituality.

If his [the saint's] spirituality were there, one would not think of other things. My heart at times suggests that I should marry. Okay, even if my family arranges my marriage, by the way I am engaged, I am asked for by my aunt's family. ... I say that I will not get married but I also believe in fate. I am not able to say, right, what if fate turns me over, who knows what it makes of me? ... If I do something, like marriage etc., a girl or something, or it may be that he [the saint] sends a girl; there is actually one that he has sent [*Dost laughs*].[29]

In these very personal reflections, Dost had affirmed the idea that being oriented toward a saint is to pursue the promise of certain objects even if one's destination is not always in clear sight. He revealed a capacity for self-doubt, a questioning of his choices, leaving open the question of his future. But his circumstances had changed by the time we were to meet again. In returning to this conversation a year later, I was looking for the dynamism that was eventually lost to certitude in the aftermath of Murad's scandal. The malleability of his earlier views stood in sharp contrast to the argument he had with his peers just the other night. Now an initiated fakir at the lodge, Dost had come to view his fakir path in more certain and fixed terms. If Zaheda's struggle over the years had led her from reasonable confidence to a place of insecurity and growing loss (see chapter

3), Dost's trajectory demonstrated a remarkable shift from the doubting position of an aspiring fakir to one who was firmly grounded as a *talib*, a desirer-seeker. The events of 2013 had led to a consolidation of Dost's earlier diverging views. His position on fakir marriage, celibacy, and saintly companionship were especially firm. Dost and his peers, despite the hot disagreements, the ongoing arguments, the divergences in their positions I had observed in 2013, had come to derive meaning and purpose from Murad's scandal.

The vacuum that Murad had once left behind felt remarkably fresh even in 2018 when I returned to the lodge after a long break. It had been almost five years since the scandal and there was no prospect of Murad's full return to favor. Living on the outskirts of Lahore, he had visited the shrine a few times only to pay his respects. The fakirs he had mentored over the years had maintained some measure of contact with him, mostly over the phone. Dost had since found a purpose in his fakir pursuit. And just as his mentor once did, he was also seen breaking into long orations. Unfortunately for Dost, however, he neither had the fortune of his mentor's charm nor could garner the same following as Murad. Interestingly, though, Murad had a principal role to play in this coming-of-age story. The training and tutelage he offered to Dost had proven to be as instrumental as the space his departure created for Dost to flourish on his own.

Love over Loyalty

During the time that the *kafi* was abuzz with the news about Murad, I also found my first opportunity to interview its custodian, Nur-Shah. I had tried several times earlier, with fakirs putting in a word for me, but all such meetings had been brief, at best an exchange of greetings and pleasantries. Though we hadn't really interacted, he was nonetheless present in the conversations. He was after all the spiritual master of the many fakirs I had spoken to at the lodge over the years. Also, that I was spending extended periods of time at the lodge could not have happened without his tacit consent.

When he finally agreed to be interviewed, it was during the final days of my stay in 2013. Things at the lodge were in flux, as I have explained. Murad, one of his most special fakirs, was no longer with him. The daily management of the shrine and the lodge was also changing hands. While Murad was known to be the teacher to young initiates, the lodge's everyday affairs, especially the distribution of tasks and the management of the shrine's daily income and fakir expenses, were in the hands of another fakir who held the office of *wado-fakir*, literally big or senior fakir.[30] As it turned out, the same year that Murad left the lodge for the love of a woman, the *wado-fakir* established a romantic liaison with another woman at the shrine, also a disciple of the custodian. They were eventually married. In contrast with Murad's, this match, however, had met the approval of the master. And while it meant that the *wado-fakir* would have to give up his chief role at the lodge, settling for a lesser position, he had, unlike Murad, managed to salvage his membership in the fakir fraternity. This interview took place at a time when the old guard of the lodge was being replaced by somewhat younger fakirs. Dost, for example, was acquiring a reputation for speaking on matters of faith, and another young fakir was dealing with new and greater responsibilities of managing the administrative affairs of the lodge.

Nur-Shah met me in the dimly lit front yard of his house, situated right across from the shrine of Bodlo. As soon became clear in our interaction, there were no opportunities to pose any questions. He had already made up his mind on the issues he wished to address, steering the conversation rather forcefully into a direction of his choice. As per his directions, the interaction was not recorded on a mechanical device. He, however, permitted me to take notes. That night Nur-Shah was to present a narrative that was as unsettling as the current state of affairs at the lodge. His discourse, I reckoned, was a premeditated response to the recent developments, in particular the question of fakir marriages. Even more interesting is that he did so in relation to the life of Bodlo, the saint whose legacy, material as well as spiritual, he represented. Given his unquestionable moral and spiritual authority over fakirs of the lodge, his position on the matter was understandably of great interest to me.

That Bodlo was a celibate figure was an uncontested matter in Sehwan. This wasn't just popular narrative, it was endorsed by the official discourse of the lodge. Nur-Shah's family have long maintained that since Bodlo was indeed celibate, as present-day custodians of the shrine, they were in fact the direct descendants of his brother. This idea of direct lineage is, more critically, the same legal reasoning through which the shrine of Bodlo, despite its economic viability and promise, was secured back through a court case when the Pakistani state had sought to take control of the shrine under the Department of Auqaf. Moreover, fakir ideals of celibacy at the lodge were built upon Bodlo's celibacy. All this, to my utter disbelief, would now be put into question, as Nur-Shah portrayed Bodlo anew as a married saintly figure.[31] He did not offer a detailed account of the event, nor had I the opportunity to intervene, but by casually mentioning the occasion of Bodlo's marriage to a noblewoman, Nur-Shah was effectively turning an established discourse on its head while casting marriage as acceptable in both Islamic legal and mystical ways.[32] None of the elite sayyid figures of Sehwan I have spoken to over the years have categorically denied or discounted the possibility and permissibility of marriage for their fakir initiates. Yet each one of them stressed that an engagement with or a pursuing of profane and corporeal pleasures was bound to fundamentally affect the capacities and powers of a fakir, the very position Dost had taken with regard to Murad's case. Their point was that loyalty to one's *murshid* and complete devotion to a saintly figure precluded the pursuit of other intimacies, rival attachments, and competing orientations.

The problem, it seemed, wasn't solely a question of marriage or of abandoning the ideal of celibacy and sexual abstinence, as it had first appeared.[33] It was in fact a taking up of an object of desire, which threatened the very pact of unquestionable submission that inaugurates fakir life at the lodge. As fakirs are initiated at the *kafi*, they are believed to pass through death to a newly born status. This passage is marked by ceremony and ritual. These are intimately conducted, private affairs, though some fakirs have described to me parts of what takes place.[34] As part of the preparations, the initiate must shave his body entirely, upon which he is given a ritual bath by a senior fakir, just as the dead are washed before burial. Then dressed in just a loincloth, he is presented to the *murshid*. He first prostrates himself, expressing his complete submission, then, placing one thumb on the other, the initiate stands in the audience of his master. He returns born anew, as it were, equipped with a red garment, a new name, and a reformed status as a confirmed fakir. At other lodges in Sehwan, a hot seal is applied on the fakir's arm. With it, a pact of hierarchy between the master and fakir is also sealed (see fig. 4.3).[35] In another account narrated to her by a fakir of the lodge, Delphine Ortis (2020, 317) recounts how the fakir body "is first of all rid of its erotic potential by shaving the hair … and then humiliated by earth put on his head." In her reading, these acts symbolize the fakir's freedom from both his virility and pride. These also prepare him to wear the *langot*, the garment that Murad had once mentioned, the "sex-cover" as Ortis calls it, or "a symbol of the sexual abstinence [the fakir] is committed to." From this moment on, in her view, the fakir "has neither past nor future." As a first symbolic act, the new fakir is sent to beg in the surrounding areas, sealing his status of servitude. As a token of

FIGURE 4.3
A fakir pays respects to his sayyid master at another *kafi* in Sehwan, 2012.

this new master-disciple relationship, she notes, the novice is given a secret word or unique formula for meditation (Ortis 2020, 317). Details may
slightly vary across fakir accounts and descriptions, though what's consistent is that the spiritual birth of the novice comes with a pact of complete
submission, uttered in words and acted out in ritual. As clay ready to be
molded, the fakir novice, here comparable with "newborns who need the
suckling of their masters," accepts the doubly gendered role of the *murshid*
as procreator and nurturer, father as well as mother, which according to
one reading is an infantilizing and feminizing of oneself as the willing and
passive receptacle (Malamud 1996, 96). Ortis (2020, 319), however, suggests that it is the servile condition of the wife that better corresponds to
the status of the male fakir in relation to his spiritual masters. Its gendered
connotations aside, prostration completes a fakir's final act of total submission to his protector lord in Sehwan.

In Murad's own words, he had no will of his own. In referring to his
own ceremony of initiation, he described Nur-Shah as his owner: "Whatever I am today, it is because of him. He is my *murshid*; he is my god. I have

prostrated to him."[36] Murad's independent decision to pursue a woman without the approval of his master is a failure to take his *murshid* as his arbitrator and intercessor for matters both worldly and spiritual. Margaret Malamud (1994, 434) has described the relationship between a *murshid* and *murid* (master and disciple) as "intensely personal," encompassing domains both spiritual and mundane, so much so that submitting to the will of the *murshid* is considered a "step in learning to surrender to the will of God." A *murid* or a disciple in this sense is one who not only opens up his inner states and conditions to the scrutiny of his guide, he must turn over "the governance of his worldly affairs and control over his body to the direction of his master" (Malamud 1994, 434). Shahzad Bashir has evocatively described such total voluntary submission to Sufi masters through the corporeal metaphor "corpses in morticians' hands" (2011, 187). It is precisely this ideal of the *murid* that Murad had failed to live up to. In so doing, Murad had abandoned his pact of submission and lost the right to remain under the protection of his patron, his *murshid*. It is not simply marriage but Murad's defiance that cost him dearly. There were fathers and married fakirs at the lodge, after all. The *wado-fakir*, for instance, had married with the approval of the *murshid* and so, despite the change in rank, he was able to retain his *wardi* and with it a place among fakirs.

Fakir intransigence was rarely tolerated, and patrons were known to excommunicate wayward fakirs, although this was not reported in Murad's case. It was the giving up of the *wardi* that had become the shorthand for his story. Taking off the shroud-like garment is a symbolic occasion of return to straight paths of the social. In departing from the *kafi*, Murad reentered the world of the living, for without a shroud he is less likely to be read as (socially) dead. By desiring and pursuing a woman, Murad upset a pursuit of mystical objects ascribed to him as a *talib* (seeker-desirer). Murad was now on his own trying to settle in a new city, finding ground at a different shrine. He was distressed with how things had unraveled. In a conversation on the phone in 2013, Murad sounded unsettled and insecure; he longed for Sehwan and his peers, he told me. His ties to his home *kafi* could never be severed, in his view, nor could those to his *murshid*, whom he had on numerous occasions described as his god and creator (*rabb*) and whose love he had compared to that of a mother. Many at the lodge expected his return to favor, but none could speculate when and how that trust would eventually be restored. Even if Murad, as it were, had not managed to live up to the ideals he had once held and disseminated, his ideas as well as his personality had had a deep impact on young fakirs at the lodge. In one of our meetings, Murad had said in verse, "You are of here and here you shall remain / but I, a fragrance diffused into air."[37] And so it had come to be. Though no longer at the lodge, he remained, throughout my time in the field, the most talked-about fakir, his presence most palpable in the lives he had affected and touched—this notwithstanding the arguments his marriage and subsequent departure had sparked among his peers or the ensuing conflict with his master whom he had served for about twenty years. Fakir disagreements on intimacy opened up a way to understand how spirituality is not always in antagonistic relation to sexuality, but rather, the two are complexly conversant. Whether fraying or thriving, be it with a saint or not, intimacy's ability to usurp or displace other relations or upset futures was also reaffirmed in the aftermath of the scandal, especially for fakirs at the lodge who were left to make sense of Murad's veering love for a woman. In the greater tale of saintly intimacy and unstraight affordances, however, the story of Murad stands in for the idea that saintly bonds, even when secured through rites of initiation and afforded by spiritual masters, can come undone or show signs of disaffection, especially in the face of rival intimacies and competing objects of desire.

In the final of five settings, I turn to a graveyard in Sehwan. With fakir accounts of contesting authorities in a haunted place, I illustrate how fakir experiences and feelings of intimacy are complexly structured, which alongside the saint feature the company of (other) dead, the more-than-human, material bodies as well as spiritual beings. More importantly, it takes a spatial turn to augment the greater argument that intimacy and its unfolding or a worlding with saints is as much curbed by local conditions and politics as it is enriched by sedimenting histories in and of place. In other words, it sets the last act that stages how grove, shrine, courtyard, lodge, and graveyard are intimate settings, not only because fakirs dwell in these sites or their lives unfold in these places, but also because these bring fakirs into critical intimacy with greater histories and the polysemic imaginations of Sehwan itself.

5

Worlding
Fakirs, Fairies,
and the Dead

"Here in Sehwan, the unrevealed [*ghaybat*] are plenty"—Jamal prepares the ground to tell a long tale. He is describing not djinns, he says, but ghost-spirits (*bhoot*) that haunt this very place. The setting of this tale is no less special than its telling. It is after dark in a graveyard on the north-ernmost edge of Sehwan. Suitably remote, this part of town is steeped in legend, Sehwan's everyday frenzy lost to its quiet and solitude. On a No-vember night in 2013, Delphine and I are sitting under a *kikar* tree, a fakir dwelling amid old graves where Jamal resides. With his audience in place and an audio recorder in sight, Jamal embarks on a performance with his usual mix of word, song, and dance. It's not his first, and it won't be the last time Jamal will break into theatrics as he describes his extraordinary en-counters in the graveyard. I particularly recall one whereby he had come to unearth the tombs of two fairies, now a shrine of which he is a self-appointed custodian. In this moment, however, the site he is describing is not the graveyard itself but the fabled hill that overlooks it, what locals call the "inverted city" (*ulta sheher*) or "fortress of the infidels" (*kafir-qila*).

FIGURE 5.1
Jamal in the graveyard by night, 2013.

Jamal points to a section of the dreaded hill and says, "There, inside, is a figure made of fire; it is a figure of fire that sings *bhajan*; *bhajan* of the Hindus you know!" In no time, he rises from his seat and sings aloud a Hindu devotional song. Before we know it, he is dancing: *dhig, dhig, dhig, dha*; he utters musical notes as he moves, imitating rather poorly postures of Hindu deities.

Under a single incandescent bulb, this bright spot serves as a perfect stage in an otherwise dark theater of the graveyard. Fittingly enough, he is in costume. He is wearing a stunning multicolored vest that he patch-worked himself (see fig. 5.1). As he resumes his seat and the story, Jamal identifies the fiery spirit as Devraj, a powerful figure that protects a grand treasure in the depths of the hill. For good reason, Devraj is watchful of Jamal's presence. His closeness to the fairies is also why Jamal must face demons of the nearby fortress. In one of their encounters, when Devraj appears to him, he promises Jamal boons and bounty as well as power over the unseen should Jamal fulfill his demands. Jamal's thrill is palpable in this instance. He continues the tale with much fervor: "I asked him, 'What are your terms?' He said, 'Drink this blood of the buffalo.' I was like ... oh, he's going to make me drink blood!? I said, 'I won't drink blood.'" At this point Jamal declares his loyalty to the family of the Prophet (*ahl-e bayt*). By invoking rival saintly forces, he cites a conflict of moral authorities. "'If you do not drink blood,'" Devraj continues, "'then chant the name of Lord Krishna.' I asked, 'How?' He replied, '*Om namaste deva*' [Hindu salutation to a god]. I said, 'If I were to do *om namaste deva*, wouldn't I upset my Lord?'" Just when we are curious to hear how Devraj responds, Jamal pauses. One can hear the silence of the graveyard, as if that too were joining in to add effect. Then in hushed tones, he resumes, but in a different vein: "Now I am certain, *hazrat* Isa [Jesus] is about to return. His time has come. The signs have appeared in the world." That night, Jamal's performance would last more than an hour, leaving Delphine and me exhausted, struggling as always to keep pace with the many figures and story lines he routinely cites in his tales.

Complex, polyvocal, and incoherent at times as Jamal's stories are, his present-day accounts of the graveyard are accounts of Sehwan over time. His regular encounters with Hindu gods and Muslim saints, with white souls from the "time of the English," as he puts it, and with spirits of an ancient world are part of the ways in which deeper ecologies and sedimented histories of a place like Sehwan become manifest in everyday forms. More importantly, these reveal not only how a sacred-spatial imagination of Sehwan takes felt and enfleshed shapes but also how its experience is anchored in local ecologies and complex temporalities of affect. Interestingly enough, even in the remoteness of the graveyard, Jamal isn't the only one claiming such experience. Not far from where we were sitting that night lived Shah-Bibi, a woman fakir who in fewer years than Jamal has managed to deepen her presence on the site. This chapter, though featuring two fakirs with competing claims to a single site, also engages the many contestations that haunt the historical imagination of Sehwan as well as the memory of the saint. In the final of five episodes, so to speak, we come closer to understanding why Sehwan, for fakirs, is that place where saintly histories feel at arm's length. More precisely, the graveyard offers a heterotemporal view into how intimate ties with saints expand fakir social and historical horizons, an unfolding by which they come to reappraise their place in the world. It is worth recounting that fakirs are persons who, in everyday parlance, reject the world or renounce the worldly. Their unworlding figures are least likely to be read as futural or aspirational. Yet the graveyard tells a different story: fakir ties to the living and the worldly are made dense through their affective attachments with its deceased and displaced actors. To this end, I take the position that there isn't a pregiven world or reality that fakirs approach from an outside, but, as Anderson and Harrison (2010, 8) have noted, the term *world* points us rather to the context or background against which particular things take meaning or accrue significance, in their words, "a mobile but more or less stable ensemble of practices, involvements, relations, capacities, tendencies and affordances." This chapter then is also about how fakirs mobilize such worlds or turn worldly as a result of their embroilment in human-nonhuman knots, sacred enmeshments, and saintly historical affordances, a process I further elaborate as *worlding with saints*.

Unlike most people who are drawn to it, I was not directed to Sehwan in a dream. No particular vision, I say, has determined my journey to the pilgrimage town, though Murad, my fakir interlocutor, once insisted that not being able to recall a dream is no proof of its nonoccurrence. The point is that for most of my interlocutors, fakirs or otherwise, arriving in and departing from Sehwan was always contingent upon Lal's approval. In fact, each time my plans for a weekend break in Karachi would alter at the last minute, my fakir interlocutors were quick to remind me how the decision to leave or return wasn't mine to make in the first place. Soon enough, in the company of believers, I learned to appreciate that the magical was veiled by the mundane, that there were signs to look out for, and that everyday utterances and ordinary sights required mindful consideration. Being in Sehwan required recognizing a condition of receptivity; it meant being actively implicated in constant streams of exchange between beings and across realms. Not only was Sehwan of the fakirs a passage for winged horses and hybrid creatures, mythic giants and fairies, Shi'i imams and those befriended by Allah (*walis*)—figures and phenomena Jamal had referred to in the plural as *ghaybat*—they were remarkably, for some, at accessible distance. That what counts as unrevealed, even hidden, in fakir stories refers not to the absent or the imaginary but the yet-to-be-revealed. These are participants who might be differently present in a situation or figurations whose apprehension, visibly or otherwise, depends on heightened modes of knowing that fakirs strive for or gain through an intimacy with saints. What this also means is that there exists a correspondence, a slippage if you will, between physical contours of a place, its topographic or architectural features, and its nonmaterial knowledge, that is to say, its dialogical and visionary potentials. Pointing to a capacity for suturing worlds, especially in relation to religion's "multiplicitous affairs with notions of the divine," scholars describe affect as an "indistinct yet critical volume" that discretely impinges but also concretely and "animatingly moves through, between, or alongside other volumes and engages its subjects in dialogue across invisible borderlands" (Kasmani et al. 2020). This indeed resonates with Amira Mittermaier's idea that understandings of saintly places are "incomplete unless they are conceptualized within a notion of space that includes both the material and the imaginary" (2008, 48).[1] Fakir pursuits also confirm such a view: The sequence of visions that pulls Baba-Akram in search of the enigmatic figures of the dream is also the blueprint for an eventual fakir dwelling outside Sehwan; Amma's dealing with fakir spirits is inseparable from the spatial politics of the saint's durbar, in particular her claim to the men's prayer space where she sits every day. Similarly, Murad's loss of the fakir garment signals a surrendering of place in the commune; and Zaheda's condition of disorientation involves an ongoing struggle to reground herself in the saint's courtyard and beyond the space of the family. However, to accentuate how, in the wake of affective ties, fakirs move and are also moved in terms of thoughts and feelings, I turn to Ann Armbrecht's work on pilgrimage in Nepal. I think with her notion of *thin places*, in her words, "places where one's nerve endings are bare" (Armbrecht 2009, 204), to explore how through strands of feeling and emotion, a place such as this graveyard is rendered a diaphanous site of heterotemporal feeling. Insofar as such porosity of place signals "spectral depth, affective input, and emotional traffic," it ought to inflect the place's temporal orders, because "thin reminds us that there is a clearing outside linear time, that every now and then, an opening is created for feeling and knowing, knowing by feeling" (Kasmani 2019b, 35). I read the graveyard as a porous setting where social relations encompass more than those between humans and where Sehwan's multiple histories find routine copresence. Fakir narrations of the graveyard are, in this sense, actively and continually historicizing narrations of Sehwan. These are also hauntological citations of that which remains submerged or traces of the graveyard's displaced actors and agencies. In Jan Slaby's terms, we might appreciate these as *sustained affective textures* through which a sense of the historical is carried over into the present. The felt and bodied experience of fakirs in and of the graveyard in this chapter reveals how "the past ... lingers on, individually and collectively, within the depths of corporeal comportment and within material texture of social, institutional, worldly formations" (Slaby 2020, 174). By focusing on two fakirs in a single graveyard, this chapter inquires into the ways in which layered ecologies of time and space are imbricated in a *worlding with saints* and how such complex historical figurations shape fakir circumstances in the present as well as their visions of the future.

Two Fakirs and a Graveyard

Shah-Bibi is a fakir woman who has made her home amid the dead of Sehwan. I was first introduced to Bibi in 2011, though only in passing and while speaking to Jamal in the graveyard. She was then new to the place and still on good terms with her fakir neighbor. After that, I approached her many times for an interview. According to Bibi, she needed to consult her "sources" on whether or not to allow me access. The other hurdle was posed by Tony: not only would the dog not approve of my presence anywhere near her, but part of the graveyard that it guarded had turned off-limits for me. By the time I was able to overcome such obstacles, interestingly enough, Bibi's relations with Jamal had already soured.

This first interview of ours was long in coming. It was early evening and the sun hadn't set yet. We were sitting inside Bibi's home. Though simply laid out, its sprawl and structure were much more elaborate than Jamal's spot under the tree. Propped against its southern boundary wall, on slightly raised ground, Bibi had cordoned off an entire section of the graveyard (see fig. 5.2). Where there were once wild bushes now stood a two-room mud structure. Much of it was still dominated by a tree. Around it, in what could be described as her living area, Tony and I made for a small but focused audience. I was particularly interested in learning how she had come to live in the graveyard. As Bibi spoke, right across from us, in an outdoor kitchen, was an old man she then introduced to me as her second husband. He was busy preparing the evening meal. Though, to stay true to my notes from the day, in the same sitting she also described him as her wife, pointing to his daily duties of cooking, cleaning, and caring for her. This wasn't just making light of the situation. Bibi used this example to bolster her claim that she was indeed a true man in terms of her spiritual caliber. Interestingly, though, like Amma of the mosque, she felt the need to remind me how her case was not like that of ordinary women or that her relationship with her husband did not involve sex. Conversely, she needed him around in order not to draw suspicion, given her more-than-domestic circumstances in the graveyard. In other words, despite her spiritual prowess, Bibi was faced with an ascribed femaleness of her pursuit, a point I have elaborated in the previous two chapters.

FIGURE 5.2
Bibi's former dwelling in the graveyard, 2012.

Life among the dead wasn't easy. Bibi's situation in the graveyard came with its own demands, after all. In order to endure the spirits and demons local to the site, Bibi followed a strict regime of prohibitions that determined codes of diet, dress, and sexual practice, all part of her fakir dis/guise or *bhes*. She was always dressed in a plain all-white *shalwar-kamiz*. The masculine cut of her garment was unusual for women to wear. Still, she covered her head with a long white drape additionally customized with a colorful patchwork cap on top. The many rings on her fingers and a studded necklace accessorized her simple outfit to fakir standards. In short, Bibi's unusual circumstances required equally unusual measures. To my questions regarding her past, she would bring up a number of things: a whole series of dramatic and turbulent times stretched between her former life in Karachi and the one she was beginning to establish in Sehwan. Central to this was her experience of being a mother to eleven children as well as running a business since the death of her first husband. She spoke of her early affinity for spiritual matters, especially her initial training in the care of her fakir grandfather. At one point during our interview, in midsentence, Bibi turned quiet. She closed her eyes and pointed her index finger toward the sky. I saw her experience a continuous wave of yawns. She shivered and shuddered as she freed herself of the trembling motion. The entire episode lasted just a few minutes. Upon reciting a silent prayer, she eventually regained her composure and was ready to resume our conversation. The brief disruption, as she would explain to me, was due to otherworldly beings whose routine passage across the Sehwan skies, once at dawn and again at dusk, would affect her in this manner. In a sense, Bibi was conveying to me the extent of her knowledge of the place's hidden or more-than-visible dimensions, claims that sounded much like what I had heard from Jamal. Like him, though minus the theatrics, she too spoke at length about the special nature of the soil on which we were sitting, the dead that inhabited the earth below us, the more-than-living beings that looked on from above. I was suddenly beginning to see how her growing affective ties to the graveyard and its transference in narrative could dislodge Jamal's claim to the site. For a long time, Jamal was a lone figure, with an entire graveyard to himself. When he first set foot on it almost ten years ago, he established a home under a eucalyptus tree, where a few blankets on the ground and some earthen pots still mark his presence. The site, as per Jamal, was then a neglected place, and only in time would he discover its true character. The earth in Sehwan is made transparent in Jamal's evocative descriptions of the site. In his words, it is a graveyard made of glass, such that he is able to communicate with its inhabitants:

> Once a year, there comes a moon; … once every year there is a moon such that in the full moon all of them come out of their graves, with their shrouds. I do not understand their language [*laughs*]; I am surprised at what language they speak. … One says, my home is there and the water [of the river] has destroyed it; "retrieve the sign of my home so that I may sleep in peace." … For this reason, I mark the places of these innocent [people], and I water these [graves].

Over the years and based on numerous visions like these, Jamal has unearthed a great number of lost graves, restoring in a way a large part of the site, though the primary vision that would confirm his purpose and duty in the graveyard was a distinct one. Two fairies, originally from the fabled mountains of Qaf (Koh-Qaf) appeared to him one night, who, according to Jamal's narrative, had once arrived in Sehwan in their amorous pursuit of Lal.[2] These figures, whom he refers to as Jiji, which is a Sindhi title of respect for women, identified their hidden tombs to him and charged him with their care. Pointing to where he usually sleeps in the graveyard, Jamal described this early encounter with the fairies in great detail:

> Here, when I fell asleep ... and while sleeping I noticed the sound of young children [makes different indiscernible sounds]. I thought, how come I hear children's sound here in the graveyard? I told myself, get out of bed and see, what if someone has left an unwanted child somewhere around here; this also happens here. When I opened my eyes and sat up, would you believe me, these graves that you see, the innocent persons, all in their shrouds, were standing in front of me, on both sides, all around me. Then I said, I think I'm dead [in great trouble]. They were speaking to each other. I was seeing them, all of them dressed in shrouds. I was reciting [Quranic verses] but to no effect, so I attempted to run. This wall wasn't there at the time. I thought, if I run [on] that side, by the time I reach there, they would get hold of me, devour me. And if I were to run [on] this side, at least Bodlo is nearby. This other shrine is close too. When I stood up and was ready to run, so I saw this light from here. As I stood up to see, a light came and stood before me. A human being, but appearing as light, illuminated from head to toe, drawing close to me. It kept coming toward me and came as close as, let's say, the distance between you and me. Then to me, it said, "Don't be scared, fakir! I'm Jiji-pak, the veiled one." I told Jiji, "You are not human. A human being would not appear like light; how can it be? Is a human being like that?" I said, "Either you are a *hoor* [houri; virginal figures in Islamic paradise] or a fairy but even more beautiful than a fairy, prettier than *hoor*s you are! But human you are not!" So, she said, "I'm Jiji-pak, the veiled one; no human to this day has held me in sight. The situation has now crossed limits and for this reason I beckon you. From this day on, you are the custodian of my home; establish my sign [*nishan*]."

The two tombs now stand as a twin shrine to the fairy sisters, a testimony also to Jamal's fakir labor over time. If Jamal considered his place in the graveyard a bestowal, Bibi hadn't just accidently ended up there either. As she revealed to me, she had been directed to Sehwan and particularly to this site through a series of dreams and visions. Sehwan, according to her description, was one among three vertebrae that hold the earth in place, Karbala and the Hijaz being the other two. Hijaz is the region of Arabia where the sacred Islamic cities of Mecca and Medina are located. Karbala is another holy site, revered especially by Shi'i Muslims, where Hussayn (the grandson of the Prophet) was martyred in the seventh century CE. The three are extremely hard fragments of the earth, Bibi explained, so hardened by the axial character of their function that these necessitate the direct reign of Mawla (a reference to Ali, holiest of Shiʻi figures). In her words, "If he [Ali] were not to govern this piece of land, only God knows what would become of it." Her statement is reflective of what some in Sehwan believe, which is that Lal, the saint of Sehwan, is a placeholder for Ali, if not an avatar of Ali himself. This correspondence of saintly character is embedded in a landscape of imagination that surrounds the figure of Lal, a point to which I return later in the chapter. For now, Bibi's hard-core understanding of Sehwan serves at once as a sign of its power reserves and the urgency of its taming by an all-powerful patron. Choosing the English term *main tower*, a reference to telecommunications masts and structures, she emphasized the high status of Sehwan as a site of divine reception. Of the shrine of Lal, she said, "There exists an atmosphere where all are present: the ones made of light, made of fire, angels—of the entire universe. Friends/allies of Allah, prophets, all of them ... every *qutb, ghaws, wali, pir*, fakir [categories of saintly figures]. Let me tell you this one thing, that this is the main tower!"

That neither Sehwan nor this place was ordinary was hardly news to me. The nearby hill is laden with miraculous legends associated with the saint. The solemn memory of Lal's wrath was etched in its topography, where he was believed to have turned on its head what was once an ancient settlement. It was also where the dense fabric of the living surrendered to the marshes, a spot so uninhabitable in reality and so dreadful in legend that it was perfect for fakir seclusion. When Jamal first welcomed Bibi into the folds of the graveyard, he might have imagined a different outcome or, at least, he did not expect her to stay long in the unwelcoming conditions of a graveyard. But Bibi's deepening presence was unsettling, to say the least. Soon enough, she was drawing a small following. I too observed her offering spiritual guidance and praying over materials and substances as part of a burgeoning healing repertoire. Clearly, Jamal wasn't impressed. He was critical of her growing reach, what he had come to consider an encroachment on the graveyard. He was also unconvinced of Bibi's claims of spiritual expertise, which he attributed to dark, demonic forces as opposed to saintly sources. Bibi was no fan of Jamal either. Tensions were soon simmering in the graveyard, each fakir accusing the other of false pretense and black magic. In fact, they both confirmed to me on different occasions that they had fought verbally as well as through spiritual means. Each accused the other of involving proxy spirits that they both had at their disposal.

Jamal's reservations about Bibi weren't completely unfounded. In all the years that I've known her, I too have at times found her stories hard to grapple with, if not baffling. Extraordinary accounts were routine when it came to my encounters with fakirs. That wasn't the issue; rather, Bibi, as a matter of fact, was full of intrigue. For one thing, at the time of our first meeting, she claimed to be 105 years old when one would've guessed her to be fifty at the most. She insisted that she is currently living through a second cycle and hence appears younger than her cumulative age. And if that wasn't confounding enough, in addition to her spiritual pursuits, she claimed to work for a transnational anticorruption task force. She even carried a somewhat official-looking ID in her pocket, an organization I wasn't able to find a trace of through internet searches. The precise details of her role in this job were hardly comprehensible, though I did spot her a few times with a retired army officer, whom she described as her boss. I had many a time entertained the popular belief that fakirs also make for perfect information-gathering agents for the state. The mystery surrounding Bibi's so-called work on the side made the purpose of her disguise (*bhes*) all the more intriguing. Her association with a former officer of the Pakistan Army, and my brief and rather strange meeting with him, had reified some of my doubts. So confounding were her circumstances that I sometimes referred to her as *spy-amma* in my field notes, also to distinguish her from Amma at the shrine (see chapter 2). Retrospectively, I have also wondered if the "sources" that had approved of my "case," as she put it, were at all spiritual, when she agreed to invite me to her dwelling in the graveyard.

The circumstances that had led her to Sehwan were no less dramatic. While she emphasized that she was predisposed to a fakir life, she turned to it only by accident. According to this account, she was married off to her cousin at a young age. Upon her husband's untimely death, she was left with eleven children and a blanket-manufacturing business to take care of. When a deadly fire accidentally burned the factory down, she was forced to flee from Karachi in order to escape a criminal legal case. She then lived in hiding for a few years in a village in Sindh, where she met her second husband before arriving as a fakir in Sehwan. In the meantime, she managed to negotiate a deal with the families of the deceased workers (in the factory), and the case was eventually withdrawn. Captivating as her accounts were, their most stunning instance was yet to come. When I returned to Sehwan in 2013, two years after that first interview, Bibi was still living in the graveyard but with a different man. To my utter disbelief, she now referred to the man she had once introduced to me as her second husband as a mere servant of hers, reminding me of how he used to cook and clean for her. And the new man in the graveyard was supposed to be her original husband, who in this latest version of Bibi's life wasn't dead but had in fact returned from a fifty-five-year period of ascetic wandering. This cast a long shadow of doubt on everything I had gathered from her, yet I remained all the more invested, riveted in fact.

Regardless of the gossip on the street, Bibi was firmly grounded in the graveyard. In our new encounters, she revealed to me how she had identified, through another vision, the exact location of her and her husband's future graves. In one of our meetings, she explained that she had elaborate plans to carry out the reorganization of space according to these visions. In a particular dream, she was shown where the new entrance would be, where precisely the two would be buried, and even the space where pilgrims to their graves would gather in the future. So detailed was this dreamed layout that she was also able to point out where the water dispenser would be placed. Stunning as her future plans were, Bibi wasn't the only one deepening her presence on the site. In a sense, both Jamal and Bibi were invested in long-term physical modifications of the graveyard. In fact, when the fairies identified their lost tombs to Jamal, they also brought to his attention the hidden graves of many others. These, as Jamal explained, had been devoured over the years by the encroachments of the adjacent shrine and fakir lodge. As a lone fakir with no means, Jamal was in no position to pick a bone with the powerful sayyid patrons of the neighboring complex. But soon a subsequent and alarming vision would compel him into action.

As I slept, would you believe me, I say I saw in my sleep that I am asleep in the graveyard. There is moonlight, light of the full moon. I am looking at the moonlight and from within the moonlight emerged a cloud. ... As I am watching this, I say to myself, see how the moon is breaking now. The gas from the moon is emanating, like gas, like a smoke, like a cloud it appeared. It came and came, and as I watched, it came downward. As it came down, I noticed that one of its wings stretched from here to there. The other wing, I knew not, stretched from here to where? And you know the Zuljanah [the legendary horse of Hussayn in the battle of Karbala]? The body is all Zuljanah, the head is that of my

Jiji! Whose head is it? It is Jiji's! If only it would strike, I would die like an ant would. Then the third day as I woke up, I went straight to them [the neighbors].

The vision that Jamal describes here was for him a critical reminder that the situation in the graveyard needed urgent addressing. Disparate beings—a fairy and the horse of an Islamic holy figure—were not only combined in hybrid form but were powerful allies on his side. The sayyids would eventually withdraw from the site, but this was neither quick nor easy. It would take years of insisting and a series of visions on Jamal's part and misfortunes on the sayyids'. In their eventual retreat from a section of the graveyard, in drawing anew the boundaries between the two sites, Jamal's command over the hidden features of the place was firmly and materially established. Since his arrival, he had reclaimed part of the graveyard and had almost created anew the shrine of the fairies. He had also repopulated the place by restoring graves of the dead while securing the northern and eastern peripheries of the graveyard with a low wall.

Jamal received visions while sleeping in the graveyard, and Bibi was led to it through a series of dreams and visions.[3] It is however clear that both Bibi and Jamal have articulated their claims in relation to their experiences and interaction with extraordinary beings local to the site. While the foundations of their claims rest on experiences and interactions that occur in what Mittermaier (2008) calls the dialogical dream space, these take very tangible forms and often result in physical modifications of space, its ownership, and its usage. The physical and material aspect of the place in question is intimately lined with extraordinary imagination and experience. Like the grove, the first in this book's series of five settings, the graveyard is no doubt peripheral. Its distance from the shrine of the saint and, in that sense, the center of state action affords distinct possibilities. The graveyard that Bibi and Jamal describe is not a static space of buried corpses; instead, it is animated by souls from below and above, beings from within and without, though even in such remoteness and solitude, the place was not free of the greater politics of Sehwan. We might note that compared to Baba-Akram's dwelling in the grove, Jamal and Bibi were not directly affected by bureaucratic decisions of the state, since the graveyard is not subject to Department of Auqaf administration. That said, Jamal's place in the graveyard was borne of his refusal to be initiated in a fakir lodge and put him regularly at odds with the neighboring sayyids. Similarly, it may be argued that the difficult and invasive labor that women fakirs must do in order to obtain a place where place is not given was not so different in the graveyard after all.[4] In a sense, what Amma performs at the shrine under the eyes of the state is what Bibi must carry out on her own in the seclusion of the dead.

On my last visit in 2018, eight years since I first came to the graveyard, it felt much the same, and yet I knew it was constantly changing. As I met with Bibi and her husband, we were no longer sitting around a tree. A more elaborate concrete structure, though unfinished, had come to replace the simple mud dwelling of earlier years. Tony was dead, and Bibi, it seemed, was preparing for eventual death. The new space was laid out around what she foresaw as a tomb hall. Her dream had taken physical form, and her aspirations in the graveyard were extending into a posthumous future. Jamal's dwelling under the tree, however, was as bare as it had always been, though since our last meeting, he too had intervened in parts of the graveyard. He had managed to carve out from a section of the site a raised platform of sorts. A large carpet now marked a place for gathering on this flattened piece of land. On another day during the same field visit, Jamal pointed to a couple of new graves. Some of the unidentified bodies from the deadly attack at the shrine in 2017 had been laid to rest here. As Jamal spoke of the horrors of that night, one sensed how its figures and features might eventually find a place in his narrativization of the site. I was yet again reminded that the graveyard was after all one of those places where Sehwan's ancient and newer histories came face to face. It had also been the setting for the saint's miracles. Some of its long-term inhabitants, once contemporaneous with Lal himself, be they spirits, fairies, the dead, or demons endure through fakir narratives in the present. To grasp the affective scopes and textures of the graveyard, we ought to thus also apprehend the greater context of saintly memory and narrative in which the place is embroiled.

Narrative Geographies of Sehwan

Only a few hundred meters from the graveyard is the shrine of Bodlo. This is the fakir setting that I engaged in chapter 4. Both these sites lie in the shadow of the fabled fortress, environs that are additionally storied through its place in saintly legend (see fig. 5.3). It is commonly narrated in Sehwan that Bodlo, the saint's favorite fakir, once signaled the impending arrival of Lal.[5] Or that Bodlo, with his endlessly long beard, would call out the saint's name every day while sweeping clean the alleys of Seh-

FIGURE 5.3
A view of Sehwan from the old fortress featuring the two domes of the shrines of Lal and Bodlo, 2012.

wan. Irked by the constant nuisance, the prince residing in the overlooking fortress ordered that Bodlo be killed. But each time Bodlo was killed, he would return to the streets the next morning, preparing as usual for the saint's arrival. After six failed attempts, the prince ordered that Bodlo be dismembered. He was to be cut into pieces, his flesh mixed with animal meat and then sold at the local butcher's. As Lal set foot in the city, he called out for his beloved fakir. Returning the call of the master, each and every piece of Bodlo's butchered body rose from the skulls of those who had consumed him. Bodlo then stood resurrected in the presence of his master. So furious was Lal that to invoke divine punishment, he turned his cup over, causing in effect the fortress and its environs to be turned on their head.[6] Today, lining the northern limit of the town, the site of Bodlo's killing and the saint's manifestation of divine fury is remembered as the inverted city or the fortress of the infidels. It is this that overlooks the graveyard and it is here that Devraj resides, the powerful Hindu demon of Jamal's narrative. In other words, fakir stories of the graveyard are not isolated experiences or imagined encounters. They are in fact tied to greater histories of the place itself.

The graveyard is one among several other locations that bespeak the memory of the saint.[7] One of these is the Indus River. The saint's relationship and rivalry with the river is well established in legend though best enshrined in the fact that the saint is known as Jhule Lal, a name originally directed at the river deity of the Indus.[8] A crucial interface of varying divine forces find a confluence in the river: in the figure of Lal, the Quranic river saint Khizr meets an Indic fish god.[9] Such coming together in ritual and legend, however, is not without conflict. Though the river is believed to be compliant with Lal's hierarchical position, it has on several occasions punished others who fail to recognize its independent right to reverence. As per local legend, the water-facing shrine of Juman-Jatti, walking distance from the graveyard, is one such site in Sehwan where the wrath of the river king (*darya-badshah*) is continually made manifest. As the story goes, Juman-Jatti, a saint in his own right, would regularly pay his respects at the doorstep of Lal, the chief saint of Sehwan. Every time he would return from his visit to the shrine, he would withdraw walking backward, observing a custom of saintly reverence. But this meant that he would invariably have his back toward the mighty river. The repeated destruction of his river-facing shrine due to flooding and its half-fallen edifice in contemporary times is explained as an act of displeasure on the river's part and a reaction to Juman-Jatti's irreverence toward it.[10] The affected architecture of the shrine is a concrete reminder of how an old river god continues to thrive in altered registers of divinity.[11] The other major site associated with the saint's memory is the garden of Lal, or Lal-bagh, the wooded grove where Baba-Akram once established a fakir dwelling (see chapter 1). A few kilometers south of the city, the area is known to have been the contemplative environs where the saint camped before making his way into the town. While still at a distance, his impending arrival in town had made not just the prince but also local saints anxious. According to one legend, the holy men of the town felt threatened by his decision and demanded that he prove the merit of his spiritual achievements. Lal asked them to join him for a prayer at the river. As the men arrived, they were astonished to see that Lal had spread open his prayer mat on the surface of the river itself while remaining afloat. None were able to follow suit, and so they quietly acquiesced.[12] The following excerpt from a special publication to mark the saint's fair in 1968 details another of Lal's many encounters with the established holy men of the town:

They sent to him a bowl of milk filled up to its brim. This was an implicit sign that this city is already filled with people of Allah [saints]. There is no space left for you in the city. Just like there is no more space in this bowl of milk, you must also go and live elsewhere. Qalandar Shahbaz [Lal] floated a flower in the bowl and had it sent across to them. His response therefore was that just as this flower has made its place in the bowl full of milk, for me too a similar place will emerge. Not only will there be space, but in fact the way in which this flower is floating above the milk, I too, God willing, will always remain superior to you.[13]

Many in Sehwan believe that where the shrine of Lal now stands is where the high temple of Shiva once stood.[14] In a different version, however, the location of his tomb marks the stretch of land where Lal is said to have rested on his arrival in town. In one legend, when the saint expressed his wish to settle down, the owner refused to give up his claim on the property. Lal struck him dead with single blow of his staff. When questioned about the incident, the saint declared that he had merely killed a dog. Unconvinced, the family of the deceased man dug up the grave to indeed find a dead dog. In yet another version, he first arrived in the quarter of the city that at the time was inhabited by sex workers. On the night of his arrival, the women and their male clients were overcome by an extraordinary aura. None of the men that night, it is said, were able to perform sexually. It was only the next morning that people were able to explain what had occurred the night before. The charisma of a powerful saint had started to take effect. Equally enigmatic stories abound when it comes to the burial of the saint's body, a year after he arrived in town. While I had also heard the story from other locals, Amma, my fakir interlocutor at the shrine, once described that when the time came to bury the saint, the mullahs of the city decided to give him a funerary bath. As they began undressing him, there were layers and layers of cloth tied to his groin. Every time they would remove a layer, another would surface. That the truth of his genitals was never revealed is proof for many that the saint was fiercely celibate. Then came a mysterious voice that asked for the body to be veiled from all sides. When the curtains were finally lifted, a miraculous tomb was already in place. Today, hundreds of funerary sheets drape the tomb of the saint, so numerous that no mortal has ever seen the surface of the tomb itself, it is widely claimed in Sehwan. Citing this legend, many fakirs and prominent sayyid figures in Sehwan do not refer to the shrine as a tomb; instead they call it the throne of Lal (*takht*).

Locals also boast that Sehwan is a sacred geography with 125,000 shrines or that it has forever been a place of pilgrimage.[15] Whether perpetually holy or not, saintly memory attests that it is a place profoundly altered since the time a wandering mystic in the thirteenth century camped in a jungle outside its southernmost limit. Whether in a violent combat with a despotic ruler or a triumph over idol worship, in quiet defeat of prostitution or a steady prevailing over established saints, Lal in local remembrance is a force to be reckoned with.[16] In the turning upside down of a fortress, in his emasculating impact in acts of sex, in the floating metaphor of the brimming cup, in his prevailing over the river as well as in his takeover of territory is a remaking of place: the place of Lal.[17] None of this is out of joint given that the power and influence of Muslim saints (or *walis*) is tied to the master concept of *wilayat*: a particular confluence of saintly and spatial authority. The Islamic notion of sainthood "encapsulates the range of complex ideas defining the charismatic power of a saint," writes Pnina Werbner, "not only over transcendental spaces of mystical knowledge but as sovereign of the terrestrial spaces into which his sacred region exists" (1998, 27).[18] It stems from the premise that saints are friends and allies of Allah, entitling their persons as instruments of divine favor and fury. It is exactly this that affords Lal the power to invite godly wrath and turn the fortress upside down over the killing of Bodlo.

In a fascinating account of deviant dervishes and the construction of antinomian piety in Ottoman Aleppo, Watenpaugh (2005, 549) pursues the argument that spatial activity is instrumental to the construction of a mystical self.[19] He identifies the conceptual demarcation that existed between the built environment, regarded as the domain of conventional Islam, and the wilderness, the domain of the antinomian saint, "each endowed with opposite social meaning yet dependent on each other" (536). He suggests that the tension between inhabited urban space and wilderness was performed and maintained in the figure of the itinerant, deviant dervish.[20] While my reading of the graveyard is interested less in demarcating realms than in its porous condition, such ideals acquire particular significance insofar as fakirs model their spatial behavior after an antinomian mystic like Lal.[21] Fakir predilection for alternate habitats cites vagrant forms of Sufi piety, where ascetic mastery is given in explicitly spatial forms: peregrination, perpetual cycles of pilgrimage, even hermetic seclusion.[22] For a chapter set in a graveyard, it is also worth noting that dwelling among the dead is a spectacular embodiment of the Prophetic injunction

"Die before you die" and stands for the negation of the self among anti-nomian Sufis (Karamustafa 2015, 118).[23] Fakirs of this book, however, are not strictly vagrant figures. Their orientations in the contemporary are distinct from their historical models or predecessors. Many are in fact emplaced in specific locales even if their pursuits might once have involved journeying or periods of peregrination. Similarly, it can be argued that Jamal and Bibi's habitation in the graveyard is both a confirmation and a customization of an ascetic norm. And yet to render it exclusively in terms of social death—an unworlding—fails to capture how the two are implicated in local constellations and contestations of power. Their divisive perception of place aside, Jamal and Bibi, on the one hand, "co-exist in the world of the narrative and its vision of local sacred geography" (Green 2004b, 226). On the other hand, conflicts, contests, and disputations as well as their affective narrativization of those experiences are altered citations of legends associated with the saint himself. In fact, what we observe in the contemporary labors of Jamal and Bibi in the graveyard is not too distant from how Lal, too, in local narratives is portrayed. The saint is at the forefront of a struggle for spatial and imaginative dominion. He is more than a world-rejecting, miracle-making figure. What is remembered of Lal in Sehwan oscillates between accounts of seclusion and public confrontation. Whether itinerant or meditation-loving hermit confined to caves and retreats, Lal's portrayal is deeply implicated in the social and political life of the town. He fights the old order with miraculous conduct, strikes down his foes, and lays the foundation for new communities and institutions: fakirs, especially with their communities and lodges as detailed in chapter 4, are an example of such new founding in Sehwan. In the several sites attributed to his miracles and feats is in fact an etching of a new political order. I maintained in the earlier part of this book that the history of the saint of Sehwan is at best a patchwork of brief references, some found in sparse historical accounts, some in other saints' hagiographies. I have also argued that Lal, even if historically evasive, is a recurring figure of abundance. As Sehwan's narrative geographies of the saint make plain, Lal's presence feels a lot firmer in legends. These are stories of the saint that cross-shape with his imprint on the place itself. Lal and Sehwan are inseparable figures, always in narration.[24]

Sehwan is an archetype, writes Michel Boivin. It is, in his words, "the most significant place for the observation of"—and might I add, also feeling—"the medieval religious legacy in Sindh" (2008, 39). If Sehwan, to rely on Boivin's terms, is a historical continuum, it is also one that resists any straight access to a singular or paramount history. Like the dismembered body of Bodlo in legend, Sehwan's divergent pasts and plural orientations require a constant recalling, a re-membering of fragments scattered, forgotten in other forms, strewn across expanses of time and space. The graveyard is one instance whereby such a multitude is concentrated and felt. What ties fakir labors, despite their different stories, their conflict in the present, and their divergences on the question of the graveyard's future, is the place's affective capacity to bring them into intimate contact with the saintly. Intimacy here is not captured by, or directed toward, a single locus of devotion, an object of reverence like the tomb of the saint, but by greater conditions of spatiality: the place's sacred histories and metaphysical portals. Be it Jamal's bottomless tales of the extraordinary, Bibi's white shroud-like garment, his work with the fairies or her strict dietary regime, their ways of habitation in the graveyard reference places beyond Sehwan, an Elsewhere in Mittermaier's (2012) terms. These also imbricate times other than the contemporary moment, what Anand Taneja (2017, 60) calls *elsewhen*. Fakir capacities to see through a graveyard made of glass and beyond material textures of place confirm Armbrecht's view on *thin places*. She notes that invisibility does not always equal absence insofar as what is not readily visible to our eyes has to do with what no longer is valued by the world in which we live (Armbrecht 2009, 215). In this sense, tales of fakir mastery in the graveyard have to count for more than a retelling of historical legend or saintly memory. These point also to a worlding insofar as such remembering enfolds a diverse historical experience into the contemporary and renders it valuable and credible through distinctly felt and enfleshed modes. *Worlding with saints* hence refers to an ongoing process, an ensemble of mutual affordances through which a world accrues significance or its particular and less-ordinary mobilization is made concrete: just as fakirs turn worldly or perceptive with saintly beings, saints too, through fakir acts and feelings, find their bearings in the world as the more-than-living. To be so embroiled, I would hasten to add, does not overwrite fakir disdain for, nor their desires for maintaining a critical besideness to, the world. It is about how fakirs grow affectively sharp through saintly companionship and are able to craft their roles as healers and guides who know better. So long as intimacy is a revelation, such worlding involves a making present through shared feeling and knowing, not so much what is absent as that which goes unnoticed or acts sub rosa. It is also a reminder that coming close in Sehwan means fakirs being privy to secrets of place, or that relations involve a heightened awareness by means of being raw and exposed. Also, that fakirs apprehend in affective terms what matter enfolds; they see what remains overlooked in place; and they command and tame, like saints before them, the manifold spatial and temporal textures of the world.

To the extent that fakirs work with displaced actors and agencies or reveal the submerged narratives of the graveyard, their performances capture a sense of what Lisa Blackman calls embodied hauntologies. Though her call "that one should look for something more than now" has to do with scholars' affective implications in their contexts of research, in my specific rendering, it helps figure how "a distributed or mediated form of perception" animates, stages, and enables fakir persons "to 'see' what might usually exceed conventional modes of perception" (2015, 26). Sufi forms and norms of domesticating space, it follows, are best observable in how fakirs in the contemporary draw near to, or gain intimate knowledge of, affective textures of place. It is also such mastery that enables fakirs to perform, narrativize, and authorize their roles as able spiritual guides and healers. Their command and control of their environments extends to the place's unrevealed or extralocal constituents as well as its heterotemporal fabric. These manifest in accounts of encounters with differently corporeal beings that bear distinct histories, in the taming of the natural world, and equally in their ability to intervene in material environments and carry out physical modifications of space. Not only that; the imaginative and dialogical realms of dreams and visions flow seamlessly into fakir worlds, opening up continuities that are otherwise "foreclosed by the spatial and temporal restrictions of waking life" (Mittermaier 2008, 48). In this book's more critical terms, this would suggest that what transpires in the graveyard and what it affords individuals—by means of relations, knowings, and obstinacies—are tied to histories that do not sit straight with singular Islamic pasts. Intimacy here involves fakirs' simultaneous relations with more-than-human forces, mythical figures, and spiritual beings across Shi'i, Hindu, and Sufi registers. Such plural orientations, in this instance, do not work against their intimacy with Lal, but rather complement both his sparse historical record and his dense presence in local narrative. Viewed another way, intimacy serves as that felt mode of knowing through which multiple, at times unstraight or irreconcilable, histories are channeled, and in whose wake fakirs gain a complex and layered affective consciousness of the place and, by such virtue, also of their place in the world. Insofar as *wake* also means consciousness, such worlding in the wake is about how fakirs act on, in, and against, at times alongside, their feelings; how they grow perceptive, resist, make amends, or continually review their place in the world as it weighs upon them, alters, adapts, and transforms with and around them over time. To the extent that intimacy is an unfolding, fakir stories of the graveyard, be they life accounts or the miraculous feats of others, are threads through which their ties to the world are densely made, unmade, and remade. These are also ways in which a sense of thinness prevails: a porous worlding, so to speak, that is critically intimate with its many pasts and affectively continuous with other places. It follows that Sehwan of the fakirs is a not singular or fixed setting, but rather a richly structured mobilization in correspondence with other spatial-temporal realms. An intimacy with, or a mastery of, the graveyard's particular ecological, topographical, and imaginary features is thus also a coming close to Sehwan's less-visible processes, its dis/closing histories and futures. Jamal's and Bibi's prospective plans and more-than-material investments in the graveyard reveal that as fakirs draw close to the saintly in Sehwan, they also seek to embed themselves in long-standing affective textures of place.

This chapter, though set in a single graveyard, has engaged a greater geography of Sehwan. It is one that surfaces across contemporary lives and their historical extensions, involves traffics of dreams and spirits. It unfolds in the solitude of the dead and yet in the company of more-than-human figures. The graveyard as a place ridden with struggles stands as a mirror to Sehwan's own troubling present and contested histories, reminding us in every instance how critical intimacies with the past involve their active mobilization into the present.

CODA

Queer
Forward Slash
Religion

صحبت | *suhbet*
(Urdu, from Arabic) Companionship, conversation,
cohabitation, spiritual meeting, sex

In another coda, in a different book, Kadji Amin (2017, 183) invites us to
consider what meanings might adhere to *queer* if we were to journey with
it; more precisely, what happens when queer, as imagined in a single location, takes on life in other historical, geopolitical, conceptual, and cultural
settings. When it comes to this book, the will to treat a saint's shrine in Pakistan or ascetically drawn lives as critical epistemic grounds of queer—not
mere satellite sites to confirm its presence or absence elsewhere—is driven
by a specific intellectual want. What epistemic obstinacies might we come
up against or which lines of interpretation are to unfold if we were to read
religious lifeworlds, in this instance Islamic ones, not just queerly, or with
the aim of queering religion? More still, faced with congealed volumes of
queer and affect studies' respective and joint theoretical constitutions, how

might we learn to read queer religiously? Such ambition, I reckon, cannot be satisfied by queer-jacketing religion, that is to say, forcing our reading of religion to fit queer intellectual apparatuses or tailoring the field to a queer cut. This, then, is also not a call for Islamicizing queer.[1] In fact, it demands of scholars a methodical attentiveness to the possibility that queer ordinarily lurks through religious ecologies and lifeworlds. A move such as I am proposing correlates with Donovan Schaefer's (2015) overtures on "queer religious ecologies," grounds that hitherto remain underexplored in affect theory, even though there is, as he so compellingly establishes in *Religious Affects*, much to be gained from religious studies' inheritances. Having navigated comparable lacunae, this book with its coda speculates a desiring between analytically disinclined objects, religion and queer. A forward slash (/), or what is otherwise the divide symbol in programming, a switch in command line syntax, or the sign that separates the elements of a path in internet addresses, is here an inclined figure of orientation. It is a gesture by which one object draws toward a disparate other, possibly to arrive at a companionship.

In a religion-conscious reading of Ann Cvetkovich's (2012) book *Depression: A Public Feeling*, Schaefer identifies not just religious vocabulary but also its paraphernalia. He points to practices of altar making and evocations of ritual and healing, in his words, "affects, which in spite of her atheism, she understands as religious" (Schaefer 2015, 110–11). The "religious shapes" that queerly shine through or rise up in Cvetkovich's "Depression Journals" are "affective ligatures" that in Schaefer's reading compulsively tie the writing to a Catholicism of her childhood. Evocative for sure, such residues however do not quite equal an embracing or valuing of religion as a critical reserve for queer intellectual thought, certainly not in ways I am here calling for. As a matter of fact, my own scholarly endeavors have drawn in my religious history, as is made plain in the autobiographical indulgences that pervade the introduction to this book. However, to take up queer religiously as I have attempted is a distinct project. It not only affirms Schaefer's statement that "religion is a bloom space" (2015, 217) but also ensures that religious histories neither come up as gingerly made confessions nor are relegated to a closet space in queer thinking. The more remarkable albeit involuntary insight here is a different one. Schaefer's sub-rosa account of queer affect in religious ecologies makes one wonder how taking on queer elsewhere, a Sufi-Islamic lifeworld in this case, can come up against a predominantly even if unembraced Christian heritage of queer scholarship. This is not best remedied by simply transplanting queer in another place when we know that concepts also bear forth historical and methodological biases, in this case, of Western psychoanalysis. How then might we proceed in the face of un-outed bodies of intellectual histories or find grounding in quintessentially secular sites of queer theory that are predominantly shaped by religion's presumed absence? What pathways exist for theoretical and methodological forgetting and moving on that Arondekar and Patel (2016, 159) call for in light of queer studies' established analytical habits?

This ethnography on saintly intimacy in Pakistan has engaged a religious-intellectual universe not as just setting nor mere background but as *bloom space*. Hermeneutic efforts to cull queer value from diversely sacred aesthetics, Islamic-spiritual inheritances, and religious affect, as I have here pursued, is not the same as searching for indigenous queers or rehabilitating queers of faith. *Queer Companions* has contended that affective bonds with a saintly object can enfold unstraight prospects of the public and the political in Pakistan.[2] Queer, then, more than a designator for nonnormative gender and sexualities, is that device by which we come to question whether queer history is always only a history of queer activism (narrowly defined, gay rights and so on). Or can we think more capaciously, a history of queerness per se, that makes space for, and is made up of, differently alternate ways of being in the world? Fakirs, the ascetically drawn protagonists of this book, show us precisely that: they reveal how taking up a religious yet socially oblique object of desire means risking one's investments in familiar and familial lines in hope of certain others; or that in bonding and binding themselves with otherwise historical figures, fakirs articulate a critical being beside established norms in the present. In betraying what is socially inherited, such persons also align themselves anew to less-dominant religious histories; and if not transgressing, they make themselves less amenable to reproductive rhythms, economies, futures. Such paths are neither slick nor smooth, as they accompany a range of obstinacies, social as well as spiritual. One of the contentions this book has advanced is that saintly orientations also affect one's sense of being historical. Fakir lines of relation to historically distant figures often cannot persevere in straight or linear forms in that these tend to involve multiple and unstable inheritances or insofar as being close to saints affords embodied and affective ways of knowing that render such persons at a temporal slant to official knowledge (Freeman 2019, 16). Across five chapters and through several life stories, the book has laid out various ways in which fakir relation to the world is altered through felt and enfleshed modes of coming close to a thirteenth-century saintly figure. I have argued that Islamic saints expand as much as they complicate the ambit of one's social-historical ties. More central to this book, however, is the idea that coming close to saints involves a tarrying with intimacy's dis/closures: critical affective relations, knowings, as well as obstinacies. These are unstraight affordances, in terms of this book, that figure in intimacy's bloom. These are also learnings that, beyond individual fakir lives, carry value for queer scholars and those who study religion. Fakirs know well, and also illustrate for us that in facing certain directions and in following certain lines, other destinations invariably fall behind them, behind us. In the words of Sara Ahmed, "following lines also involves forms of social investment," and "such investments 'promise' return (if we follow this line, then 'this' will follow), which might sustain the very will to keep going" (2006, 17). Giving up lines of social investment for fakirs—or analytical habits, theoretical genealogies, and epistemological economies in the case of scholars—risky as it sounds, may also mean that new or other futures are made possible (Ahmed 2006, 21), or that we might well arrive at intellectual nodes less familiar or grounds hitherto unexplored. Fakir lines in this book are orientations as much as invitations, calling us to open ourselves up to queerer horizons. What oblique objects might we find along less likely routes? Which paths will unfold if we were to allow ourselves a veering off the straight of queer? What affective investments and orientations are we willing to question or give up in hope of new ones?

Uneasy bedfellows has served as one descriptor for the relation between the categories of queer and religion (see Scherer 2017). I, however, re/turn to the Urdu concept of *suhbet* to envisage a possible companionship between the two. *Suhbet* first appears in the introduction to this book as part of the constellation of Sufi terms of intimacy. I have mainly relied on the concept of *qurb* to explain and explore fakir intimacy with saintly objects, places, and figures as well as the affective dis/closures such coming close entails. The term *suhbet*, to which I now turn, bears meanings that can range from an auspicious meeting to an ordinary conversation; it audaciously folds discourse with intercourse: to do *suhbet* means to converse or come into dialogue, especially in its Persian usage, though in Urdu it can additionally be a euphemism for sharing a bed, a polite word for sex, a suggestion of carnal knowledge.[3] From Arabic and shared across

Turkish, Persian, and Urdu languages, *suhbet* is a truly expansive concept that denotes friendship, a coming together and staying with. It is also the term for spiritual communing and learning. The close companions of the Prophet Muhammad, for instance, are *sahabah*, that is to say, those who were routinely present in his *suhbet*. In Sufi contexts, it captures an intimate occasion marked by the audience of a holy figure or the transmission of spiritual love and knowledge between masters and disciples. Given the affective bonds and knowings it involves, *suhbet*, I contend, bears the potential to transform strangers into lovers, and lovers into kin. One is known by the *suhbet* one keeps, I often heard my mother remark as I was growing up. A digitally assembled photograph of the saint and myself, if readers recall the opening pages of this book, had turned into a contentious issue at home. If the image conjured up my parents' worst fears that I might be believing in the saint, by appearing in his company by way of collage, I was also overwriting my family's critical history with Sufi saints and shrines. Just as *qurb*, the term for saintly intimacy in this book, names that which circulates in the in-between of close bodies, *suhbet* refers to the altering condition of being in company. It refers to a companionship, no matter and especially between stranger bodies, in whose wake their sense of intimate knowing is altered as much as it inflects the public terms by which those bodies are known. How, then, might we imagine a *suhbet* between queer studies and the study of religion, Islam in particular?[4] What blooms might such affective companies yield? What figures and inheritances can be conjured up, transmitted, and shared across bodies (of knowledge)? What intimacies, loves, and kin making might unfurl in the process? More critically, how might each alter the other's forms of knowing or risk its own terms of being known?

Doing *suhbet*, whether as conversation or sex, does not, however, assume an absence of difference or the flattening of power hierarchies. In *Touching Feeling*, Eve Sedgwick articulates a politics of being beside. Any child, she notes, "who's shared a bed with siblings" knows that *beside* does not depend "on a fantasy of metonymically egalitarian or even pacific relations," but rather includes, among other relations, paralleling, differentiating, rivaling, leaning, desiring, attracting, withdrawing, and so on (Sedgwick 2003, 8). Sedgwick's interest in *beside* is a way of thinking outside the hermeneutics of *beneath*, *behind*, or *beyond* or avoiding topoi of depth, hiddenness, origin, or telos. In this work, however, *beside* has helped me articulate fakir relations to established norms, whereby their betrayal of the straight troubles and expands seams of Islamic histories, yet it does not dispense with that world entirely. Furthermore, *beside* as "at the side of" something can be a figure of careful attendance, even affinity, or as "next to" can suggest simply a physical nearness. It allows us to conceive of a being-with such that the provocation that queer and religion might gain from being bedfellows need not imply always amicable relations or an all-out salacious affair between the two. Rather, sharing fields for historically disinclined objects can be about an attentiveness to the other's tactile presence, a feeling for their moves, a cautious give and take of leanings, a push and pull of affects. More critically, *beside* helps us think of tandem arrangements, keeping a check on the other's tendencies, even tender rivalries, but such that one triumphing over the other—queering religion or Islamicizing queer—are no longer desirable outcomes.[5]

In the editor's introduction to *Queer/Religion*, a special issue of *Scholar and Feminist Online*, Elizabeth Castelli invites readers "to think in more complex and layered ways about the meeting place of queerness and religiosity—a space that is not only conflictual but also potentially generative" (2017). As part of the same issue, Nikki Young's (2017) essay explores the parallel, symbiotic, and liberative potentials of religion and queer studies by proposing both "as methodologies of freedom that confront and dismantle technologies of normalization." She further notes that "queer studies forces us to consider, evaluate, and create meanings through a lens of what *could* be" and that it "makes room for imaginative possibility to serve as the foundation for understanding what *is*." Religion's orientation to the cosmos, she argues, requires a similar and "constant dismantling of boundaries that divide what is from what *might be*." Such a take on the queerness of religion, more critically, signals a move from habituated lines of thinking a relationship of irreconcilable antagonism. In an account of religion within transgender circles in Pakistan, Claire Pamment (2019b) has revealed how pious performance works hand in hand with trans visibility and political activism. Reading religious performance across public protests, electioneering campaigns, electronic media, and everyday devotion in homes and shrines, as well as the community's reliance on Sufi idioms for transgender terms of identity, Pamment argues that pious acts "offer an embodied outlet for negotiating multiple axes of exclusion" as well as "provide a potent force for trans activism in Pakistan, further strengthening access to rights" (2019b, 310).[6] Also worth mentioning here is Lucinda Ramberg's (2014) meditation on the sexuality of religion. In an ethnography that traverses queer embodiment and Hindu ritual imaginaries, she describes how sacred marriage—the South Indian practice of dedicating girls (at times also boys) to a goddess—has implications for the disposition of sexuality and gender as well as kinship.[7] Ramberg in fact turns to sex as a way to question what counts as religion.

If scholars of religion have explored overlaps of sexual and religious identities, queer challenges to theological traditions can also be traced.[8] Ali A. Mian's (2019, 115) transgenre reading of same-sex desire across European and Islamic discourses is a compelling example of "the resourcefulness of 'the erotic' as an analytical category" for grasping affective dimensions of religious tradition. Works like Mian's aside, the scholarship on same-sex desire in Islamic sociohistorical contexts has barely dealt with the criticality of queer. It has predominantly concerned itself with doctrinal and jurisprudential issues surrounding sexuality, sexual difference, and alterity (see Jahangir and Abdullatif 2016; Kugle 2010b; El-Rouayheb 2005). This bent of knowledge, especially within religious studies, echoes the reparative work that has been undertaken as part of gay Christian theology, which either assumes a queer core to religion that requires an uncovering or suggests, apologetically at best, that sacred texts are much queerer than religious tradition might have us believe (Schippert 2011, 71). When it comes to the study of Islam, such desirous return to sources is best exemplified in the scholarship of Scott Kugle. In *Homosexuality in Islam*, Kugle (2010b) turns the common perception that same-sex desire is anathema to Islam on its head and offers a radical rereading of scriptural sources and doctrinal history. More relevant to the theme of this book, however, is Kugle's (2007) earlier work. In *Sufis and Saints' Bodies*, he offers a meticulous analysis of sacred corporealities and transgressive desire by focusing on various bodily parts of different saintly figures across Islamic geographies and history.[9] Even a rich and thorough study such as Kugle's eventually succumbs to the trope of queer origins and their historical loss, not least the binary of an apparently queer-bodied and sexuality-affirming good (Sufi) Islam and a body-averse, sexuality-repressing bad Islam.[10] Whether liberationist or reconciliatory, the politics of such scholarship in my view is curbed by the fact that it seeks to recover if not also idealize the lost futures of a past from the perspective of a queer present. Valuable as Kugle's work is to conversations in Sufi studies or to queers of faith, and to my own understanding of the unstraight politics of saintly bodies, the *suhbet* or grounds of meeting that I am here rooting for are not invested in queer's rehabilitation in religious tradition, less so in a project of queering.[11] In fact, overreading scripture or a motivated queering of religious histories carries with it the risk of what I call queer-jacketing religion. The proposition that we learn to read queer religiously should not be seen as an argument for "'religion-ing' lesbian, gay, bisexual and transgender subjectivities and histories" (White 2017).[12] The point rather is to explore whether queer theorizing can find other lives in the epistemological reserves and affective resources that religious ecologies and lifeworlds have to offer.

Reading queer religiously is as much an opening up of queer to more-than-secular or differently coded archives and genealogies as it is a call for its methodical consideration: to do a thing religiously is to do it with consistent and conscientious regularity. Its analytical moves would require that figurations of unstraight desire and sexual alterity are refracted through a wider social and interpretive frame, an intellectual universe, which includes and culls value from its workings with sacred aesthetics and religious affect. It also involves mining and exploring the possibilities that emerge with significant intellectual dislocations, or considering its ethical issues and methodological limits; for instance, to what extent might we term—or not—religious lives as in/adequately queer? How might we trouble queer's secular histories or query what we inherit as queer? More still, what makes a thing religiously queer or queerly religious? It is likewise a being open to what queer perspectives and thinking bring to the study of religion, if not also to the possibility of religious studies' further undisciplining or the unraveling of religion itself as a colonial category of knowledge.[13] More critically, we can come to appreciate how, through geopolitically determined modes of circulation but also by exclusion, queer as an episteme accrues hegemonic value. *Suhbet* means that not only would we encourage a conversation where little exists but in each other's affective company also learn to question "the theoretical emphases and epistemological assumptions" through which we come to know sexuality, its objects, history, and geography (Babayan and Najmabadi 2008, vii).

This book is set at an ancient site of devotion in Pakistan. Across a number of life stories, we learn how fakirs deal with queer dis/closures of intimacy or what endures as individuals draw affectively close to the historical figure of Lal. He is a thirteenth-century antinomian mystic whose tomb-shrine is located in Sehwan. *Queer Companions* has argued that as saintly intimacy blooms, it lays bare otherwise futurities so to speak, emergent leanings into new or previously less-available possibilities of life with saints. Be it at public shrines or in the solitude of graveyards, as part of ascetic lodges or through singular acts of seclusion and wandering, found in dream space or waking life, fakir pursuits are, in terms of this book, spatiotemporal forms of extending into the world with affect. Ruminating on the queer affects of saintly intimacy, it has considered the futures such being intimate dis/closes as well as the existing sociohistorical relations that saints frustrate and eventually expand. Fakir lives compel us to reappraise our own understandings of proper religiosity, ethical self-fashioning, and projects of a moral life.[14] Precisely the fact that what counts as properly religious among fakirs cannot entirely be explained in normative, doctrinal, legalistic, and scriptural terms has empowered this work to portray aesthetic-affective modes of religious world making and trouble ethnographic knowledge concerned with what it means to be Muslim, pious or not. Through queer analytics of intimacy and futurity, I have argued that fidelity to saints or attachment to their tombs does not always equal a recoiling from the worldly. Instead, fakir lives, loves, and labors in Sehwan reveal a becoming worldly by affective means. More critically, affective bonds with saintly figures help fakirs overcome conditions of the present in that these afford individuals historically expansive modes of being social that not only reorder what has been, but also seek to reconfigure what might come to be.[15] It is tied to the book's notion of unstraight affordances, which helps articulate how individuals tarry with saintly relations, knowings, and obstinacies that dis/close in intimacy's wake. I would here reiterate that to be afforded a thing does not reduce individuals to passive or reactive agents. It rather refers to a reciprocal interplay that hangs on how intimate partners perceive the qualities of the other or come to recognize the possibilities on offer. I have therefore argued that just as fakirs turn perceptive through saintly bonds, saints too are afforded an affective bearing in the world through such processes. I have accordingly called Islamic saints queer companions, if only as provocation, to bring home the otherwise-ing forms in which their intimate companies guide and inflect believers' ways of being historical, an unfolding, which always also includes affect's forward endurance in time.

To the extent that coming close to one object involves departing from another, this book has explored the ethical and political stakes of intimacy involving Islamic saints. By expanding on the Urdu term *qurb*, it has described intimacy with saints as affective bonding that blooms in the critical interstice of being near a thing and being nearly that thing, suggesting in a way that intimacy hangs on notions of critical distance. On the formations of intimacy or its elaboration over time, the book has inquired what takes place when saints' affection or a striving for saintly contact is premised on a body leaving its usual, socially assigned or proper place. Which imaginal and affective genres trigger and accompany such dislocations? What bodily grammars are involved in grounding alongside the saintly or, more precisely, what constitutes the gendered labors of taking place where place is simply not given? Also, what follows when arduous pursuits of the saintly fail or falter, or when saintly ties become abundant and begin to feature rival objects of desire? Such betrayals of the straight, this kind of going astray with saints, whether eventually rewarded or not, are in this work unstraight affordances, dis/closed in the unfolding of intimacy. The many elements that make up the greater argument of this book on saintly intimacy and futurity can be regathered here as three conceptual clusters, namely, saintly governance, intimate corporealities, and worlding with saints.

One of the contentions this book has advanced is that saintly vitality in Pakistan thrives on orders of the state. By this I mean that intimacy with saints, even if experienced in inward registers, constitutes a public genre sustained by the material-affective infrastructures of saintly governance. The cross-reading of affect and governance that I have pursued in this work is tied to how I understand the Pakistani state's relationship with saints. In this particular regard, I have pointed to the often inseparable dynamics of governing saints and governing with saints. The book has considered how an administrative presence of the Pakistani state at saints' shrines like Sehwan extends into wider imaginal modes of dream, song, and image and whose overlapping pull draws fakirs, and also other pilgrims, to find an advanced affective access to the saintly. What this has meant for the larger argument on unstraight affordances is that fakir futuring amid impaired conditions or against the expected course of things as well as the crises of inheritance that are stirred up as a result of intimacy with saints are not just saintly affects but are propelled in part by stately infrastructures of the imaginal. I have further elaborated how the state's interest in saints' places or its motivations to govern saints have entailed a limited democratization of shrine space. This is particularly salient for women's spiritual careers, which, though doubly impaired, both by patrilineal transmission of saintly authority and an ascribed femaleness to their bodies, are to some extent secured by the state's arbitrating role at public shrines. Saintly governance more provocatively suggests that as fakirs come close to the saintly in Pakistan, they also draw nearer to the state.

With intimate corporealities, we can gather and reflect on the manifold felt and enfleshed modes of coming close to saints that the book has identified across fakir life stories, a bodiliness I have described in detail through the fakir concept of dis/guise (*bhes*). I have argued that saintly intimacy hinges on critical performances of the body insofar as one's closeness with saintly figures and locations is corporeally afforded or to the extent that such bodiliness validates one's being out of step with straight rhythms of the social. Dis/guise also helps us understand the modulating interface between inward feeling and the public unfolding of intimacy. If to be a fakir, as this book has contended, is to pursue saintly objects as well as to remain committed to otherwise futurities such desiring ushers in, it is a public performance of fakir dis/guise that sanctions the body's departures from socially inherited objects and situations. On its felt modes, the book has contended that unstraight affordances not only support otherwise ways of being in the world, but that these can equally work against intimacy. Saintly bonds, as I have illustrated, even when secured through rites of initiation and afforded by spiritual masters, can come undone or show signs of disaffection, especially in the face of rival intimacies and competing objects of desire and devotion. Conflicts around intimacy reveal how sexuality and sacrality are complexly conversant in fakir bodies, along with the linkages that exist between saintly love and marriage or the ways in which ideas around sexual intimacy shape fakir understandings of saintly relations.

Last, worlding with saints conveys the idea that intimacy involves forms of affective knowing through which one's ties to the world are sutured anew. Coming close to saints affords fakir individuals an elaborate sense of time and place, not necessarily deeper or precise knowledge per se but a heightened awareness, a growing conscious by way of feeling intimate. It has informed my decision to render fakir lives in tandem with particular settings in which these unfold. Taken up especially in the discussion on saintly spatiality, I have described how intimacy serves as that interface through which multiple, at times unresolved or irreconcilable, histories world together; or how in the company of more-than-living beings and mythic creatures, fakirs acquire an affective hold on complex ecologies and by such virtue also on their place in the world. Multiple historical figurations shape fakir circumstances in the present as well as their visions of the future. No matter whether unstable or often indistinct, such elaborate knowing by way of feeling is tied to fakir reputations as persons who know more or better. Fakirs move and are moved through affective knowing, or tarry with unstraight affordances that saintly bonds dis/close or bring to bear, and which, more broadly considered, constitute the queer affects of saintly companionships.

This book has not invested itself in reparative or recuperative labors like scholarship that seeks to anachronistically restore queerness to non-Western histories and global South contexts. Furthermore, it has refused a minoritization of both queer and Pakistan in epistemological terms. On the one side, queer remains, at least to anthropologists of religion, a label reserved for nonnormative sexuality and LGBTQIA+ subjects. Debates in the anthropology of Islam are comfortably oblivious to conversations in queer theory. On the other side of this equation is queer studies' blind spot for histories and figurations of queerness elsewhere, a geopolitical bias that determines why places such as Pakistan and settings like religious shrines do not strike us as sites for queer thinking. Such disregard isn't simply a symptom of queer theory's fraught relationship with area studies. The key to understanding elsewheres is that these are also temporal figurations, that is, the else of here is also the not-yet-here of queer.[16] In that sense, the intellectual labors of this book have also reaffirmed a contention I make in a different work, that queerness "is not in any way more here than there, more now than before; that it is tied to the logic of cities and secularities in a way that it is unmappable in religious or non-metropolitan life-worlds" (Kasmani 2019b, 36). Thus, an attentiveness to a minoritized geography like Pakistan, left-behind sites such as Sehwan, bypassed locations beyond the metropole, or places that in Arondekar's (2020, 3–4) terms are "inherently non-recuperative, not discovered (again)" warrants that we do more to unmoor straight, progressive, or linear temporal idealities attached to queer, and in so doing also shake off our settled habits of theorizing and politicizing sexuality in such places.

This book on fakir lives and saintly intimacy has no doubt delved into very particular lifeworlds. It has taken up questions distinct to a religious tradition, even if one that is plurally conceived and complexly configured. It has, however, also journeyed elsewhere. Its epistemic thrust has ventured beyond discursive frames of Islam or Pakistan. Here, the underlying will has been to unstraighten anthropological shapes of devotional Islam or Islamic devotion but also to pose the question, how and in what terms can intimate relations with Islamic saints or commitment to an ostensibly religious object be of value to queer forms of thinking, knowing, and world making? The book's will, like all desire, is lined also with hope: that so tarrying will make other knowings blossom, that new and queer companionships might bloom in the wake.

Introduction

1   Some scholars prefer *faqir* (from its Arabic root *faqr*). My interlocutors in Sehwan have additionally defined the term in relation to *fikr*, meaning thought and reflection.

2   My reading of intimacy as an interface of public and private worlds learns from existing scholarship but is made distinct by virtue of its religious formations and archives. On the entanglements of imperial and intimate formations or the ways in which sexual arrangements and colonial governance corresponded in late nineteenth- and early twentieth-century Indonesia, see Stoler (2010). On understandings of intimacy within liberal logics of settler colonies in the United States and Australia, see Povinelli (2006).

3   *Queer* is neither a figure of identity politics in this work nor an exclusive reference to my interlocutors' sexualities.

4   For more on intersections of queer theory and religion, see Schippert (2005, 2011), Wilcox (2009).

5   *Lal* (red, dear one) or *La'l* (ruby, gem), though different words and both ascribed to the saint, are indistinguishable in Sehwan since there is no difference in pronunciation.

6   According to the provisional data of the 2017 census, the population of greater Sehwan including neighboring villages was about 269,291 people, out of which 104,239 were town residents.

7   On Bodlo's shrine and his importance for fakir devotion, see chapter 4.

8   My childhood in the 1980s was synonymous with top-down Islamization

during the military dictatorship of General Zia. Regressive legislative measures like shariah courts, state-sanctioned persecution of Ahmedis, and women's social marginalization through the infamous Hudood Ordinances were introduced.

9   For hierarchies of divine friendship, see Bashir (2011, 85–95). For a detailed study on Islamic saints as friends of God, see Renard (2008).

10   Critiques of saint veneration find ordinary circuiting through religious sermons, popular literature, television serials, men's reformist gatherings, and women's domestic prayer circles, also via social media platforms (see also Malik 1998).

11   For more on Islamic arguments and debate in Pakistan, see Marsden (2005), Sökefeld (1999), Metcalf (1987). On Islamic mysticism in South Asia, see Bennett and Ramsey (2012), Green (2012b), Rozehnal (2007), Ernst (1992, 1997). On Sufism and society, see Curry and Ohlander (2012).

12   Ahl-e Hadis is a religious reform movement that emerged in northern India in the mid-nineteenth century. Most Pakistanis identify with the Hanafi school of jurisprudence while maintaining an adherence to the Barelvi or Deobandi movements of religious reform in South Asia. On Islamic piety movements and the Tablighi Jamaat in Pakistan, see Khan (2016, 2018), Metcalf (1998, 2002); for sectarianism in Pakistan, see Zaman (1998). On Shi'i religious identity in contemporary Pakistan, see Fuchs (2019).

13   *Futurity* is distinct from *future* (temporality) in that it refers to the capacity of a thing to advance and endure in forward time.

14   On women and Sufi healing, see Bellamy (2011), Callan (2008), Flueckiger (2006); on performances of ritual drumming and *dhamal*, see Frembgen (2012a) and Wolf (2006); on Sufi literature, devotional music, and narrative, see Mir (2006), Abbas (2002), Qureshi (1986); on devotional objects and images, see Frembgen (2012b), Boivin (2011), Flood (2009), Zaidi (2009). For Sufi emotion and embodiment, see Werbner and Basu (1998); on Sufi shrines, see Strothmann (2016), Currie (1989), Troll (1989), Kurin (1983), Eaton (1982). For pilgrimage, see Boivin (2012a), Werbner (2003).

15   Meaning way or path, *tariqat* forms the second in a four-stage journey of the Sufi: *shari'at, tariqat, ma'rifat, haqiqat*.

16   Women's public circumstances are less suspect at shrines, tempered by the dual protection of the saint and the state. On Pakistani women's spheres, see Ring (2006), Ahmed (2005), Grima (2004). On middle-class piety among women in Pakistan, see Maqsood (2017); on women and religious revivalism in Pakistan, see Ahmad (2009).

17   This refers to the West Pakistan Waqf Properties Ordinance (1959). For more on *auqaf* in Pakistan, see Ibad (2019), Philippon (2016), Strothmann (2016), Malik (1990). For crossovers of Sufi pilgrimage, shrine markets, and political economy in Sehwan, see Delage (2018).

18   As descendants of the Prophet, sayyids enjoy historical, material, and spiritual privilege unlike other spiritual figures in Sehwan; see chapter 2. On religious

and political authority of sayyids in South Asia, see Fuchs (2020), Gautier and Levesque (2020), Ansari (1992).

19   More than twenty-five shrines have been targeted since 2005 (Ibad 2019, introduction). On the tragedy at Sehwan, see Kasmani (2017c).

20   For guidance and discipleship at an Indian shrine, see Pinto (2006); see Raj and Harman (2006) for vow making at South Asian shrines.

21   See chapter 2. On women and spirits in South Asia, see Bellamy (2008), Callan (2008), Gold (1988).

22   Digby particularly refers to the Delhi sultanate during the thirteenth and fourteenth centuries.

23   A world order whereby the Sufi and the sultan are both kings necessitates the division of their spheres of authority; for more, see Anjum (2011). On saints, communal conflict, and interfaith harmony, see Bigelow (2010).

24   Christina Sharpe's multifold notion of "the wake" depicts the ways in which transatlantic chattel slavery is "an event that is still ongoing" (2016, 20). She proposes a staying in the wake, "a form of consciousness," under prevailing conditions of Black non/being (15).

25   For affordance in design, see Norman (1988, 1999); for approaches to materiality, see Bauer (2019), Knappet (2004); on affordance and terrorism, see Taylor (2012).

26   He observes this for affordances that relate to animals and other persons.

27   My use of *queer* and *unstraight*, each with its own distinct capacities, is not to distinguish between what is properly queer or not, sexual or otherwise.

28   She evokes the Islamic notion of *sirat-e-mustaqim*, a guiding principle that informs the notion of living an ethical life in her discussion on gender/sex change in Iran.

29   For the emergence of *qalandar* as a trope in Sufi poetry, see Ewing (2006, 233–39). For *qalandar* groups in South Asia, see Digby (1984).

30   On renunciation and social deviance, see Karamustafa (2006, 13–23).

31   *Qalandar*s as a distinct group of deviant dervishes formed in the thirteenth century. Their existence as a mode of religiosity is evidenced in Persian literature (*qalandar* as topos) and Sufi theoretical treatises as early as the eleventh century; see Karamustafa (2006, 32).

32   For more on affective texture, posture, and situatedness, see Slaby (2020).

33   Custodian families in Sehwan take the position that the saint's actual name was most likely Shah Hasan and not Usman, the latter commonly associated with the Sunni. The title Lal Shahbaz as reference to the saint is first recorded in late seventeenth-century textual sources (Boivin 2011, 20). For a detailed biography of the saint (in French), see Boivin (2012b).

34   According to the Suhrawardi Sufi tradition, the saint was initiated in Multan by Baha'uddin Zakaria (Boivin 2011, 18). Boivin (2012b, 105) notes that custodians in Sehwan claim a loose affiliation with some Qadiri strands though no formal initiations into the order are made. For more on the saint's history, see chapter 1.

35   Available archaeological evidence does not confirm the claim (see Collinet 2008). However, historians believe that overlaps are likely (see Boivin 2011, 96; Schimmel 2003, 355).

36   According to *Tarikh Mazhar Shahjahani,* a seventeenth-century account of Sindh translated from Persian into Urdu (Namkin [1634] 2009, 160), on the eve of the festival Shivratri, every Hindu man and woman of Sehwan would bathe at Chhoti Nali, one of the springs associated with the saint on the outskirts of town.

37   According to Boivin (2012b, 43), the Indus was worshipped under the name Udero Lal, depicted as an incarnation of Varuna, the Vedic deity of waters. Other references include Amar Lal, Darya Shah, Darya Nath, Zinda pir, Shaykh Tahir, and the Quranic figure (Khwaja) Khizr. For more on Jhule Lal, see Parwani (2010), Khan (2008).

38   Boivin (2008, 37) refers to the Chinese pilgrim Huein Tsang's seventh-century account, which portrays Sehwan as a stronghold of the Shivaite sect Pashupatas before the region's Arab conquest at the beginning of the eighth century. Arab geographers have called it Sadusan and Siwistan (variants: Shiv-asthan, Shiv-astano). The British Army engineer and archaeological surveyor Alexander Cunningham identifies Sehwan as Sindomana, one of two places mentioned in the time of Alexander's conquest. He notes that the Greek name Saindhuwan (or the abode of the Saindhavas) is the origin of the name Sehwan (Cunningham 1871, 266). For historical accounts of Sindh, see Asif (2016), Cook (2008), Khuhro (1981), Burton (1851), Burnes (1837).

39   In his address to the annual conference at the saint's fair in November 1969, Sindhi nationalist leader G. M. Syed (2012) traced features of shrine ritual and fakir practices to Shivaite forms.

40   For a historical sketch of the shrine, see chapter 2.

41   For a complex and considered relationship between Sufi and Shivaite in Sehwan, see Boivin (2008).

42   In her book *The Powerful Ephemeral,* Carla Bellamy (2011) describes as "ambiguously Islamic" those Muslim shrines that have complex religious histories and involve an interfaith following.

43   For more on *suhbet,* see the coda.

44   For Sufi masters and disciples, see Bashir (2011), Malamud (1996); for homoerotic desire in Sufi contexts, see Mian (2019), Kugle (2007); for intimacy in Sufi discourse, see Shaikh (2012).

45   The poem he refers to is "The Qualities of Lovers" by Hilali Jaghatai (d. 1529).

46   See Urdu Lughat, http://www.udb.gov.pk/, accessed March 2021.

47   She notes that saintly dreams and visions expand spheres of action to an Elsewhere, affective ties and dialogic relations that remind believers "of the very condition of being with and continuously being acted upon" (Mittermaier 2012, 253; see also Mittermaier 2011). On affective politics across religious contexts, Kasmani et al. (2020) note that engagements with the Elsewhere always involve an unsettling of the here and now.

48   Intimacy harbors consequences for all parties involved. Donna Haraway speaks of companion species and poses the question, "How is *becoming with* a practice of becoming worldly?" (2008, 35). Such *becoming with* ties and reties partners through reciprocal action and affection, in her terms, attachment sites of world making.

49   The gerund *worlding* shifts attention from world as an extant thing to a generative ontological process (for more, see Stewart 2010, 2014; Haraway 2008).

50   On the inwardness and publicness of intimacy, see Berlant (1998, 281).

51   Gender-variant persons in Sehwan refer to themselves in varying registers, like *khadra* (in Sindhi), *khwaja-sara* (in Urdu), or simply *fakir*. My research with such fakirs is better detailed in an article that discusses transgender politics in Pakistan (see Kasmani 2021).

52   Some of my earlier work has engaged her notion of becoming, from which I have since turned away (see Kasmani 2016b, 2017b).

53   The term *Shiʿi* is so gingerly present in the book that it doesn't even appear in the index. He notes that adducing non-Sunni examples is not antithetical to the project; however, he explains his deliberate choice of Sunni sources in these words: "I have done this simply for the pragmatic reason that I do not want to facilitate the facile objection that I am conceptualizing Islam on the basis of marginal or non-representative phenomena" (Ahmed 2016, 104).

54   Scholarly focus on Sehwan is fairly recent. For notable examples, see Ortis (2017, 2020), Kasmani (2012, 2015, 2017b, 2019a), Delage (2018), Jaffer (2018), Frembgen (2012a). Frembgen's (2011) book offers reflections and field notes from Sehwan's annual pilgrimage. For works in French, see Ortis (2019), Delage (2016), Boivin (2012b). For publications in Sindhi, see Kandhro (2011), Advani (2010), K.-M. Sehwani (2009), Abbasi (2002).

55   For asceticism and renunciation in broader South Asia, see DeNapoli (2014), Salgado (2013), Khandelwal (2004), Burghart (1983).

56   Nile Green (2012b, 2) has noted that privileging of the mystical neglects the social and overlooks Sufi investment in the tangible realm of physicality. For comparable critiques on the piety turn in the anthropology of Islam, see Mittermaier (2012), Schielke (2010), Soares and Osella (2009).

57   See, for example, Fuchs (2019), Haq (2019), Ibad (2019), Philippon (2016), Strothmann (2016), Khan (2012), Jalal (2000), Ansari (1992), Malik (1990).

58   For religion in Ann Cvetkovich's work, see Schaefer (2015, 109–11).

59   Notable examples include Scott Kugle's (2007) monograph on saints' bodies and desire, the study of sexual diversity in the Muslim world by Vanja Hamzić (2016), and the volume *Islamicate Sexualities* edited by Babayan and Najmabadi (2008).

60   A first fieldwork was carried out in the framework of my master's degree project at the Institute for the Study of Muslim Civilisations in London. I returned subsequently in 2009 and 2010 as part of the French Interdisciplinary Mission in Sindh led by Michel Boivin. To work around my limitations in accessing his

works in French, I spent a few days in Chambéry, France, to interview Michel Boivin in July 2013.

61 I mostly stayed at the rest house of the Department of Antiquities, Sindh.

62 The greater material involves twenty-four fakirs, an almost equal number of men and women and a few transgender persons. This included resident, visiting, and journeying fakirs that I met and interviewed on a regular basis.

63 During my first stay, I relied on my friend Marvi Mazhar to facilitate access to women at the shrine. My presence among women drew less attention over time.

64 See Narayan (1993, 673). For positionality and dynamics in the field, see Kalir (2006), Bloch (1998), Abu-Lughod (1990). On fieldwork and travel, see Clifford (1996).

1. Infrastructures of the Imaginal

Sections of chapter 1 appeared in "Pilgrimages of the Dream: On Wings of State in Sehwan Sharif, Pakistan," in *Muslim Pilgrimage in the Modern World*, ed. Babak Rahimi and Peyman Eshagi (Chapel Hill: University of North Carolina Press, 2019), 133–48.

1 Death anniversaries of saints are celebrated in Pakistan, marking their union with the divine. These are called *'urs* (Arabic for *wedding*) or simply *mela* in Sehwan, meaning fair. For impressions of Sehwan's annual fair, see Frembgen (2011), Passow (2005).

2 According to Michel Boivin (2011, 20), it is in late seventeenth-century textual sources that the title "Lal Shahbaz" as reference to the saint is first recorded.

3 For more on dreams and the imaginal, see Mittermaier (2011), Corbin (1997), Chittick (1993, 1994).

4 In rendering Baba's story in English, I adopt the gender-neutral pronouns *they, them, their* to record Baba's distinct subjectivity. When speaking, Baba interchangeably relied on feminine and masculine speech registers.

5 On the role of dreams in Sufi contexts, see Mittermaier (2011), Ewing (1990, 2006), Green (2003).

6 On dreams and visions, Anand Taneja refers to *elsewhen* or "times other than the contemporary moment" (2017, 60).

7 For more on intersections of the ghostly and the temporal in Islamic South Asia, see Taneja (2017), Khan (2006).

8 For comparable insights, see Kasmani (2019a).

9 For a different discussion on the lyrical and the political, see Kasmani (2017a).

10 In a study of shrines of Awrangabad, India, he identifies the dual spheres in which saintly places existed in the seventeenth century, spanning their discursive and material dimensions.

11 From the construction and survey report titled "Redevelopment of the Mazar of Hazrat Lal Shahbaz Qalandar at Sehwan Sharif." No date of publication is

mentioned. I accessed a copy of this report in the personal collection of Michel Boivin in Chambéry, France, in July 2013.

12   At least six films between 1969 and 1975 featured songs in praise of the saint. For the saintly and the cinematic in India, see also Taneja (2017).

13   The other date is 1251 (see Boivin 2012b, 83).

14   Sources do not indicate why Lal was headed to India. However, according to Michel Boivin (2012b, 80–83), he is likely to have first arrived in Multan in 1263. He stopped in places like Makran, Lahut-lamakan, Panjgur, and Pasni in Balochistan as well as Naing, Lake Manchhar, and Sehwan in Sindh.

15   According to this claim, Lal is associated with Raja Bharthari, a prince who renounced his throne and established a hermitage in Sehwan. The figure is also known as Raja Virag by Hindus of Sindh. According to Michel Boivin, it is possible that Lal established himself on this site or that his tomb was built there. For more, see Boivin (2011, 19; 2012b, 122).

16   Sehwan at this time was also under the influence of the Isma'ilis (Boivin 2012b, 85), which might explain Lal's arrival in the region or his choice to settle in Sewhan.

17   The other three figures are Baha'uddin Zakaria (d. 1267) of Multan, Fariduddin Ganjshakr (d. 1266) of Pak-Pattan, and Jalaluddin Surkhposh Bukhari (d. 1291) of Uchh. Their shrines are spread across southern Punjab in Pakistan. Chothanbi, a revered site between Lal-bagh and Sehwan that pilgrims visit, is believed to be their place of meeting.

18   For more on Savi, see Karamustafa (2006, 39–44).

19   The observance of the fourfold shave (the shaving of the head and all facial hair, including the moustache, beard, and eyebrows) is an ascetic practice characteristic of qalandari piety (see Karamustafa 2006, 19). For symbolism of hair among Persian qalandars, see Ridgeon (2010).

20   State institutions like the Department of Culture or the Sindhi Adabi Board routinely publish books and brochures dedicated to the saint's life as well as to Sehwan's history and heritage (for examples, see Kandhro 2011; Shauq 2011; Andhar 2010; Manjhi 2010).

21   Excerpts from the dream account in this chapter are part of a recorded interview from November 2013.

22   *Baba* (lit. father) is an honorific used for saints and spiritual masters. I have used *baba* in lowercase to distinguish the reference from the main protagonist (Baba) of this chapter.

23   Baba uses the Urdu word *shadi* instead of the Arabic '*urs*, both meaning wedding.

24   Intersex as well as feminine-identified, gender-variant persons assigned male at birth (locally, *khwaja-sara, hijra, khadra, khusra, transgender, fakir*) assume a distinct subjectivity in Pakistan. Some of these terms are now disfavored in urban Pakistan and only situationally adopted by gender-variant persons and communities themselves.

25   According to the department's website, its aims and objectives include the

management of shrines and mosques, providing pilgrim facilities like community kitchens and rest houses. For more on the history and development of the Department of Auqaf, see Ibad (2019).

26 The state collects pilgrim donations offered to saints at shrines and also generates revenue from *waqf* properties through work contracts, rents, and leases, which it claims to repurpose for the maintenance and reconstruction of old shrines and other religious endowments. For a financial review of Auqaf, its budgets and finances, see Ibad (2019, chapter 4). For an account of the distribution of shrine revenues and the economic dimension of a Sufi shrine in Lahore, see Strothmann (2016, chapters 5 and 6).

27 For more on saints and the modern Pakistani state, see Ewing (2006, 65–90).

28 This was observed in two prominent state-run journals, *Nayin Zindagi* and *Mehran*, published by the Information Department, Ministry of Information and Broadcasting, Sindh, and the Sindhi Adabi Board, respectively.

29 Starting in the 1960s, the Sindhi-language newspaper *Daily Ibrat* (published in Hyderabad) started to report the '*urs* at Sehwan in great detail.

30 New migrants claimed the southern part of the city lying below the old highway, which until then had consisted mainly of graveyards and old cemeteries.

31 The German filmmaker Martin Weinhart collaborated with the German ethnologist Jürgen W. Frembgen for the film *Der rote Sufi: Rausch und Ekstase in Pakistan* [The red Sufi: Intoxication and ecstasy in Pakistan] (Westdeutscher Rundfunk, 2011). Frembgen, who also appears in the film, accompanies pilgrims on a train journey to Sehwan.

32 For religious sectarianism in Pakistan, see Zaman (1998). For Shi'i identity and politics, see Fuchs (2019).

33 The construction report "Redevelopment of the Mazar of Hazrat Lal Shahbaz Qalandar in Sehwan Sharif" (no date) names Khomeini's Square in Isfahan, Iran, the Alhambra in Granada, Spain, and the Taj Mahal in Agra, India, in addition to shrines of imams and saints in Iran and Iraq as sources of inspiration from Islamic architecture. It can be assumed that the document was prepared between 1989 and 1992, corresponding with the first government of Benazir Bhutto.

34 Annemarie Schimmel (2003, 355) mentions the presence of a Shiva lingam close to the saint's tomb (see also Boivin 2011, 96).

35 Explicitly Sunni inscriptions like names of the first four caliphs were introduced in the tomb hall in 2013. These, however, were no longer present when I visited the shrine in 2018, possibly removed when parts of the tomb hall were repaired after the suicide attack of 2017.

36 This is aided by a mediatized circulation of the saint's persona in texts and songs, annual commemorative booklets, and brochures.

37 For more on the confluence of political and spiritual authorities in Islamic history, see Auer (2012), Curry and Ohlander (2012), Anjum (2011), Green (2004a).

38 For more on *khwaja-sara* life in Pakistan, see Khan (2016), Pamment (2010,

2019b). For *hijra* in India, see Reddy (2005), Nanda (1999). For manliness in the Punjab, see Pfeffer (1995).

2. Her Stories in His Durbar

1   For gendered politics of place making and women as "space invaders," see Puwar (2004). For women and Shi'i piety in South Asia, see Ruffle (2011), Hegland (1998).

2   Many fakirs in Sehwan claim that the shrine's original heirs were in fact ascetic followers of the saint.

3   For the historical role of sayyids and their social status in South Asia, see Gautier and Levesque (2020); on sayyid social and political roles in Sindh, see Ansari (1992).

4   A former association with the shrine and its revenues explains their material well-being and upward social circumstances in the present.

5   According to Boivin, the rift between the two families dates back to the British period (Michel Boivin, email message to author, September 1, 2014). For more management of the saint's spiritual authority, see Boivin (2003).

6   The ritual on Friday morning is more elaborate and considered auspicious, given the religious significance of the day.

7   For more on fakir relations with sayyid masters, see chapter 4.

8   The *ghusl* or bathing of the saint is considered an intimate event that requires privacy. The presence of women inside the durbar during the ceremony is discouraged. This explanation was provided by the custodian of the Bodlo shrine in response to my friend and fellow anthropologist Delphine Ortis's request to witness the event.

9   The minor shrine in question is the tomb of one of the earliest disciples of Lal.

10 While the ceremony and the participation of *kafis* remained consistent, the precise manner of conducting it cannot be said to be identical. Differences in style can occur due to change in officials. Also, certain services were discontinued; for instance, the cleaning and lighting of five lamps (*chiraghi*) was no longer observable by 2013. During my last visit in 2018, the ritual had become a completely private affair.

11 Monetary offerings to the saint are either collected in donation boxes or distributed among shrine workers on duty.

12 On spirits and their mediums, see Saniotis (2004).

13 The verb *milna* (to meet, to receive, to find) is used for fakir spirits as opposed to *charhna* (to mount) for djinns. For a typology of possessing djinns in the case of *zar* among Hofriyati women, see Boddy (1988, 10; see also 1994).

14 For the role of *pir*s in South Asia and charismatic Islam, see Pinto (2006), Lindholm (1998), Landell-Mills (1992), Mayer (1967).

15 For example, a quick survey of the markets surrounding the shrine revealed that a large number of rented shops in the market adjacent to the shrine are owned by various members of the custodian families.

16 Rarely do nonsayyid figures feature in this system. If so, they are either nominated by or closely aligned with custodian families. Only one in a system of fourteen *kafi*s of Sehwan is owned and headed by a nonsayyid *sajjadah-nashin*.

17 For more on Shi'i sayyid authority in South Asia, see Fuchs (2020).

18 Reference to Ali b. Zayn al-Abidin, one of the Shi'i imams.

19 Excerpt from an interview, recorded November 24, 2013.

20 For women's dealing with patriarchy, see Kandiyoti (1998). On illness and embodiment, see Das and Das (2007), also Csordas (1988, 2002, 2011).

21 Recorded interview, July 2009.

22 On gender-ambiguous performance and spirituality, see Kugle (2010a); for women Sufis, see Hill (2010), Pemberton (2010); on the feminine in Islamic mysticism, see Elias (2008), Mernissi (1977).

23 For women as spiritual guides, see Pemberton (2006). On gendered expressions of religion in South Asia, see Appadurai, Korom, and Mills (1991); for women saints in South Asia, see Ramanujan (1982).

24 In a study of women and poverty in parts of Sindh and Punjab, Lubna Chaudhry notes how unmarried girls in their teens and early twenties are most vulnerable. She points to discriminatory food portions within the family and limited access to health care, in addition to a lack of share in economic resources, even those that involve their labor.

25 Sarah Lamb (2005, 228) has observed that women after menopause, or whose children are married, and even widows are subject to fewer restrictions relating to impurity and thereby enjoy better mobility and access. On women and pollution, see also Blanchet (1984).

26 As a single exception, I met a young initiate who shadowed her fakir aunt in Sehwan.

27 Abba's perceptiveness on the matter was exceptional. He understood Amma's situation, perhaps because he had witnessed his wife's process and had also participated in its accomplishment.

28 Citing the figure of Lal-kunwar or the bride of Lal, some locals claim that the Hindu custom of ritual marriage with the saint of Sehwan was part of the ceremonies of the annual fair up until the mid-twentieth century (see also Boivin 2012b, 123–26). On the crossovers of devotion and marriage in the Hindu tradition, see Ramberg (2014, 2016), Kinsley (1981).

29 Women fakirs that I spoke to shared the cultural opinion that other (nonfakir) women must observe purdah and should not be seen unnecessarily in public.

3. In Other Guises, Other Futures

1 For more on *dhamal* in Sehwan, see Frembgen (2012a).

2 On the limitations and possibilities of women *pir*s in South Asia, see Pemberton (2006).

3   On the moral geography of public space at Egyptian shrines, see Samuli Schielke (2008).

4   For historiality, see discussion in chapter 1 or Rheinberger (1994).

5   In her research with Buddhist nuns of Sri Lanka, Salgado (2013) interprets similar "not woman" claims as female renunciants' understanding of themselves and their roles as defying or going beyond gender. Her point, however, is that in doing so, such women refuse to be understood through liberal feminist frameworks.

6   Interview with Zaheda, July 2009.

7   Instructions from the saint can be tied to ideas of fidelity, or why the saint doesn't like his female fakirs to have any conjugal ties with their husbands.

8   Excerpt from field diary, November 14, 2013.

9   Excerpt from field diary, November 25, 2013.

10   Zafar, recorded in field diary, July 31, 2012.

11   Zaheda, recorded in field diary, November 24, 2013.

12   Zaheda, recorded in field diary, November 24, 2013.

13   Recent years have witnessed several suicide attacks on major shrines in Pakistan; see discussion in the introduction.

14   Recorded in field diary, November 24, 2013.

15   Medina here is a metaphor for a holy center; the quotation was recorded in the field diary during our last conversation.

16   Recorded in field diary, November 24, 2013.

17   Recorded in field diary, November 24, 2013.

18   Zaheda was not allowed to reveal the name of the other saint in question.

4. Love in a Time of Celibacy

1   *Wardi* (lit. uniform) serves to stress the idea of duty to the saint and distinguishes fakirs in visible ways; see discussion on fakir dis/guise in chapter 3.

2   Bodlo, or Bodlo-bahar (in full), is a curious figure in that he is hardly traceable through classical Sufi histories. Boivin (2012b, 121) is of the opinion that the Sindhi name Bodlo, meaning innocent young boy, even Buddha, and *bahar*, which means spring, are possibly signs that the figure bears other histories but survives in a Sufi guise. For affection between Lal and Bodlo, see N. Sehwani (2009).

3   The feature of the Sufi lodge (elsewhere *khanaqah, zawiyah*), according to Zeynep Yürekli (2012), is characteristic of the historical development of Sufism.

4   Its present-day custodians were able to fight a case against the state in the courts back in the 1960s, successfully arguing that the shrine of Bodlo was in fact a legitimate family inheritance.

5   Michel Boivin holds the view that the prototype of *dargah* (Sufi shrine) better suits what I have here described as the *kafi* of Bodlo. I consider this site a hybrid category. While the shrine of Bodlo has a central role in the economic

and community life of its lodge, I take the position that both prototypes of fakir space are equally present and observable at the site in question.

6   I return to the legend in chapter 5 as part of how Lal is remembered in Sehwan.

7   For the role of Sufi lodges in urban transformation and construction of spiritual authority in medieval Anatolia, see Wolper (2003).

8   It explains to some extent why fakir initiates at Bodlo's lodge are predominantly Punjabi speaking, drawn from outside the region of Sindh.

9   Mian's observations on desire and sexuality are concerned with a single community of Muslims, namely the Deobandis of modern South Asia.

10 The younger fakir clearly identified as a woman, although the senior fakir, whom she introduced as her aunt, sometimes adopted masculine speech or switched genders when referring to themselves.

11 For a detailed account of fakir duties and responsibilities at the Bodlo *kafi*, see Ortis (2020, 321–26).

12 Recorded in field diary, July 28, 2012.

13 This practice, fakirs of the lodge explained, goes back to the time of Lal. According to local legend, Bodlo's she-camel, a gift from Lal, would itself leave the lodge each evening to collect food for its fakirs. For more details on fakir collection and preparation of food at the lodge, see Ortis (2020, 323).

14 Nilam was the horse used in the annual Muharram processions. It is dressed up as Zuljanah, the legendary steed of Imam Hussayn in Karbala, inviting the devotion and reverence of onlookers.

15 Recorded in field diary, November 15, 2011. For more on the fakir garment as a shroud for the dead, see Ortis (2020, 320).

16 Excerpt from an interview, June 2012.

17 Recorded in field diary, July 30, 2012. For more on sexuality and chastity among fakirs of Bodlo, see Ortis (2020, 319).

18 For more on antinomian piety, see Karamustafa (2006), Watenpaugh (2005).

19 Such veiled disclosures may also have to do with the fact that they were speaking to a cis-male researcher. Men and transgender persons were equally careful with their references.

20 While its suffix *satti*, or seven, refers to the number of Sehwani saints in a scheme of celibate mystics, *jatti*, if one is allowed a conjecture, must stand for an idea of celibacy, even the condition of being virgin. However, as per my observation in Sehwan, the word *jatti* is never used by itself.

21 *Nafs* usually refers to ego or self in Sufi-Islamic contexts.

22 The terms he used were *muzakarr-un mawla* and *mu'annus ud-dunya*.

23 She briefly adds that love and desire directed toward same-sex human beings is not entirely unthinkable in the writings of Ibn 'Arabi (see Shaikh 2012, 192). On Sufi mysticism and sexuality, see also Hoffmann-Ladd (1992).

24 For homoerotic and queer depictions of love between Sufi masters and disciples, see Kugle (2007).

25 Excerpt from field diary, November 19, 2013.

26 According to Karamustafa (2006, 14), the accoutrements characteristic of fakirs in the Middle Period of Islamic societies (1200–1550 CE) could include "woollen or felt garment or animal hide, cap, begging bowl, pouch, spoon, club, belt, bell, hatchet, lamp or candle, razor, needle, flint stone, and musical instruments (commonly tambourine, drum and pipe)."

27 Excerpt from field diary, July 30, 2012.

28 Excerpt from interview, November 14, 2013.

29 Excerpt from interview, July 27, 2012.

30 For more on fakir hierarchy and duties at the lodge, see Ortis (2020, 325).

31 I wondered if I was indeed witnessing firsthand the remaking of the Bodlo story or whether this account was targeted at more immediate concerns, given the changes at the lodge.

32 In an interesting and somewhat related development, only weeks before this interview, Nur-Shah himself had contracted a second marriage in Karachi. Fakir conditions on marriage do not apply in equal measure to custodian figures like Nur-Shah, who must produce male heirs in order to maintain lines and systems of routinized spiritual authority.

33 Another point of difference to consider is that the *wado-fakir* had wished to marry a female disciple who was currently residing at the lodge. In this sense, it was an internal affair, and the fakir's interest in the woman would not necessarily lead him away from the lodge itself.

34 While this was a privately conducted ritual that I did not have direct access to in terms of participation, my fakir interlocutors at the lodge described the ceremony to me so that I could record it in my field diary.

35 Fakirs of Bodlo are exempt from this practice. As per local legend, since fakirs of the other lodges had colluded with each other and killed Bodlo's camel, Lal ordered that they henceforth be marked with a seal to distinguish them from fakirs of Bodlo.

36 Recorded in field diary, January 17, 2012.

37 Recorded in field diary, November 15, 2011.

5. Worlding Fakirs, Fairies, and the Dead

An early incarnation of chapter 5 appeared as "Grounds of Becoming: Fakirs among the Dead in Sehwan Sharif, Pakistan," *Culture and Religion* 18, no. 2 (2017): 72–89.

1 For Mittermaier, that notion is an Elsewhere. For a theory of religion and space, see Knott (2008), Tweed (2006).

2 According to local lore, Koh-Qaf, or the peaks of Qaf, refers to a mountainous setting of the fairies and demons, believed by some to be located in the Caucasus.

3 This makes her claim not so much a choice as a being chosen, a feature common to less-normative spiritual careers like those of women and gender-

variant fakirs; for more, see chapters 1–3. On gender and divine agency, see Hollywood (2004).

4   For women's invasive labors of place, see Puwar (2004). For gendered geographies, see Raju (2011). More generally on space and place making, see Cresswell (2002, 2009), Massey (1999, 2005).

5   Since Bodlo appears not to be linked to any classical form or figures in the Sufi tradition, Boivin (2012b, 121) is of the opinion that the enigmatic figure is possibly a remnant of the region's ancient nature-based forms of worship and devotion.

6   In another version of the same legend, he used his staff instead of the cup to beckon divine punishment. Such details vary across narrations.

7   There are more sites in and around the city associated with the saint, which I do not discuss here. Prominent among these are Chothambi and the natural springs in Lal-bagh.

8   For more on Jhule Lal, see Parwani (2010). Sehwan at the time of the saint's arrival was dominated by followers of Shiva as well as Daryapanthis, who divinized the Indus River (Boivin 2012b, 40).

9   This particular description was provided by a visiting fakir from Lahore who in the autumn of 2011 was in Sehwan to perform his duty at the shrine of Lal. The conversation took place at his fakir retreat by the banks of the river. In most historical accounts, it is the figure of Udero Lal who is conflated with Khizr in Sindh (see Boivin 2012b, 43).

10   This legend and others like it are commonly told in Sehwan. The version I present is one I heard from fakirs at the shrine of Juman-Jatti.

11   Offerings to the Indus River can still be documented in the wider region of Sindh.

12   As described in Advani (2010, 14).

13   Author's translation from Sindhi. Original by M. Ahmed in *Shahbaz Qalandar*, 6–12 (Karachi: West Pakistan Government Press).

14   Annemarie Schimmel (2003, 355) briefly mentions Sehwan's Shivaite heritage. For more, see Boivin (2011).

15   For a study of saints' tombs, burial spaces, and types of dead in Sehwan, see Ortis (2019).

16   Whether one accepts that he first settled at a careful distance from the then walled city or that he arrived in the quarter of the sex workers, the alternate character of his choice of dwelling confirms a spatial inversion that is characteristic of antinomian piety.

17   According to Michel Boivin, the flower in milk is a key trope in Sufi narratives of the Indus valley and also beyond and can be witnessed in accounts of other saintly figures like Pir Shams of the Isma'ilis and also Guru Nanak, the spiritual leader and founder of Sikhism (email message to author, September 1, 2014).

18   Most relevant to this discussion is the notion that the authority of a *wali*, which stems from the saint's intimacy with Allah, is made manifest in his

ability and authority to protect a region or *wilayat*. For more on Sufi authority, see Buehler (1997). For more on *wilayat*, see Digby (1990).

19 For more on Islamic saints and locality, see Stauth and Schielke (2008), Zayed
(2008), Green (2004a, 2004b, 2012a).

20 For shrines and wilderness in Punjab, see Werth (1998).

21 *Qalandar*s are distinct in that such figures, marked by renunciation, celibacy,
antinomianism, and itinerancy, turn the idea of such spatiality into a defining
trait (see Karamustafa 2006; Watenpaugh 2005).

22 It pertains to a widely held notion that taming the wild is a key characteristic
of Sufis and Islamic saints as friends of Allah.

23 Its symbolic power aside, privileging a spatial performance of social death
risks underestimating fakirs' active interest in self-empowerment. For more,
see Kasmani (2017b).

24 For multilocality and multivocality of places, see Rodman (2003).

Coda

1 This does not entail one category taking over the other; see further
discussion.

2 *Unstraight* in this work does not characterize fakirs or saints as queer in iden-
titarian terms.

3 See *English-Urdu, Urdu-English Combined Dictionary* (Haq 2004, 1186).

4 I here refer to the study of religion in its broadest sense, which in addition to
religious studies proper also includes anthropological inquiries in religion,
especially the subdisciplines anthropology of religion and anthropology of
Islam.

5 Nikki Young (2017) has noted that both religion and queerness can be a check
on each other's tendencies. While religion, she argues, tempers queer's rush
toward individuality, queer studies can help interrogate the narratives and
meaning making of humanity that religion so readily performs.

6 For more on religion and trans in Pakistan, see Jaffer (2017). On transgender activism in Pakistan, see Khan (2016), Redding (2015), Pamment (2010,
2019a).

7 She argues that in such persons' performance as wives of goddesses but also
as male women or female-sexed sons, vocabularies of both kinship and gender are troubled.

8 For more on the Christian context, see Althaus-Reid (2001, 2003), Goss
(2002), Goss and West (2000); for the Jewish context, see Boyarin, Itzkovits,
and Pellegrini (2003); on intersex, transgender, and Christian theology, see
Sheffield (2008), Loughlin (2007); for religion and queer women, see Wilcox
(2009); for the Islamic context, see Babayan and Najmabadi (2008); for gay,
lesbian, and trans Muslims, see Kugle (2014); on religion and transgender
in Pakistan, see Pamment (2019b); for Islamic masculinities, see De Sondy
(2013).

9   These include the bones, belly, eyes, lips, and heart of both male and female spiritual figures between North Africa and South Asia (see also Kugle 2003).

10   For Kugle, this loss has to do with Islamic fundamentalism and the rise of the Wahhabi movement in contemporary Muslim societies.

11   Interpretive interventions such as these offer queer Muslims a place in the tradition as well as a much-desired route for reconciling sexuality with faith; see especially Kugle (2010b, 2014).

12   Reflecting on her work in the archives as part of a project on Protestantism and gay rights in twentieth-century America, Heather White (2017) describes her analytical move as "religion-ing" rather than "queering."

13   One of the implications that Claudia Schippert (2011, 69) assigns to queer theory in religion is that it can finally enable religious studies to become (more) undisciplined.

14   On ethics and the politics of Islamic piety in Cairo, see Mahmood (2005). For critique on the piety turn in the anthropology of Islam, see Mittermaier (2012), Schielke (2010), Soares and Osella (2009).

15   For queer and religion's dismantling of the divide between *what is* and *what might be*, see Young (2017).

16   For religious affects and politics of Elsewhere, see Kasmani et al. (2020).

AHL-E BAYT	Persons belonging to the household of the Prophet Muhammad.
'ALAM	A banner or flag, mostly a Shi'i commemorative structure marking the Battle of Karbala (680 CE).
'AMAL	Deed or act.
AMMA	Mother, a female spiritual figure or guide.
'ATA	Gift, grant, bestowal.
AUQAF	Religious or charitable endowments; sing. *waqf.*
BABA	Father, a male spiritual figure or guide.
BE-SHAR	Outside religious law or without shariah.
BHES/VES	Fakir guise, disguise.
BISHARAT	Sign or inspired word received from a divine source.
DACHI	Female camel.
DARBAR/DURBAR	Royal court of a king or saint.
DASTAR	Turban, headgear placed on a saint's tomb.
DHAMAL	Drumming ritual at a shrine.
DIDAR	A vision or sight of a beloved or holy figure.

FAKIR/FAQIR	Beggar, ascetic, person who takes up voluntary poverty.
FAKIRI	The task of conducting fakir life.
GHAYB	The realm of the hidden or the yet unrevealed.
GHUSL	Bath, ritual washing of a shrine.
HAL-VASLAH	Set of fakir accessories and objects.
HAZIRI	Presence, the ritual of experiencing spirits at a shrine.
IMAM	Divinely ordained or inspired leader and guide among the Shi'a.
'ISHQ	Passionate or divine love.
JATTI-SATTI	Local term for celibacy or chastity; seven celibate saints in Sehwan.
JHOLI	Pouch; folds of a long shirt.
JINN/DJINN	A being created from smokeless fire mentioned in the Quran.
KAFI	A fakir lodge in Sehwan; *khanaqah* or *zawiyah* in other Sufi contexts.
KHADIM	Shrine employee, the one who performs service.
KHWAJA-SARA	Urdu term for transgender, intersex, gender-variant person.
LANGOT	Garment covering a man's loins.
MACHH	Fireplace around which fakirs gather.
MAWLA	Protector; a reference to Ali ibn Abi Talib, cousin of the Prophet and a prominent figure of Islamic devotion, in particular among the Shi'a.
MELA	Fair, saint's festival.
MUHARRAM	The first and also holy month in the Islamic calendar; a period of mourning for Shi'i Muslims.
MURID	A disciple of a Sufi master, mostly initiated.
MURSHID	A Sufi master or guide.
NAFS	Carnal self.

PANJATAN	The five (holy) bodies of the Prophet's family, namely, Muhammad, Fatima, Ali, Hassan, and Hussayn.
PIR	A spiritual guide, most often a Muslim healer.
QALANDAR	An antinomian Sufi, wandering mystic.
QARIB	Close, intimate, proximate.
QURB	Closeness, intimacy.
SAJDAH-GAH	A round tablet made of earth (ideally from Karbala) that Shi'i Muslims use for prostration during daily prayer.
SAJJADAH-NASHIN	Successor to a spiritual position or shrine, mostly a male biological descendant; head of a *kafi* in Sehwan.
SAYYID	Descendant of the Prophet Muhammad.
SHALWAR-KAMIZ	The pair of loose trousers and long shirt worn by Pakistanis.
SHARI'AT	Islamic law.
SUHBET	Companionship, spiritual meeting, conversation, sex.
TALIB	Seeker on a mystical path.
TARIQAT	Mystical path or Sufi order.
'URS	Death anniversary of a saint, interpreted as a saint's wedding to God.
WADO-FAKIR	Senior fakir.
WALI	A friend of God, saint; pl. *auliya'*.
WARDI	Uniform, fakir costume.
WILAYAT	An area or region under a saint's authority.
ZIYARAT	Pilgrimage, viewing a relic or visiting a holy place.

Abbas, Shemeem Burney. 2002. *The Female Voice in Sufi Ritual: Devotional Practices of Pakistan and India*. Austin: University of Texas Press.

Abbasi, Noor M., ed. 2002. *Muhammad Usman Marwandi: Hazrat Lal Shahbaz Qalandar*. Hyderabad: Shahbaz.

Abu-Lughod, Lila. 1990. "Can There Be a Feminist Ethnography?" *Women and Performance* 5 (1): 7–27.

Advani, Bhiromal M. 2010. "Makhdum Qalandar Lal Shahbaz." In *Qalandar Lal Shahbaz: Ahwal'ayn Asar*, edited by Muhammad Ali Manjhi, 11–26. Karachi: Department of Culture, Government of Sindh.

Ahmad, Sadaf. 2009. *Transforming Faith: The Story of Al-Huda and Islamic Revivalism among Urban Pakistani Women*. Syracuse, NY: Syracuse University Press.

Ahmed, Amineh. 2005. "Death and Celebration among Muslim Women: A Case Study from Pakistan." *Modern Asian Studies* 39 (4): 929–80.

Ahmed, M. 1968. "Qalandar Lal Shahbaz." In *Shahbaz Qalandar*, 6–12. Karachi: West Pakistan Government Press.

Ahmed, Sara. 2006. *Queer Phenomenology: Orientations, Objects, Others*. Durham, NC: Duke University Press.

Ahmed, Shahab. 2016. *What Is Islam? The Importance of Being Islamic*. Princeton, NJ: Princeton University Press.

Alam, Fakhrul. 1972. "In the Name of Qalandar Give!" *Herald*, November.

Althaus-Reid, Marcella. 2001. *Indecent Theology: Theological Perversions in Sex, Gender, and Politics*. New York: Routledge.

Althaus-Reid, Marcella. 2003. *The Queer God*. New York: Routledge.

Alvi, Anjum. 2013. "Concealment and Revealment: The Muslim Veil in Context." *Current Anthropology* 54 (2): 177–99.

Amin, Kadji. 2017. *Disturbing Attachments: Genet, Modern Pederasty, and Queer History*. Durham, NC: Duke University Press.

Anderson, Ben, and Paul Harrison, eds. 2010. *Taking—Place: Non-representational Theories and Geography*. Farnham, UK: Ashgate.

Andhar, Hafiz A. 2010. "Hazrat Usman Marwandi muta'lliq Riwayatun" [The narratives concerning Usman Marwandi]. In *Qalandar L'al Shahbaz: Ahwal 'ayn Asar*, edited by Muhammad Ali Manjhi, 143–14. Karachi: Department of Culture, Government of Sindh.

Anjum, Ovamir. 2012. "Mystical Authority and Governmentality in Medieval Islam." In *Sufism and Society: Arrangements of the Mystical in the Muslim World, 1200–1800*, edited by John Curry and Erik Ohlander, 71–93. New York: Routledge.

Anjum, Tanvir. 2011. *Chishti Sufis in the Sultanate of Delhi, 1190–1400: From Restrained Indifference to Calculated Defiance*. Karachi: Oxford University Press.

Ansari, Sarah. 1992. *Sufi Saints and State Power: The Pirs of Sind, 1843–1947*. Cambridge: Cambridge University Press.

Appadurai, Arjun, Frank Korom, and Margaret Mills. 1991. *Gender, Genre, and Power in South Asian Expressive Traditions*. Philadelphia: University of Pennsylvania Press.

Armbrecht, Ann. 2009. *Thin Places: A Pilgrimage Home*. New York: Columbia University Press.

Armitage, Susan H., and Sherna Berger Gluck. 2002. "Reflections on Women's Oral History: An Exchange." In *Women's Oral History: The Frontier's Reader*, edited by Susan H. Armitage, Patricia Hart, and Karen Weathermon, 75–86. Lincoln: University of Nebraska Press.

Arondekar, Anjali. 2020. "The Sex of History, or Object/Matters." *History Workshop Journal* 89 (Spring): 207–13. doi:10.1093/hwj/dbz053.

Arondekar, Anjali, and Geeta Patel. 2016. "Area Impossible: Notes toward an Introduction." *GLQ: A Journal of Lesbian and Gay Studies* 22 (2): 151–71.

Asif, Manan Ahmed. 2016. *A Book of Conquest: The* Chachnama *and Muslim Origins in South Asia*. Cambridge, MA: Harvard University Press.

Auer, Blain. 2012. "Intersections between Sufism and Power: Narrating the Shaykhs and Sultans of Northern India, 1200–1400." In *Sufism and Society: Arrangements of the Mystical in the Muslim World, 1200–1800*, edited by John Curry and Erik Ohlander, 17–33. New York: Routledge.

Babayan, Kathryn, and Afsaneh Najmabadi, eds. 2008. *Islamicate Sexualities: Translations across Temporal Geographies of Desire*. Cambridge, MA: Harvard University Press.

Bashir, Shahzad. 2011. *Sufi Bodies: Religion and Society in Medieval Islam*. New York: Columbia University Press.

Bauer, Alexander A. 2019. "Itinerant Objects." *Annual Review of Anthropology* 48:335–52.

Bellamy, Carla. 2008. "Person in Place: Possession and Power at an Indian Islamic Saint Shrine." *Journal of Feminist Studies in Religion* 24 (1): 31–44.

Bellamy, Carla. 2011. *The Powerful Ephemeral: Everyday Healing in an Ambiguously Islamic Place.* Berkeley: University of California Press.

Bennett, Clinton, and Charles Ramsey. 2012. *South Asian Sufis: Devotion, Deviation and Destiny.* London: Continuum.

Berlant, Lauren. 1998. "Intimacy." *Critical Inquiry* 24 (2): 281–88.

Berlant, Lauren. 2006. "Cruel Optimism." *differences: A Journal of Feminist Cultural Studies* 17 (3): 20–36.

Berlant, Lauren. 2011. *Cruel Optimism.* Durham, NC: Duke University Press.

Berlant, Lauren, and Lee Edelman. 2014. *Sex, or the Unbearable.* Durham, NC: Duke University Press.

Bigelow, Anna. 2010. *Sharing the Sacred: Practicing Pluralism in Muslim North India.* New York: Oxford University Press.

Blackman, Lisa. 2015. "Researching Affect and Embodied Hauntologies: Exploring an Analytics of Experimentation." In *Affective Methodologies: Developing Cultural Research Strategies for the Study of Affect,* edited by Britta Timm Knudsen and Carsten Stage, 25–44. London: Palgrave Macmillan.

Blanchet, Thérèse. 1984. *Women, Pollution and Marginality: Meanings and Rituals of Birth in Rural Bangladesh.* Dhaka: University Press.

Bloch, Maurice. 1998. *How We Think They Think: Anthropological Approaches to Cognition, Memory, and Literacy.* Boulder, CO: Westview.

Boddy, Janice. 1988. "Spirits and Selves in Northern Sudan: The Cultural Therapeutics of Possession and Trance." *American Ethnologist* 15 (1): 4–27.

Boddy, Janice. 1994. "Spirit Possession Revisited: Beyond Instrumentality." *Annual Review of Anthropology* 23:407–34.

Boivin, Michel. 2003. "Reflections on La'l Shahbaz Qalandar and the Management of His Spiritual Authority in Sehwan Sharif." *Journal of the Pakistan Historical Society* 51 (4): 41–74.

Boivin, Michel, ed. 2008. *Sindh through History and Representations.* French Contributions to Sindhi Studies. Karachi: Oxford University Press.

Boivin, Michel. 2011. *Artefacts of Devotion: A Sufi Repertoire of the Qalandariyya in Sehwan Sharif, Sindh, Pakistan.* Karachi: Oxford University Press.

Boivin, Michel. 2012a. "Guthe Sufi Centre of Jhok Sharif in Sindh (Pakistan): Questioning the Ziyarat as Social Process." In *South Asian Sufis: Devotion, Deviation and Destiny,* edited by Clinton Bennett and Charles Ramsey, 95–110. London: Continuum.

Boivin, Michel. 2012b. *Le Soufisme antinomien dans le sous-continent indien: La'l Shahbâz Qalandar et son heritage, XIIIe–XXe siècle* [Antinomian Sufism in the Indian subcontinent: Lal Shahbaz Qalandar and his heritage, 13th–20th centuries]. Paris: Cerf.

Boivin, Michel, and Matthew Cook, eds. 2011. *Interpreting the Sindhi World: Essays on Society and History.* Karachi: Oxford University Press.

Boyarin, Daniel, Daniel Itzkovits, and Anne Pellegrini, eds. 2003. *Queer Theory and the Jewish Question*. New York: Columbia University Press.

Buehler, Arthur. 1997. *Sufi Heirs of the Prophet: The Indian Naqshbandiyya and the Rise of the Mediating Sufi Shaykh*. Columbia: University of South Carolina Press.

Burghart, Richard. 1983. "Renunciation in the Religious Traditions of South Asia." *Man* 18 (4): 635–53.

Burnes, Alexander. 1837. "On Sind." *Journal of the Royal Geographical Society of London* 7:11–20.

Burton, Richard. 1851. *Sind and Races That Inhabit the Valley of the Indus*. London: W. H. Allen.

Butler, Judith. 1988. "Performative Acts and Gender Constitution: An Essay in Phenomenology and Feminist Theory." *Theatre Journal* 40 (4): 519–31.

Butler, Judith. 1990. *Gender Trouble*. London: Routledge.

Callan, Alyson. 2008. "Female Saints and the Practice of Islam in Sylhet, Bangladesh." *American Ethnologist* 35 (3): 396–412.

Castelli, Elizabeth A. 2017. "Introduction: At the Intersection of Queer Studies and Religion." *Scholar and Feminist Online* 14 (2). https://sfonline.barnard.edu/queer-religion/elizabeth-castelli-introduction/.

Chaudhry, Lubna. 2010. "Women and Poverty: Salient Findings from a Gendered Analysis of a Quasi-Anthropological Study in Rural Punjab and Sindh." In *Pakistani Women: Multiple Locations and Competing Narratives*, edited by Sadaf Ahmad, 47–119. Karachi: Oxford University Press.

Chishti, Muhammad A. 2008. *Syed Usman Marwandi al-Maruf Hazrat Lal Shahbaz Qalandar: Hayat, Afkar-o-talimat* [Syed Usman Marwandi popularly Lal Shahbaz Qalandar: Life, thoughts and teachings]. Lahore: Haq.

Chittick, William C. 1993. "Meetings with Imaginal Men." *Sufi*, no. 19, 8–13.

Chittick, William C. 1994. *Imaginal Worlds: Ibn al-'Arabi and the Problem of Religious Diversity*. Albany: State University of New York Press.

Clifford, James. 1989. "Notes on Travel and Theory." In *Inscriptions*, vol. 5: *Traveling Theories, Traveling Theorists*, edited by James Clifford and Vivek Dhareshwar, 177–88. Santa Cruz, CA: Center for Cultural Studies.

Clifford, James. 1996. "Anthropology and/as Travel." *Etnofoor* 9 (2): 5–15.

Collinet, Annabelle. 2008. "Chronology of Sehwan through Ceramics (the Islamic Period)." In *Sindh through History and Representations*, edited by Michel Boivin, 3–21. Karachi: Oxford University Press.

Cook, Matthew, ed. 2008. *Observing Sindh: Selected Reports*. Karachi: Oxford University Press.

Corbin, Henri. 1997. *Alone with the Alone: Creative Imagination in the Sufism of Ibn 'Arabi*. Princeton, NJ: Princeton University Press.

Cresswell, Tim. 2002. "Theorizing Place." In *Mobilizing Place, Placing Mobility: The Politics of Representation in a Globalized World*, edited by Ginette Verstraete and Tim Cresswell, 11–31. Amsterdam: Rodopi.

Cresswell, Tim. 2009. "Place." In *International Encyclopedia of Human Geography*, edited by Rob Kitchin and Nigel Thrift, 1–9. Oxford: Elsevier.

Csordas, Thomas. 1988. "Elements of Charismatic Persuasion and Healing." *Medical Anthropology Quarterly* 2 (2): 121–42.

Csordas, Thomas. 2002. *Body/Meaning/Healing*. New York: Palgrave.

Csordas, Thomas. 2011. "Embodiment: Agency, Sexual Difference, and Illness." In *A Companion to the Anthropology of the Body and Embodiment*, edited by Frances Mascia-Lees, 137–56. Oxford: Wiley-Blackwell.

Cunningham, Alexander. 1871. *The Ancient Geography of India*. London: Trubner.

Currie, P. M. 1989. *The Shrine and Cult of Muʿin al-Din Chishti of Ajmer*. New Delhi: Oxford University Press.

Curry, John, and Erik Ohlander, eds. 2012. *Sufism and Society: Arrangements of the Mystical in the Muslim World, 1200–1800*. New York: Routledge.

Cvetkovich, Ann. 2012. *Depression: A Public Feeling*. Durham, NC: Duke University Press.

Das, Veena, and Ramendra Das. 2007. "How the Body Speaks: Illness and the Life-world among the Urban Poor." In *Subjectivity: Ethnographic Investigations*, edited by João Biehl, Byron Good, and Arthur Kleinman, 66–97. Berkeley: University of California Press.

Delage, Rémy. 2016. "L'espace du pèlerinage comme 'territoire circulatoire': Sehwan Sharif sur les rives de l'Indus" [Pilgrimage space as "circulatory territory": Sehwan Sharif on the River Indus]. *Les Cahiers d'Outre-Mer*, no. 274, 77–102. https://doi.org/10.4000/com.7863.

Delage, Rémy. 2018. "Sufism and the Pilgrimage Market: A Political Economy of a Shrine in Southern Pakistan." In *Pilgrimage and Political Economy: Translating the Sacred*, edited by Simon Coleman and John Eade, 59–74. New York: Berghahn.

DeNapoli, Antoinette Elizabeth. 2014. *Real Sadhus Sing to God: Gender, Asceticism, and Vernacular Religion in Rajhastan*. New York: Oxford University Press.

De Sondy, Amanullah. 2013. *The Crisis of Islamic Masculinities*. London: Bloomsbury Academic.

Digby, Simon. 1984. "Qalandars and Related Groups: Elements of Social Deviance in the Religious Life of the Delhi Sultanate of the Thirteenth and Fourteenth Centuries." In *Islam in Asia*, edited by Yohanan Friedmann, 60–108. Jerusalem: Magnes.

Digby, Simon. 1990. "The Sufi *Shaykh* and the Sultan: A Conflict of Claims to Authority in Medieval India." *Iran* 28 (1): 71–81.

Eaton, Richard. 1978. "The Profile of Popular Islam in Pakistan." *Journal of South Asian and Middle Eastern Studies* 2 (1): 74–92.

Eaton, Richard. 1982. "Court of Man, Court of God: Local Perceptions of the Shrine of Baba Farid." In *Moral Conduct and Authority: The Place of Adab in South Asian Islam*, edited by Barbara Metcalf, 333–56. Berkeley: University of California Press.

Elias, Jamal. 2008. "Female and Feminine in Islamic Mysticism." In *Sufism: Critical Concepts in Islamic Studies*, vol. 2: *Hermeneutics and Doctrines*, edited by Lloyd Ridgeon, 298–315. Abingdon, UK: Routledge.

El-Rouayheb, Khaled. 2005. *Before Homosexuality in the Arab-Islamic World, 1500–1800*. Chicago: University of Chicago Press.

Ernst, Carl. 1992. *Eternal Garden: Mysticism, History and Politics at a South Asian Sufi Centre*. Albany: State University of New York Press.

Ernst, Carl. 1997. *The Shambhala Guide to Sufism*. Boston: Shambhala.

Ewing, Katherine P. 1990. "The Dream of Spiritual Initiation and the Organization of Self: Representations among Pakistani Sufis." *American Ethnologist* 17 (1): 56–74.

Ewing, Katherine P. 2006. *Arguing Sainthood: Modernity, Psychoanalysis, and Islam*. 2nd ed. Durham, NC: Duke University Press.

Flood, Finbarr B. 2009. *Objects of Translation: Material Culture and Medieval "Hindu-Muslim" Encounter*. Princeton, NJ: Princeton University Press.

Flood, Finbarr B. 2014. "Bodies and Becoming: Mimesis, Mediation, and the Ingestion of the Sacred in Christianity and Islam." In *Sensational Religion: Sensory Cultures in Material Practice*, edited by Salley M. Promey, 459–93. New Haven, CT: Yale University Press.

Flueckiger, Joyce. 2003. "Narrative Voices and Repertoire at a Healing Crossroads in South India." *Journal of American Folklore* 116 (461): 249–72.

Flueckiger, Joyce. 2006. *In Amma's Healing Room: Gender and Vernacular Islam in South India*. Bloomington: Indiana University Press.

Freeman, Elizabeth. 2019. *Beside You in Time: Sense Methods and Queer Sociabilities in the American Nineteenth Century*. Durham, NC: Duke University Press.

Frembgen, Jürgen. 2011. *At the Shrine of the Red Sufi: Five Days and Nights on Pilgrimage in Pakistan*. Karachi: Oxford University Press.

Frembgen, Jürgen. 2012a. "Dhamal and the Performing Body: Trance Dance in the Devotional Sufi Practice of Pakistan." *Journal of Sufi Studies* 1: 77–113.

Frembgen, Jürgen. 2012b. *The Friends of God: Sufi Saints in Islam, Popular Poster Art from Pakistan*. Karachi: Oxford University Press.

Fuchs, Simon Wolfgang. 2019. *In a Pure Muslim Land: Shi'ism between Pakistan and the Middle East*. Chapel Hill: University of North Carolina Press.

Fuchs, Simon Wolfgang. 2020. "Legalised Pedigrees: Sayyids and Shi'i Islam in Pakistan." *Journal of the Royal Asiatic Society* 30 (3): 489–504. doi:10.1017/S1356186320000036.

Gautier, Laurence, and Julien Levesque. 2020. "Introduction: Historicizing Sayyidness: Social Status and Muslim Identity in South Asia." *Journal of the Royal Asiatic Society* 30 (3): 383–93. doi:10.1017/S1356186320000139.

Geertz, Clifford. 1998. "Deep Hanging Out." *New York Review of Books* 45 (16): 69–72.

Gibson, James. 1979. *The Ecological Approach to Visual Perception*. Boston: Houghton Mifflin.

Gold, Ann. 1988. "Spirit Possession Perceived and Performed in Rural Rajasthan." *Contributions to Indian Sociology* 22 (1): 35–63.

Gordon, Avery. 2008. *Ghostly Matters: Haunting and the Sociological Imagination*. Minneapolis: University of Minnesota Press.

Goss, Robert. 2002. *Queering Christ: Beyond Jesus Acted Up.* Cleveland, OH: Pilgrim.

Goss, Robert, and Mona West, eds. 2000. *Take Back the Word: A Queer Reading of the Bible.* Cleveland, OH: Pilgrim.

Green, Nile. 2003. "The Religious and Cultural Roles of Dreams and Visions in Islam." *Journal of the Royal Asiatic Society,* 3rd ser., 13 (3): 287–313.

Green, Nile. 2004a. "Geography, Empire and Sainthood in the Eighteenth-Century Muslim Deccan." *Bulletin of the School of Oriental and African Studies, University of London* 67 (2): 207–25.

Green, Nile. 2004b. "Oral Competition Narratives of Muslim and Hindu Saints in the Deccan." *Asian Folklore Studies* 63 (2): 221–42.

Green, Nile. 2006. *Indian Sufism since the Seventeenth Century: Saints, Books and Empires in the Muslim Deccan.* New York: Routledge.

Green, Nile. 2012a. *Making Space: Sufis and Settlers in Early Modern India.* New Delhi: Oxford University Press.

Green, Nile. 2012b. *Sufism: A Global History.* Sussex: Wiley-Blackwell.

Grima, Benedicta. 2004. *The Performance of Emotion among Paxtun Women: "The Misfortunes Which Have Befallen Me."* Karachi: Oxford University Press.

Hamzić, Vanja. 2016. *Sexual and Gender Diversity in the Muslim World: History, Law and Vernacular Language.* London: I. B. Tauris.

Hamzić, Vanja. 2019. "The *Dera* Paradigm: Homecoming of the Gendered Other." *Ethnoscripts* 21 (1): 34–57.

Haq, Abdul. 2004. *English-Urdu, Urdu-English Combined Dictionary.* New Delhi: Star.

Haq, Farhat. 2019. *Sharia and the State in Pakistan: Blasphemy Politics.* Abingdon, UK: Routledge.

Haraway, Donna J. 2008. *When Species Meet.* Minneapolis: University of Minnesota Press.

Harriss, Kaveri. 2010. "Gender and the Poetics of Chronic Ill-Health: British Pakistani Experiences." In *Pakistani Women: Multiple Locations and Competing Narratives,* edited by Sadaf Ahmad, 163–93. Karachi: Oxford University Press.

Hegland, Mary. 1998. "The Power Paradox in Muslim Women's Majales: North-West Pakistani Mourning Rituals as Sites of Contestation over Religious Politics, Ethnicity, and Gender." *Signs: Journal of Women in Culture and Society* 23 (2): 391–428.

Hill, Joseph. 2010. "'All Women Are Guides': Sufi Leadership and Womanhood among Taalibe Baay in Senegal." *Journal of Religion in Africa* 40 (4): 375–412.

Hoffman-Ladd, Valerie J. 1992. "Mysticism and Sexuality in Sufi Thought and Life." *Mystics Quarterly* 18 (3): 82–93.

Hollywood, Amy. 2004. "Gender, Agency, and the Divine in Religious Historiography." *Journal of Religion* 84 (4): 514–28.

Ibad, Umber bin. 2019. *Sufi Shrines and the Pakistani State: The End of Religious Pluralism.* London: I. B. Tauris. Ebook.

Ingold, Tim. 2000. *The Perception of the Environment: Essays on Livelihood, Dwelling and Skill*. London: Routledge.

Ingold, Tim. 2016. *Lines: A Brief History*. London: Routledge.

Jaffer, Amen. 2017. "Spiritualising Marginality: Sufi Concepts and the Politics of Identity in Pakistan." *Society and Culture in South Asia* 3 (2): 175–97.

Jaffer, Amen. 2018. "A Drama of Saintly Devotion: Performing Ecstasy and Status at the Shaam-e-Qalandar Festival in Pakistan." *TDR: The Drama Review* 62 (4): 23–40.

Jahangir, Junaid, and Hussein Abdullatif. 2016. *Islamic Law and Muslim Same-Sex Unions*. Lanham, MD: Lexington.

Jalal, Ayesha. 2000. *Self and Sovereignty: Individual and Community in South Asian Islam since 1850*. London: Routledge.

Kalir, Barak. 2006. "The Field of Work and the Work of the Field: Conceptualising an Anthropological Research Engagement." *Social Anthropology* 14 (2): 235–46.

Kandhro, Anwar S. 2011. *Tazkirah Qalandar Lal Shahbaz*. Karachi: Department of Culture, Government of Sindh.

Kandiyoti, Deniz. 1998. "Bargaining with Patriarchy." *Gender and Society* 2 (3): 274–90.

Karamustafa, Ahmet. 2006. *God's Unruly Friends: Dervish Groups in the Islamic Later Middle Period, 1200–1550*. Oxford: Oneworld.

Karamustafa, Ahmet. 2015. "Antinomian Sufis." In *The Cambridge Companion to Sufism*, edited by Lloyd Ridgeon, 101–25. New York: Cambridge University Press.

Kasmani, Omar. 2012. "Of Difference and Discontinuity: Gender and Embodiment among Fakirs of Sehwan Sharif." *Oriente Moderno* 92 (2): 439–57.

Kasmani, Omar. 2015. "Women [Un-]Like Women: The Question of Spiritual Authority among Female Fakirs of Sehwan Sharif." In *Devotional Islam in Contemporary South Asia: Shrines, Journeys and Wanderers*, edited by Michel Boivin and Rémy Delage, 47–62. Abingdon, UK: Routledge.

Kasmani, Omar. 2016a. "Fakir Her-Stories: Women's Spiritual Careers and the Limit of the Masculine in Pakistan." *TRAFO—Blog for Transregional Research*, May 26. https://trafo.hypotheses.org/4243.

Kasmani, Omar. 2016b. "Off the Lines: Fakir Orientations of Gender, Body, and Space in Sehwan Sharif, Pakistan." PhD diss., Freie Universität Berlin.

Kasmani, Omar. 2017a. "Audible Specters: The Sticky Shia Sonics of Sehwan." *History of Emotions: Insights into Research*, October 2017. doi:10.14280/08241.54.

Kasmani, Omar. 2017b. "Grounds of Becoming: Living among the Dead in Sehwan Sharif, Pakistan." *Culture and Religion* 18 (2): 72–89.

Kasmani, Omar. 2017c. "May Your Boats Come Ashore." *Friday Times*, February 24.

Kasmani, Omar. 2019a. "Pilgrimages of the Dream: On Wings of State in Sehwan Sharif, Pakistan." In *Muslim Pilgrimage in the Modern World*, edited by Babak Rahimi and Peyman Eshagi, 134–48. Chapel Hill: University of North Carolina Press.

Kasmani, Omar. 2019b. "Thin Attachments: Writing Berlin in Scenes of Daily Loves." *Capacious: Journal for Emerging Affect Inquiry* 1 (4): 34–53.

Kasmani, Omar. 2021. "Futuring Trans* in Pakistan: Timely Reflections." *TSQ: Transgender Studies Quarterly* 8 (1): 96–112.

Kasmani, Omar, Nasima Selim, Hansjörg Dilger, and Dominik Mattes. 2020. "Introduction: Elsewhere Affects: Politics of Engagement across Religious Lifeworlds." *Religion and Society* 11 (1): 92–104.

Khan, Arsalan. 2016. "Islam and Pious Sociality: The Ethics of Hierarchy in the Tablighi Jamaat in Pakistan." *Social Analysis* 60 (4): 96–113.

Khan, Arsalan. 2018. "Pious Masculinity, Ethical Reflexivity, and Moral Order in an Islamic Piety Movement in Pakistan." *Anthropological Quarterly* 91 (1): 53–78.

Khan, Dominique S. 2008. "Jhulelal and the Identity of Indian Sindhis." In *Sindh through History and Representations: French Contributions to Sindhi Studies*, edited by Michel Boivin, 72–81. Karachi: Oxford University Press.

Khan, Naveeda. 2006. "Of Children and Jinn: An Inquiry into an Uncertain Friendship during Uncertain Times." *Cultural Anthropology* 21 (2): 234–64.

Khan, Naveeda. 2012. *Muslim Becoming: Aspiration and Skepticism in Pakistan*. Durham, NC: Duke University Press.

Khandelwal, Meena. 2004. *Women in Ochre Robes: Gendering Hindu Renunciation*. Albany: State University of New York Press.

Khuhro, Hamida. 1981. *Sind through the Centuries: Proceedings of an International Seminar Held in Karachi in Spring 1975 by the Department of Culture, Government of Sind*. Karachi: Oxford University Press.

Kinsley, David. 1981. "Devotion as an Alternative to Marriage in the Lives of Some Hindu Women Devotees." In *Tradition and Modernity in Bhakti Movements*, edited by Jayant Lele, 83–93. Leiden: Brill.

Knappett, Carl. 2004. "The Affordances of Things: A Post-Gibsonian Perspective on the Relationality of Mind and Matter." In *Rethinking Materiality: The Engagement of Mind with the Material World*, edited by Elizabeth DeMarrais, Chris Gosden, and Colin Renfrew, 43–51. Cambridge: Cambridge University Press.

Knott, Kim. 2005. "Insider/Outsider Perspectives." In *The Routledge Companion to the Study of Religion*, edited by John Hinnells, 243–58. New York: Routledge.

Knott, Kim. 2008. "Spatial Theory and the Study of Religion." *Religion Compass* 2 (6): 1102–16.

Kugle, Scott. 2003. "The Heart of Ritual Is the Body: Anatomy of an Islamic Devotional Manual of the Nineteenth Century, Haji Imdadullah's *Zia al-Qulub*." *Journal of Religious Studies* 17 (1): 42–60.

Kugle, Scott. 2007. *Sufis and Saints' Bodies: Mysticism, Corporeality, and Sacred Power in Islam*. Chapel Hill: University of North Carolina Press.

Kugle, Scott. 2010a. "Dancing with Khusro: Gender Ambiguities and Poetic Performance in a Delhi *Dargah*." In *Rethinking Islamic Studies: From Orientalism to Cosmopolitanism*, edited by Richard C. Martin and Carl W. Ernst, 245–65. Columbia: University of South Carolina Press.

Kugle, Scott. 2010b. *Homosexuality in Islam: Critical Reflection on Gay, Lesbian, and Transgender Muslims*. Oxford: Oneworld.

Kugle, Scott. 2014. *Living Out Islam: Voices of Gay, Lesbian, and Transgender Muslims*. New York: New York University Press.

Kurin, Richard. 1983. "The Structure of Blessedness at a Muslim Shrine in Pakistan." *Middle Eastern Studies* 19 (3): 312–25.

Lamb, Sarah. 2005. "The Politics of Dirt and Gender: Bodily Techniques in Bengali India." In *Dress, Undress, and Difference: Critical Perspectives on the Body's Surface*, edited by Adeline Masquelier, 213–32. Bloomington: Indiana University Press.

Lambek, Michael. 1993. *Knowledge and Practice in Mayotte: Local Discourses of Islam, Sorcery, and Spirit Possession*. Toronto: University of Toronto Press.

Landell-Mills, Samuel. 1992. "An Anthropological Account of Islamic Holy-Men in Bangladesh." PhD diss., University of London.

Lindholm, Charles. 1998. "Prophets and *Pirs*: Charismatic Islam in the Middle East and South Asia." In *Embodying Charisma: Modernity, Locality and the Performance of Emotion in Sufi Cults*, edited by Pnina Werbner and Helene Basu, 209–32. London: Routledge.

Loughlin, Gerard, ed. 2007. *Queer Theology: Rethinking the Western Body*. Malden, UK: Blackwell.

Mahmood, Saba. 2005. *Politics of Piety: Islamic Revival and the Feminist Subject*. Princeton, NJ: Princeton University Press.

Malamud, Margaret. 1994. "Sufi Organizations and Structures of Authority in Medieval Nishapur." *International Journal of Middle East Studies* 26 (3): 427–42.

Malamud, Margaret. 1996. "Gender and Spiritual Self-Fashioning: The Master-Disciple Relationship in Classical Sufism." *Journal of the American Academy of Religion* 64 (1): 89–117.

Malik, Jamal. 1990. "Waqf in Pakistan: Change in Traditional Institutions." *Die Welt des Islams* 30 (1/4): 63–97.

Malik, Jamal. 1998. "The Literary Critique of Islamic Popular Religion in the Guise of Traditional Mysticism, or the Abused Woman." In *Embodying Charisma: Modernity, Locality and the Performance of Emotion in Sufi Cults*, edited by Pnina Werbner and Helene Basu, 187–208. London: Routledge.

Manjhi, Muhammad A. 2010. *Qalandar Lal Shahbaz: Ahwal 'ayn Asar* [Qalandar Lal Shahbaz: Account and traces]. Karachi: Department of Culture, Government of Sindh.

Maqsood, Ammara. 2017. *The New Pakistani Middle Class*. Cambridge, MA: Harvard University Press.

Marsden, Magnus. 2005. *Living Islam: Muslim Religious Experience in Pakistan's North-West Frontier*. Cambridge: University of Cambridge Press.

Massey, Doreen. 1999. *Power-Geometries and the Politics of Space-Time*. Heidelberg: University of Heidelberg.

Massey, Doreen. 2005. *For Space*. London: Sage.

Mayer, Adrian C. 1967. "*Pir* and *Murshid*: An Aspect of Religious Leadership in West Pakistan." *Journal of Middle Eastern Studies* 3 (2): 160–69.

Mayne, Peter. 1956. *The Saints of Sind*. London: John Murray.

Mernissi, Fatima. 1977. "Women, Saints, and Sanctuaries." *Signs: Journal of Women in Culture and Society* 3 (1): 101–22.

Metcalf, Barbara. 1987. "Islamic Arguments in Contemporary Pakistan." In *Islam and the Political Economy of Meaning: Comparative Studies of Muslim Discourse*, edited by William Roff, 131–59. London: Croom Helm.

Metcalf, Barbara. 1998. "Women and Men in a Contemporary Pietist Movement: The Case of the Tablighi Jama'at." In *Appropriating Gender: Women's Activism and Politicized Religion in South Asia*, edited by Patricia Jeffery and Amrita Basu, 107–21. New York: Routledge.

Metcalf, Barbara. 2002. "Traditionalist Islamic Activism: Deoband, Tablighis and Talibs." *ISIM Papers*, 1–24. https://openaccess.leidenuniv.nl/handle/1887/10068.

Mian, Ali Altaf. 2019. "Genres of Desire: The Erotic in Deobandī Islam." *History of Religions* 59 (2): 108–45.

Mir, Farina. 2006. "Genre and Devotion in Punjabi Popular Narratives: Rethinking Cultural and Religious Syncretism." *Comparative Studies in Society and History* 48 (3): 727–58.

Mittermaier, Amira. 2008. "(Re)Imagining Space: Dreams and Saint Shrines in Egypt." In *Dimensions of Locality: Muslim Saints, Their Place and Space*, edited by Georg Stauth and Samuli Schielke, 47–66. Bielefeld: Transcript.

Mittermaier, Amira. 2011. *Dreams That Matter: Egyptian Landscapes of the Imagination*. Berkeley: University of California Press.

Mittermaier, Amira. 2012. "Dreams from Elsewhere: Muslim Subjectivities beyond the Trope of Self-Cultivation." *Journal of the Royal Anthropological Institute* 18 (2): 247–65.

Moin, A. Azfar. 2015. "Sovereign Violence: Temple Destruction in India and Shrine Desecration in Iran and Central Asia." *Comparative Studies in Society and History* 57 (2): 467–96.

Mooney, Nicola. 2010. "Lowly Shoes on Lowly Feet: Some Jat Sikh Women's Views on Gender and Equality." In *Sikhism and Women: History, Texts and Experience*, edited by Doris R. Jakobsh, 156–86. New Delhi: Oxford University Press.

Moser, Benjamin. 2014. "In the Sontag Archives." *New Yorker*, January 30. http://www.newyorker.com/online/blogs/books/2014/01/in-the-sontag-archives.html.

Muñoz, José Esteban. 2009. *Cruising Utopia: The Then and There of Queer Futurity*. New York: New York University Press.

Najmabadi, Afsaneh. 2014. *Professing Selves: Transsexuality and Same-Sex Desire in Contemporary Iran*. Durham, NC: Duke University Press.

Namkin, Yusuf. (1634) 2009. *Tarikh Mazhar Shahjahani*. Translated by Sayyid M. A. Naqvi. Jamshoro: Sindhi Adabi Board.

Nanda, Serena. 1999. *Neither Man nor Woman: The Hijras of India*. 2nd ed. Toronto: Wadsworth.

Narayan, Kirin. 1993. "How Native Is a 'Native' Anthropologist?" *American Anthropologist*, new ser., 95 (3): 671–86.

Norman, Donald A. 1988. *The Psychology of Everyday Things*. New York: Basic Books.

Norman, Donald A. 1999. "Affordances, Conventions, and Design." *Interactions* 6 (3): 38–41.

Ortis, Delphine. 2017. "From Potent Dead to Potent Places? Reflections on Muslim Saint Shrines in South Asia." *Asia Pacific Journal of Anthropology* 18 (5): 483–98. doi:10.1080/14442213.2017.1373845.

Ortis, Delphine. 2019. "La tombe: Miroir de la destinée des morts? Analyse de différents espaces funéraires dans une ville de pèlerinage pakistanaise (Sehwan Sharīf, Sindh)" [The grave: Mirror of the destiny of the dead? Analysis of different funeral spaces in a Pakistani pilgrimage town (Sehwan Sharif, Sindh)]. *REMMM*, no. 146, 47–70.

Ortis, Delphine. 2020. "Building Up Oneself as an Ascetic in the Shadow of Devotional Artifacts: The Case of the *malang-fuqara* of Pakistan." *Journal of Material Cultures in the Muslim World* 1 (1–2): 314–30.

Pamment, Claire. 2010. "Hijraism: Jostling for a Third Space in Pakistani Politics." *TDR: The Drama Review* 54 (2): 29–50.

Pamment, Claire. 2019a. "The Hijra Clap in Neo Liberal Hands: Performing Trans Rights in Pakistan." *TDR: The Drama Review* 63 (1): 141–50.

Pamment, Claire. 2019b. "Performing Piety in Pakistan's Transgender Rights Movement." *TSQ: Transgender Studies Quarterly* 6 (3): 297–314.

Parwani, Lata. 2010. "Myths of Jhuley Lal: Deconstructing a Sindhi Cultural Icon." In *Interpreting the Sindhi World: Essays on Society and History*, edited by Michel Boivin and Matthew Cook, 1–27. Karachi: Oxford University Press.

Passow, Till, dir. 2005. *Mast Qalandar*. HFF Potsdam. Film.

Pechilis, Karen. 2012. "The Female Guru: Guru, Gender and the Path of Personal Experience." In *The Guru in South Asia: New Interdisciplinary Perspectives*, edited by Jacob Copeman and Aya Ikegame, 113–32. London: Routledge.

Pemberton, Kelly. 2006. "Women *Pir*s, Saintly Succession, and Spiritual Guidance in South Asian Sufism." *Muslim World* 96 (1): 61–87.

Pemberton, Kelly. 2010. *Women Mystics and Sufi Shrines in India*. Columbia: University of South Carolina Press.

Pfeffer, Georg. 1995. "Manliness in the Punjab: Male Sexuality and the Khusra." *Sociologus* 45 (1): 26–39.

Philippon, Alix. 2016. "An Ambiguous and Contentious Politicization of Sufi Shrines and Pilgrimages in Pakistan." In *Devotional Islam in Contemporary South Asia: Shrines, Journeys and Wanderers*, edited by Michel Boivin and Rémy Delage, 174–89. Abingdon, UK: Routledge.

Pinto, Desiderio. 2006. *Piri-Muridi Relationship: A Study of the Nizamuddin Dargah*. Delhi: Manohar.

Povinelli, Elizabeth A. 2006. *The Empire of Love: Toward a Theory of Intimacy, Genealogy, and Carnality*. Durham, NC: Duke University Press.

Puwar, Nirmal. 2004. *Space Invaders: Race, Gender and Bodies Out of Place*. Oxford: Berg.

Qureshi, Regula Burckhardt. 1986. *Sufi Music of India and Pakistan: Sound, Context and Meaning in Qawwali*. Cambridge: Cambridge University Press.

Raj, Selva, and William Harman, eds. 2006. *Dealing with Deities: The Ritual Vow in South Asia*. Albany: State University of New York Press.

Raju, Saraswati. 2011. *Gendered Geographies: Space and Place in South Asia*. New Delhi: Oxford.

Ramanujan, A. K. 1982. "On Women Saints." In *The Divine Consort: Rādhā and the Goddesses of India*, edited by John Stratton Hawley and Donna Marie Wulff, 316–24. Berkeley: Graduate Theological Union.

Ramaswamy, Vijaya. 1996. *Divinity and Deviance: Women in Virasaivism*. Delhi: Oxford University Press.

Ramberg, Lucinda. 2014. *Given to the Goddess: South Indian Devadasis and the Sexuality of Religion*. Durham, NC: Duke University Press.

Ramberg, Lucinda. 2016. "Backward Futures and Pasts Forward: Queer Time, Sexual Politics, and Dalit Religiosity in South India." GLQ 22 (2): 223–48.

Redding, Jeffrey A. 2015. "From 'She-Males' to 'Unix': Transgender Rights and the Productive Paradoxes of Pakistani Policing." In *Regimes of Legality: Ethnography of Criminal Cases in South Asia*, edited by Daniela Berti and Devika Bordia, 258–89. Delhi: Oxford University Press.

Reddy, Gayatri. 2005. *With Respect to Sex: Negotiating Hijra Identity in South India*. Chicago: University of Chicago Press.

Renard, John. 2008. *Friends of God: Islamic Images of Piety, Commitment, and Servanthood*. Berkeley: University of California Press.

Renard, John. 2009. *Tales of God's Friends: Islamic Hagiography in Translation*. Berkeley: University of California Press.

Rheinberger, Hans-Jörg. 1994. "Experimental Systems: Historiality, Narration, and Deconstruction." *Science in Context* 7 (1): 65–81.

Ridgeon, Lloyd. 2010. "Shaggy or Shaved? The Symbolism of Hair among Persian Qalandar Sufis." *Iran and the Caucasus* 14 (2): 233–63.

Ring, Laura. 2006. *Zenana: Everyday Peace in a Karachi Apartment Building*. Bloomington: Indiana University Press.

Rodman, Margaret. 2003. "Empowering Place: Multilocality and Multivocality." In *The Anthropology of Place and Space: Locating Culture*, edited by Setha M. Low and Denise Lawrence-Zúñiga, 204–23. Oxford: Blackwell.

Rozehnal, Robert. 2007. *Islamic Sufism Unbound: Politics and Piety in Twenty-First Century Pakistan*. New York: Palgrave Macmillan.

Ruffle, Karen. 2011. *Gender, Sainthood, and Everyday Practice in South Asian Shī'ism*. Chapel Hill: University of North Carolina Press.

Safi, Omid. 2000. "Bargaining with Baraka: Persian Sufism, 'Mysticism,' and Premodern Politics." *Muslim World* 90 (3–4): 259–87.

Salgado, Nirmala S. 2013. *Buddhist Nuns and Gendered Practice: In Search of the Female Renunciant*. New York: Oxford University Press.

Saniotis, Arthur. 2004. "Tales of Mastery: Spirit Familiar in Sufis' Religious Imagination." *Ethos* 32 (3): 397–411.

Sarkar, Mahua. 2012. "Between Craft and Method: Meaning and Inter-subjectivity in Oral History Analysis." *Journal of Historical Sociology* 25 (4): 578–600.

Schaefer, Donovan O. 2015. *Religious Affects: Animality, Evolution, and Power.* Durham, NC: Duke University Press.

Scherer, Bee. 2017. "Queer Thinking Religion: Queering Religious Paradigms." *Scholar and Feminist Online* 14 (2).

Schielke, Samuli. 2008. "Policing Ambiguity: Muslim Saints-Day Festivals and the Moral Geography of Public Space in Egypt." *American Ethnologist* 35 (4): 539–52.

Schielke, Samuli. 2010. "Second Thoughts about the Anthropology of Islam, or How to Make Sense of Grand Schemes in Everyday Life." ZMO Working Papers, no. 2. Berlin. https://d-nb.info/1019243724/34.

Schimmel, Annemarie. 2003. *Mystical Dimensions of Islam.* Lahore: Sang-e-Meel.

Schippert, Claudia. 2005. "Queer Theory and the Study of Religion." *Rever: Revista de Estudos da Religião* 5 (4): 90–99.

Schippert, Claudia. 2011. "Implications of Queer Theory for the Study of Religion and Gender: Entering the Third Decade." *Religion and Gender* 1 (1): 66–84.

Sedgwick, Eve Kosofsky. 2003. *Touching Feeling: Affect, Pedagogy, Performativity.* Durham, NC: Duke University Press.

Sehwani, Khair-Muhammad, ed. 2009. *Sehwan Sadyan Khaan* [Sehwan through the centuries]. Sehwan, Pakistan: Murad.

Sehwani, Nazir. 2009. "Qalandar Jo Dadlo: Sakhi Qalandar Bodlo" [The beloved of Qalandar: The generous Qalandar Bodlo]. *Hilal-e-Pakistan*, August 12.

Shaikh, Sa'diyya. 2012. *Sufi Narratives of Intimacy: Ibn 'Arabi, Gender and Sexuality.* Chapel Hill: University of North Carolina Press.

Sharpe, Christina. 2016. *In the Wake: On Blackness and Being.* Durham, NC: Duke University Press.

Shauq, Nawaz Ali. 2011. *Qalandar, Sufi 'ayn Malamati* [Qalandar: Sufi and Malamati]. Karachi: Department of Culture, Government of Sindh.

Sheffield, Tricia. 2008. "Performing Jesus: A Queer Counternarrative of Embodied Transgression." *Theology and Sexuality* 1 (3): 233–58.

Simone, AbdouMaliq. 2013. "Endurance, not Survival." *Cityscapes Magazine,* June 28. https://cityscapesmagazine.com/index.php?p=articles/endurance-not-survival.

Slaby, Jan. 2020. "The Weight of History: From Heidegger to Afro-Pessimism." In *Phenomenology as Performative Exercise,* edited by Lucilla Guidi and Thomas Rentsch, 173–95. Leiden: Brill.

Soares, Benjamin, and Filippo Osella. 2009. "Islam, Politics, Anthropology." *Journal of the Royal Anthropological Institute* 15 (1): 1–23.

Sökefeld, Martin. 1999. "Debating Self, Identity, and Culture in Anthropology." *Current Anthropology* 40 (4): 417–48.

Spadola, Emilio. 2019. "On Mediation and Magnetism: Or, Why Destroy Saint

Shrines." In *Muslim Pilgrimage in the Modern World*, edited by Babak Rahimi and Peyman Eshagi, 223–39. Chapel Hill: University of North Carolina Press.

Stauth, Georg, and Samuli Schielke, eds. 2008. *Dimensions of Locality: Muslim Saints, Their Place and Space.* Bielefeld: Transcript.

Stewart, Kathleen. 2010. "Worlding Refrains." In *The Affect Theory Reader*, edited by Melissa Gregg and Gregory Seigworth, 339–53. Durham, NC: Duke University Press.

Stewart, Kathleen. 2014. "Tactile Compositions." In *Objects and Materials: A Routledge Companion*, edited by Penny Harvey, Eleanor Conlin Casella, Gillian Evans, Hannah Knox, Christine McLean, Elizabeth B. Silva, Nicholas Thoburn, and Kath Woodward, 119–27. New York: Routledge.

Stoler, Ann Laura. 2010. *Carnal Knowledge and Imperial Power: Race and the Intimate in Colonial Rule.* Berkeley: University of California Press.

Strothmann, Linus. 2012. "Managing Piety at the Shrine of Data Ganj Bukhsh, Lahore, Pakistan." PhD diss., Freie Universität Berlin.

Strothmann, Linus. 2016. *Managing Piety: The Shrine of Data Ganj Bakhsh.* Karachi: Oxford University Press.

Syed, Ghulam M. 2012. "'Urs je moq'ey te pesh kayal khutbo" [Address delivered on the occasion of 'Urs]. *Dam Mast Qalandar Magazine*, July, no. 3, 3–5.

Taneja, Anand. 2017. *Jinnealogy: Time, Islam, and Ecological Thought in the Medieval Ruins of Delhi.* Stanford, CA: Stanford University Press.

Taylor, Max. 2012. Introduction to *Terrorism and Affordance*, edited by Max Taylor and P. M. Currie, 1–16. London: Continuum.

Terry, Jennifer, and Jaqueline Urla. 1995. *Deviant Bodies: Critical Perspectives on Science and Difference in Popular Culture.* Bloomington: Indiana University Press.

Thajib, Ferdiansyah. 2019. "Inhabiting Difference: The Affective Lives of Indonesian Muslim Queers." PhD diss., Freie Universität Berlin.

Troll, Christian, ed. 1989. *Muslim Shrines in India: Their Character, History and Significance.* New Delhi: Oxford University Press.

Tweed, Thomas. 2006. *Crossing and Dwelling: A Theory of Religion.* Cambridge, MA: Harvard University Press.

Watenpaugh, Heghnar Zeitlian. 2005. "Deviant Dervishes: Space, Gender, and the Construction of Antinomian Piety in Ottoman Aleppo." *International Journal of Middle Eastern Studies* 37 (4): 535–65.

Weiss, Anita. 2010. "Within the Walls: Home-Based Work in Lahore." In *Pakistani Women: Multiple Locations and Competing Narratives*, edited by Sadaf Ahmad, 12–24. Karachi: Oxford University Press.

Werbner, Pnina. 1998. "Sufi Regional Cults in South Asia and Indonesia: Towards a Comparative Analysis." In *Dimensions of Locality: Muslim Saints, Their Place and Space*, edited by Georg Stauth and Samuli Schielke, 25–46. Bielefeld: Transcript.

Werbner, Pnina. 2003. *Pilgrims of Love: The Anthropology of a Global Sufi Cult.* London: C. Hurst.

Werbner, Pnina, and Helene Basu, eds. 1998. *Embodying Charisma: Modernity, Locality and the Performance of Emotion in Sufi Cults*. London: Routledge.

Werth, Lukas. 1998. "The Saint Who Disappeared: Saints of the Wilderness in Pakistani Village Shrines." In *Embodying Charisma: Modernity, Locality and the Performance of Emotion in Sufi Cults*, edited by Pnina Werbner and Helene Basu, 77–92. London: Routledge.

White, Heather. 2017. "Protestant Closets and Queer Histories: Notes from an Archive-in-Process." *Scholar and Feminist Online* 14 (2). https://sfonline.barnard.edu/queer-religion/protestant-closets-and-queer-histories-notes-from-an-archive-in-process/.

Wilcox, Melissa M. 2009. *Queer Women and Religious Individualism*. Bloomington: Indiana University Press.

Wilson, Ara. 2012. "Intimacy: A Useful Category of Transnational Analysis." In *The Global and the Intimate: Feminism in Our Time*, edited by Geraldine Pratt and Victoria Rosner, 31–56. New York: Columbia University Press.

Wilson, Ara. 2016. "The Infrastructure of Intimacy." *Signs: Journal of Women in Culture and Society* 41 (2): 247–80.

Wolf, Richard. 2006. "The Poetics of 'Sufi' Practice: Drumming, Dancing, and Complex Agency at Madho Lal Husain (and Beyond)." *American Ethnologist* 33 (2): 246–68.

Wolper, Ethel Sara. 2003. *Cities and Saints: Sufism and the Transformation of Urban Space in Medieval Anatolia*. Philadelphia: Pennsylvania State University Press.

Young, Nikki. 2017. "Queer Studies and Religion: Methodologies of Freedom." *Scholar and Feminist Online* 14 (2). https://sfonline.barnard.edu/queer-religion/queer-studies-and-religion-methodologies-of-freedom/.

Yürekli, Zeynep. 2012. "Writing Down the Feats and Setting Up the Scene: Hagiographers and Architectural Patrons in the Age of Empires." In *Sufism and Society: Arrangements of the Mystical in the Muslim World, 1200–1800*, edited by John Curry and Erik Ohlander, 94–119. New York: Routledge.

Zaidi, Saima. 2009. *Mazaar Bazaar: Design and Visual Culture in Pakistan*. Karachi: Oxford University Press.

Zaman, Muhammad Qasim. 1998. "Sectarianism in Pakistan: The Radicalization of Shi'i and Sunni Identities." *Modern Asian Studies* 32 (3): 689–716.

Zayed, Ahmed A. 2008. "Saints (*awliya'*), Public Places and Modernity in Egypt." In *Dimensions of Locality: Muslim Saints, Their Place and Space*, edited by Georg Stauth and Samuli Schielke, 103–23. Bielefeld: Transcript.

fakir dwellings: Baba-Akram, 41, *42*, 49, 57–58; Bibi, 135, *136*, 143, 148; the graveyard, 147–48, 179n23; Jamal, 143, 148

fakirs, 2, 165n1, 181; affective sharpness, 22; affective textures, 18; audio recordings, 29; celibacy, 117–18, 121, 125–26, 176nn19–20; difficulties, 14; disciple-master relationships, 102–3, 126–28, 182; disorientation, 14, 100, 105, 134; Dost, 108, 118–26; durbar places, 80; epistemologies, 133; futurity, 38, 155; gendered assumptions about, 86; gendered relationship to masters, 127–28; gender politics, 24; gender-variant, 169n51, 177n3; hauntologies, 150; and historically distant figures, 154; infrastructures of the imaginal, 56; intoxication, 33; inward experience manifestation, 76; Islamic norms, 18; and the *kafi* system, 72; knowledge of spirits, 69–70; labor, 34, 105, 114, 138, 142, 148; and Lal, 12–13, 16–18, 22–23; lines, 8, 14, 93, 96, 98–106; marriage, 126, 177nn32–33; Mastani, 70–72, 80, 91; miracle retellings, 46; narrativization practices, 148, 150; objects, 27, 62, 108, 120, 177n26; and place, 151; poverty, 8; *qalandar* influences, 17–18; recognizability, 24; sainthood potential, 10; versus sayyids, 71, 73; in Sehwan, 7–9; social status, 8–9; spatial practices, 147–48, 150, 162; storytelling, 31; submission to masters, 127–28; unstraight affordances, 104; worlding, 132–33, 150–51, 154, 160. *See also* Amma; Baba-Akram; *bhes* (dis/guise); Bibi; Bodlo; fakir dwellings; fakir women; Jamal; lodges (*kafis*); Murad; saintly intimacy; Zaheda

fakir women: *bhes* (dis/guise), 91; career advancement, 93; celibacy, 79, 95, 117–18, 175n7; chosen-by-Lal narratives, 9, 69, 75–77, 94–95, 177n3; endurance, 33, 61, 103–6; exclusions faced by, 61, 72–73, 82; family relationships, 75, 118; gender-based public scrutiny, 105; invasive labors of place, 142–43; lack of support, 62, 73; menstruation, 77; narrativization practices, 31, 33, 42, 56, 75–76, 93; versus other women, 80, 174n29; postsexual self-presentation, 78; prejudices against, 94; prevalence, 24; purity instructions, 79; saintly intimacy, 80; social conflict roles, 77; and spirits, 73–74; spiritual authority, 31, 73. *See also* Amma; Bibi; Zaheda

faqirs. See fakirs

Flood, Finbarr B., 20

flower-in-milk tropes, 146, 178n17

four friends (mystics), 45, 171n17

futurity, 8, 166n13; fakirs, 38, 105, 155; intimacy, 20; queer, 27; saintly intimacy, 19, 57, 159–60

gender: assumptions about fakirs, 86; *'ata* (male charisma) versus *'amal* (women fakir acts), 72–73; celibacy politics, 118–19; and saintly intimacy, 24, 80, 121; spatial politics, 61, 90; spirit possessions, 70; spiritual guides, 86; Virasaivite saints, 94–95; Zaheda's views, 94–95, 121. *See also* gender issues; gender-variant persons

gendered segregation and exclusion: durbars, 61; innovative responses, 73; lodges, 72, 82; menstruation, 77, 174n25; ritual drumming performances, 61; shrines, 60–61; spiritual careers, 78–79, 174n26

gender issues: assumptions about *pir*s, 86; disadvantages based on, 72–73; fakirs' relationships to masters, 127–28; public scrutiny of women, 105; state administration of shrines, 64, 82. *See also* gendered segregation and exclusion

gender-variant persons, 50, 169n51, 171n24, 177n3. *See also* Baba-Akram

Gibson, James, 15–16

governance: infrastructures, 39–40; queer surpluses, 57; saints, 12, 34, 161; shrines, 33; *wali*s, 12. *See also* state administration of shrines graveyard: distance from the shrine, 142; dwelling in, 147–48, 179n23; hauntology, 134, 143–45, 150; imagination and materiality, 142; relationship to history, 149; saintly intimacy, 149; stories of, 130–32, 134; as thin place, 134, 149; worlding, 150. *See also* Bibi; Jamal

Green, Nile, 43, 51, 169n56, 170n10

Grima, Benedicta, 78

Haraway, Donna, 168n48

Harrison, Paul, 133

Harriss, Kaveri, 75

hauntologies, 134, 143–45, 150

haziri, 70–71, 182

Hazrat Usman Marwandi. *See* Lal

healers. See *pirs*

Hijaz, 138

Hinduism: Lal, 19, 40, 45, 174n28; in Sehwan, 18–19, 167n36, 168n38; shrine of Sehwan, 18–19, 55, 65, 67, 146, 172n34

Ibad, Umber bin, 52

Ibn al-ʿArabi, 37

imaginal, 37, 40, 56

Indus River, 145, 178n11

infrastructure, 39–40, 44–45, 51, 53, 56, 172n31

Ingold, Tim, 14

intersex persons (*khwaja-sara*), 24, 56–57, 61, 72, 171n24. *See also* Baba-Akram

intimacy, 1, 22; affective relations, 1–2; affordances, 16; consequences, 168n48; dis/closures, 15, 21, 155, 159; dreams, 38; ethics, 23; felt and enfleshed, 1, 16, 18, 23, 132, 149, 154–55; futurity, 20; maintenance requirements, 21; with the past, 150–51; plural orientations, 150–51; public, 19, 23; *qurb* (closeness), 1, 9–10, 21–22, 86, 183; relationality, 20; sexuality, 20; *suhbet* (companionship, sex), 20, 152, 155–56, 158–59; as unfolding, 1, 7, 10, 19, 29, 129, 151, 161–62; *uns* (spiritual love), 20; unstraight affordances, 16, 33, 80, 87, 121, 129, 162. *See also* saintly intimacy

intimate corporealities, 162

Islam: Ahl-e Hadis reform movement, 7, 166n12; anthropology of, 28, 163; disputes, 6–7; fundamentalist, 180n10; same-sex desire, 158; *sirat-e-mustaqim*, 167n28; Sunni, 7; transgressive desire, 158, 180n9

Islamic studies, 26–27, 156, 158, 169n53

Jamal (fakir): demons, 131–32; dream-visions, 141–42; dwelling, 143, 148; fairy encounters, 131, 137–38, 141; and the graveyard, 137–38, 141–42, 148–49, 151; hidden grave discoveries, 137–38, 141; narrativization practices, 143; relationship with Bibi, 135, 139–40; storytelling performances, 130–32; and the suicide attack on the shrine, 143

Jamal al-Din Savi, 45

Juman-Jatti, 145, 178n10

kafis. *See* lodges

Karamustafa, Ahmet, 17, 177n26

Karbala, 27, 41, 74, 88, 138–39, 176n14, 181, 183

Khan, Naveeda, 6, 26

khanaqah. *See* lodges

Khizr, 145, 178n9

khwaja-sara. *See* intersex persons

Koh-Qaf mountains, 177n2

Kugle, Scott, 158, 180nn9–10

Lakkiyari, 65–67

Lal (Laʿl Shahbaz Qalandar), 3; and Ali, 139; authority, 147; Baba's dream-visions, 37–38, 42–43, 46–50, 134; and Bodlo, 3–4, 110, 112, 144; celibacy, 146; fakir relations with, 12–13, 16–18, 22–23; film representations, 44; grove associated with (Lal-bagh), 41, 145; Hinduism, 19, 40, 45, 174n28; history, 18–19, 45–46, 148, 167n34, 171nn14–16; Indus river, 145; inheritance, 65; Jhule Lal, 19, 145; legend of the fortress, 112, 144, 178n6; legends (other), 144–48, 178n16; marriage, 174n28; miracle retellings, 46; miracles, 139; name, 18, 165n5, 167n33; as *qalandar*, 3, 17, 38, 40, 45–46; red, 47; and Sehwan, 133, 148;

Shi'i heritage, 18, 45–46; Shi'i popular-
ity, 40; sites associated with, 145–46,
178n7; songs praising, 40–41, 44, 46,
171n12; winged form, 36–37, 40, 44.
See also shrine of Sehwan
La'l Shahbaz Qalandar. *See* Lal
Lamb, Sarah, 77, 174n25
lodges (*kafi*s), 72, 109, 182; bonds of
dependence, 114; custodians, 72,
113–14, 127n32, 174n16, 183; gendered
exclusion, 72, 82; initiation rituals, 116,
126–27; male social obligations and
support, 109, 114; sayyid control, 72,
114, 174n16; Sehwan system, 110–11.
See also Bodlo-kafi lodge
love, 20–22, 168n45

Malamud, Margaret, 128
Malik, Jamal, 51
Malik, Veena, 36, 37
marriage: Amma's experiences, 69, 77, 79,
174n27; Bibi's experiences, 135, 140–41;
Bodlo-kafi lodge, 125, 128, 177n33;
fakirs generally, 126, 177nn32–33;
Murad's scandal, 107–10, 118–24,
128–29, 134; Zaheda's experiences,
95–97, 102–3
Mastani, 70–72, 80, 91
Mawla (Ali), 118, 139, 182
men, 117, 126, 182; *langot*s (male loin cov-
erings), 117, 126, 182. *See also* gender;
lodges (*kafi*s)
Mian, Ali A., 112, 158, 178n9
Mittermaier, Amira: dreams, 43, 142;
the Elsewhere, 23, 38, 149, 168n47,
177n1; Islamic shrines, 38; saintly
places, 134
Moin, Ali Azfar, 12
Moser, Benjamin, 35
mothers and mother figures, 76–80, 82,
174n25
Murad (fakir), 105, 107; Bodlo lodge, 110,
114–16, 124, 127–28; celibacy, 117;
dreams, 133; evasiveness about his
past, 109, 114, 116; fakir garments,
116–17; marriage scandal, 107–10,
118–24, 128–29, 134; saintly intimacy,
121. *See also* Dost

murid-murshid (disciple-master) relationships, 102–3, 126–28, 182

orientations, 104–5
Ortis, Delphine, 84, 101, 108, 115, 130, 132;
fakirs, 8, 10; lodge initiations, 126–27;
saint bathing ceremony, 173n8

Pakistan, 7, 11, 52, 165n8. *See also* Sehwan,
Pakistan; state administration of
shrines
Pamment, Claire, 157
Patel, Geeta, 28, 154
Pechilis, Karen, 73, 79
Pemberton, Kelly, 90
photography, 3–7, 36–37, 39–40, 156
pious performances, 157
*pir*s (spiritual guides and healers), 71–72,
183; gendered assumptions about, 86;
women, 90
possessions, 69–70, 173n13
public intimacy, 19, 23

*qalandar*s, 17, 167n31, 183; fakir orientation
to, 18; fourfold shave, 50, 92, 171n19;
Lal, 3, 17, 38, 40, 45–46; recognizability, 23–24; sexuality, 117; spatial practices, 179n21
queer, 165n3; affect, 35, 153; in anthro-
pologies of religion, 163; reading
religiously, 2, 28, 34, 152–59; versus
unstraight, 167n27. *See also* unstraight
affordances
queer epistemologies, 26, 28, 152
queer futurity, 27
queer governance surpluses, 57
queer history, 154
queering, 39, 158–59
queer-jacketing, 34, 153, 158–59
queer studies: criticisms of, 28; and religion, 153–54, 157, 179n5; and religious
studies, 25–26, 28, 34, 156, 179n4,
180n13
qurb (closeness), 1, 9–10, 21–22, 86, 183.
See also saintly intimacy

Ramaswamy, Vijaya, 79, 94–95
Ramberg, Lucinda, 157–58, 179n7

photography, 3–4; courtyard, 87–88, 90, 92, 134; and dreams, 43; durbar, 12, *13*, 60; expansions and renovations, 53–55, 65, 85, 88, 172n33; former custodians (*sajjadah-nashin*), 72, 174n16, 183; gender mixing, 61; Hinduism connections, 18–19, 55, 65, 67, 146, 172n34; history, 52–53, 64–65, 173n2; infrastructure, 44–45; monetary offerings, 68, 173n11; morning cleaning ritual, 65–68, 81, 173n6, 173n10; photographs, *54*; plan, *89*; political functions, 12; political patronage, 53; public interest, 44; sayyid power, 69, 72, 173n15; security, 81; Shiʻism, 3, 6, 54–55, 63–64, 87; suicide bombing and aftermath, 11–12, 31, 81–82, 87–88; Sunni inscriptions, 172n35; Sunni worshippers, 63; tomb of Lal, 3, *13*, 20, 55, 60–62, 66–69, *89*, 146; violence, 11–12, 167n19; women at, 8, 11, 166n16; Zaheda, 8–10, 13, 90, 92, 99–100, 106, 134. *See also* saint's fairs (*mela*); state administration of shrines

shrines: Bodlo's, 4, 110–12, 125, 143, 173n9; and dreams, 43; gendered segregation and exclusion, 60–61; legal status, 11; women's experiences, 60–61, 64, 66, 70–71, 88, 90, 173n8. *See also* shrine of Sehwan; state administration of shrines

Simone, AbdouMaliq, 104

Slaby, Jan, 15, 134

space: bloom spaces, 153–54; dreams, 142; imaginary-material connections, 134; mystical selves, 147–48; saintly, 12, 149, 162; *wilayat* (territorial influence), 12, 147, 178n18; women's religious careers, 90

Spadola, Emilio, 12

spatial politics of gender, 61, 90. *See also* gendered segregation and exclusion

spatial practices: fakir, 147–48, 150, 162; *qalandar*s, 179n21

spirits: cohabitating, 69–71, 73–74, 79, 173n13; encounters with, 131–32, 137–38, 141; fakir knowledge of, 69–70; fakir spirits, 70, 73–74, 173n13; fakir women and, 73–74; *haziri*, 70, *71*, 182

spiritual guides. See *pir*s

state administration of shrines: Department of Auqaf, 11, 67–69; elite family relationship, 67; evictions, 57; expansion and renovation, 65; gender, 64, 82; Hinduism, 55, 67; impacts, 50–51; limits, 69; morning ritual, 66–68; motivations, 51; popularization initiatives, 52–53; post–suicide bombing, 81; revenue disbursements, 65; saint access, 13, 55–56, 64, 82; shrine of Bodlo, 125

Stewart, Kathleen, 23

Sufism: the imaginal, 37; love, 21, 168n45; sexuality, 119, 176n23; *suhbet*, 156; vagrant forms of piety, 147, 179n22

suhbet (companionship, sex), 20, 152, 155–56, 158–59

Syed, G. M., 168n39

Taneja, Anand, 23–24, 43, 149, 170n6

Tarikh Mazhar Shahjahani, 168n36

tariqat (path or order), 9, 166n15, 183

Thajib, Ferdiansyah, 103–4

thinness, 151

thin places, 134, 149

unstraight, 16; and the beside, 18; versus queer, 167n27

unstraight affordances, 2, 15–16; fakirs, 104; intimacy, 16, 33, 80, 87, 121, 129, 162; as queer affects, 109; saintly intimacy, 16, 154–55, 160–61

unstraight anthropology of Islam, 163–64

unstraight desire, 159

unstraight heritages of shrines, 55

unstraight histories, 151

unstraight politics of saintly bodies, 158

unstraight publics and politics, 154

unstraight routes to spiritual authority, 73

unstraight tellings, 29

unstraight traditions, 45

unworlding, 27, 132, 148

ves. See *bhes* (dis/guise)

wake, the, 15, 104, 106, 151, 156, 160, 164, 167n24

www.ingramcontent.com/pod-product-compliance
Lightning Source LLC
Chambersburg PA
CBHW071740270326
41928CB00013B/2746